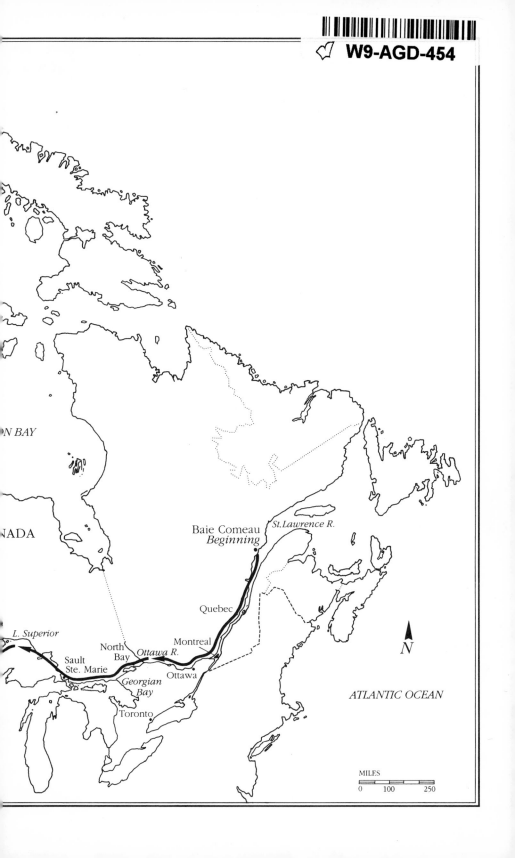

W9-AGD-454

N BAY

ADA

L. Superior

Baie Comeau
*Beginning*

St. Lawrence R.

Quebec

North
Bay
*Ottawa R.*

Montreal

Sault
Ste. Marie

*Georgian
Bay*

Ottawa

Toronto

N

ATLANTIC OCEAN

MILES

| 0 | 100 | 250 |

# GARY AND JOANIE McGUFFIN
# WHERE RIVERS RUN

Stoddart

Copyright © 1988 by Gary and Joanie McGuffin

All rights reserved. No part of this publication may be reproduced or transmitted in any form or by any means, electronic or mechanical, including photocopy, recording, or any information storage and retrieval system, without permission in writing from the publisher.

First published in 1988 by
Stoddart Publishing Co. Limited
34 Lesmill Road
Toronto, Canada
M3B 2T6


CANADIAN CATALOGUING IN PUBLICATION DATA

McGuffin, Gary
  Where rivers run:  a 6,000-mile exploration of Canada by canoe

ISBN 0-7737-2207-6

1. McGuffin, Gary.   2. McGuffin, Joanie.   3. Canoes and canoeing - Canada.
4. Wild and scenic rivers - Canada.   5. Canada – Description and travel – 1981–
I. McGuffin, Joanie.   II. Title.

GV776.15.A2M34 1988      797.1'22'0971      C88-094910-4


TEXT DESIGN: Brant Cowie/Artplus Limited

TYPE OUTPUT: Tony Gordon Ltd.


Printed in Canada

*To our parents*
*who in our earliest years*
*gave us the freedom of the wilderness,*
*the impetus to dream great dreams and*
*the courage to believe that it can all come true.*

# Contents

# Foreword

I THE EARLY SPRING of 1983, I met two young people who told me they intended to paddle across Canada. So contagious was their excitement that I did not ask the obvious questions. Like many others, I wished them light headwinds and a safe journey. I got a big hug from Joanie and a strong handshake from Gary.

I went home, looked at the map of Canada and asked myself the questions I had not asked them: Could they do it? I remembered the power of Gary's handshake and the quiet determination in Joanie's enthusiasm, and I decided yes. They could do it, and they would.

Over the next two years I followed their journey with awe and admiration.

The second question was: Why? I am one of many Canadians to whom canoeing is important, but a 6,000-mile trip, from the Gulf of St. Lawrence to the Bering Sea, is truly a daunting prospect. Why did they want to do it?

*Where Rivers Run* gives two of the answers. First, it was a challenge. Like all adventurers the McGuffins are born travelers, not tourists. Their trip could be no superficial excursion. To be worth doing it must take them along the ancient highways in the oldest and simplest of watercraft, and must show them the heart of the country. Second, their journey would bring them knowledge. They wanted to experience the vastness and the mystery of their land. They wanted to know it personally. What better way than a journey made entirely through personal exertion, a dangerous journey, a respectful journey that contained the land yet left it free.

Like the trip itself, this book is a celebration of a country, and a celebration of youth and love as well. It is as fresh as clear water. Its comments on environmental threats reflect the concern of responsible modern citizens, but its sense of wonder shines on every page, and it is the same wonder that brightened the accounts of early travelers. Through the eyes of Gary and Joanie McGuffin, all Canada is young again, and everything is possible.

Wayland Drew
Bracebridge, Ontario
1 July 1988

# Prologue

*The Missinaibi River: September 16, 1980*

The scraggly limbs of a young spruce bowed under the burden of soggy overalls and thick yellow jerseys. Dripping wool socks and laced runners decorated the crowns of knee-high saplings. In the midst of this woodland clothes closet, the warmth of a persistent flame drew us close to its heart. As we crouched, arms and hands extended for the full benefit of that delicious heat, the moisture from our drenched bodies gradually evaporated in a thin veil. A column of steam whistled through the spout of our ancient tin kettle, which balanced precariously on two crossed logs. I grasped the scorching wire handle with a damp sock and poured the tea.

"Listen!" Gary whispered. "The cranes are moving." Our eyes strained to see through the gathering gloom to the gravel bar on the far shore. The ghostlike figures of sandhill cranes were rising in flight. Gangly silhouettes filled the sky, and trumpeting cries penetrated the surrounding wilderness. Thumping waves of heavy wing beats reverberated across the flowing water. Soon quiet reigned again. Gary prodded the embers of our small fire as we recalled our travels down the Missinaibi.

Two days earlier, a frigid northern gale had brought icy sheets of sleet and snow. Through bucking waves that opposed the current, we strained at each paddle stroke. But those same winds carried a beautiful spectacle—pearly white streamers of migrating snow geese. Their resonant, melodious honking filled the sky as a portent of winter. The mystery of migration and hibernation was revealing itself. The whistle of caribou on the move, the bugling of moose in rut, the bared poplar and the raw winds that cut through our clothing all were nature's way of foretelling the season's change. The wilderness was where we felt most at home. How wonderful it would be to live out here, to paddle a canoe for endless miles down mighty rivers and across vast lakes.

*Appalachian Trail: September 25, 1981*

Scrambling over rough granite blocks, easing ourselves up cracks and through crevices, we each felt every nerve tingle with anticipation. From the mountain's south side, we emerged onto the gray lichen-encrusted moonscape sweeping out below the distant summit. Overhead, the great dome of stark blue sky stretched from horizon to horizon. A bitter wind from the north sent us staggering. It hammered at our clothes and fine ice particles stung our cheeks and noses until they shone cherry red.

Bowing our heads, we pushed on past a rock cairn and followed the snaking trail up the final slope of this great pyramidal monolith rising from the almost featureless plain below. From the horizon behind us, a bank of fish-scale-shaped cumulus clouds slid across the sky like a window blind closing. We hurried along, panting and giddy with the euphoria that long-sought achievement brings.

Finally, we stood together on the summit of Mount Katahdin, the northern terminus of the Appalachian Trail, after 2,100 miles and four-and-a-half months of backpacking from Springer Mountain, Georgia. Wordlessly we hugged one another, sharing the deep sense of pleasure brought on by the completion of a journey that was both a long-term commitment and a challenge to our physical and mental stamina.

Shrugging off our packstraps, we savored the view in every direction. Squinting eastward, we could pick out the Atlantic seaboard along the coast of Maine. Balancing on Knife Edge, a gray-black ridge that curled downward from the eastern side of the summit, we gazed south then north at the mosaic of autumn colors surrounding silver-dollar ponds and lakes. Farther north still lay Canada.

For five million steps across the backbone of eastern America, the outdoors had been our home and our classroom without walls. Here we had come to love the simplicity of life stripped to the bare essentials and to share a desire for adventure and the discovery of new places and people. Through it all, we had come to love one another.

*Rabbit Lake, Temagami: September 30, 1982*

The air was crisp and fresh with the tang of fallen birch and poplar leaves. A steady stream of blue smoke curled over the chimney, filtered out through the trees and mingled with the deep blue of the autumn sky. Laying his ax aside, Gary brushed his forearm across his brow. I rested the crosscut saw over the last few logs, then walked to his side. Surveying the cords of split birch, we felt proud to know that in eight days, we had produced an entire winter's fuel supply. It had cost us nothing more than the muscle and sweat of hours of thoroughly satisfying physical labor.

"Let's take the canoe out and cool off," suggested Gary, grabbing the paddles and life jackets.

Gliding out over the still waters of our protected bay, we rounded the point past Blueberry Island and struck out for the widest section of Rabbit Lake, known locally as "the Big Lake." Gary rested his paddle gently across the gunwales. Taking a deep breath, he mimicked the loons' wavering laughter. The reverberations from the cliffs rebounded and an answering cry came tumbling over the treetops. From the other side of the lake, more wild yodeling. Soon we were surrounded by a wilderness melody rising in crescendo.

Then, from out of nowhere, two streamlined black heads popped up beside us, ruby red eyes glinting in the sun. Our reaction was delight; the loons' response was a quick plunge back down into the dark depths. Resurfacing some distance from us, they glided away quietly and swiftly. We hesitated to paddle on.

"Shall we go now?" I asked, turning toward Gary in the stern. His dark eyes were shining with excitement. "Do you remember looking down on the blue waters in Maine?"

I nodded, replying, "And the longing we felt to finish the Appalachian Trail so we could begin another journey!"

"We've talked about a lot of canoe trips in Canada but do you think we could link them together into one long journey? One that would take us all the way across Canada, a voyage between the Atlantic and Arctic Oceans!"

Immediately a barrage of remembered challenges swirled through my mind. A moment's hesitation . . . how could we possibly? . . . but then the hesitation vanished and I replied with conviction, "I think we could!"

*Rabbit Lake, Temagami: December, 20, 1982*

Our ski tracks etched out a black ribbon behind us as we made our way back to our cosy cabin tucked in the southeast bay of Rabbit Lake. Every two weeks, we set off for supplies and mail in town 18 miles north. Each ski trek was an adventure of its own that we looked forward to with great pleasure.

In the post office that morning, our box had been stuffed, as usual, with expired grocery-store flyers. But among the flyers were responses from companies to which we had directed requests for support for our newly planned canoe expedition. We tore the letters open. They were positive replies! Ecstatically, we thrust them into the hands of the interested mail clerks who had been kept abreast of our plans. Fourteen days earlier, a short telephone conversation with Labatt Breweries had confirmed their enthusiastic endorsement. Our happiness was tempered by the sobering realization that our dream was becoming a reality.

"We won't be back for a while, will we?" I asked wistfully as we skied across the lake, not really expecting an answer. We both knew that the expedition plans could go no further in our chosen isolation. We were filled with a sense of nostalgia for the happy months we had spent here. It was time to leave our wilderness home and head back to southern Ontario. People were requesting meetings, phone calls were becoming a necessity, a canoe had to be built and, to top it off, a wedding had to be planned!

Overhead, silver, green and red fingers of the aurora borealis weaved a pulsing dance across the velvet black of the northern sky. A faint crackle and hiss pierced the crisp air, deep and still at minus 30 degrees. Suddenly, a muffled thud, then an instant later, an earsplitting rip tore across the frozen lake surface over which we traveled. Stopping in mid-stride, we listened with excitement mixed with a twinge of fear.

My mind overflowed with fond memories as we skied the final miles toward our little cabin nestled in the forest of paper birch.

The days there had been simple. Each morning we awoke to see our breath condensing in the crisp air. A loud pecking on the bird feeder attached to the porch railing urged me from the warmth of my goose-down sleeping bag. The bluejays were hungry. The sun greeted the morning as a sliver of orange between the folding hills across the lake. The gray jays soared silently on soft wings, then let out a resounding shriek. The chickadees were just as friendly, twittering and flitting from branch to feeder to hand.

Our cabin was strewn with topographic maps, books, information and pamphlets on outdoor equipment and clothing manufacturers. The plinking of manual typewriter keys and the whirring of a hand-crank sewing machine filled the air in our tiny home. At one end of the kitchen table, our only table, we had to push back yards of colored material and piles of paper before having a meal. Between writing and sewing, we filled up the wood box, collected water from a hole in the frozen bay and explored the land on snowshoes and skis. Living this wilderness life had already fulfilled one of our childhood aspirations. Now it was time to leave this life behind for a while and embark on another dream, to paddle a canoe across Canada.

# 1
## Weaving the Dream

I COULD HEAR the kindly voice of the librarian telling a group of students at the next table that it was closing time. All afternoon she had been searching through files, locating rarely read historical journals and providing a fund of information for our use in researching the journey we were planning. Two tables over, Gary was lost in contemplation. In front of him was Alexander Mackenzie's huge diary of exploration with the all-encompassing title, *Voyages from Montreal on the River St. Laurence [sic] through the Continent of North America to the Frozen and Pacific Oceans in the Years 1789 and 1793 With a preliminary account of the Rise, Progress, and Present State of The Fur Trade of that Country*. Pushing aside an atlas and a pile of maps, I tore a sheet from my notebook and folded it into a paper airplane. On the wings I wrote "Fly with your dreams!" and then I launched it toward Mackenzie's diary. It overshot its mark and hit Gary in the chest, immediately breaking the spell of his daydream.

He looked up and smiled. "Let's go home for supper. All this adventuring has given me an appetite."

We were astonished to find how quickly five hours passed in a library these days. In high school and college, we had both found studying tiresome and writing apparently meaningless essays even worse. However, we now had the opportunity to develop the keen interests we shared in Canada's geography, history, people and wild places, for the purpose of experiencing the country in a memorable and meaningful journey. We filled our winter days soaking up the diaries and journals of such renowned explorers as Alexander Mackenzie, J. W. Tyrrell, Samuel Hearne and the geographer David Thompson.

A wide variety of sources kindled our yearning to canoe through particular regions. The journey began as a collection of puzzle pieces. Small sections were arranged before the larger picture finally materialized. First of all, we wanted the journey to begin and end in salt water. The practical considerations of current flow and the ice-free seasons made travel from east to northwest the most logical choice. With the roughly mapped out route covering approximately 6,000 miles, we knew that we could not possibly traverse the country in one season unless we did nothing but paddle continuously. It would have to be undertaken in two parts. Fortunately, the majority of upstream and "big lake" paddling would take place in the first year when we were assured of a much longer ice-free season. If our plans worked out, we hoped to reach The Pas, Manitoba, by autumn, thereby covering 3,000 miles, half of the actual distance. The farther we progressed northward, the later the thaw and the earlier the freeze-up. With a possible 3,000 miles to paddle the second year, and the likelihood of only three months in which to cover the distance, it was ideal that our journey should end with the 1,100-mile downriver run on the Mackenzie River.

The next decision was to choose a starting point. We finally settled upon the Manicouagan Peninsula, upstream from Baie Comeau on the north shore of the St. Lawrence River. If we started farther east, we would be exposing ourselves to the full force of the Atlantic storms in the Gulf. Also access to the shore would be difficult unless we set off from the Strait of Belle Isle near Newfoundland. This latter option had to be abandoned when we considered the timing. We would not reach Superior in the calmest summer month, July, and we would miss two fascinating natural occurrences during early spring on the St. Lawrence — the beluga whales congregating in their calving grounds and the northward migration of the snow geese. Also, it would be a constant race to reach the expedition's proposed midway point before freeze-up if we started from the strait.

As far as we knew, no one had ever paddled from as far east to as far northwest in an open canoe. The thought of experiencing a marine ecosystem of tides and salt water was infinitely compelling. We were familiar with the presence of ten species of whales ranging from the world's largest mammal, the 100-foot blue whale, to the playful belugas, which bore some resemblance to the size, shape and color of our canoe. Early May is an especially wonderful season, because the white whales bear their young calves near the confluence of the Saguenay and St. Lawrence rivers. For us, the thought of paddling among these wise mammals of the sea was one of the most appealing aspects of the entire journey.

The north shore of Lake Superior had held great appeal for me since the year 1968, when my parents returned from their first autumn camping and canoe trip on this masterful wild coastline. Names like Pancake Bay and Wawa and colorful descriptions of endless sand beaches, blue horizons, huge curling waves and steep granite cliffs made a deep impression on my young mind.

The draw toward northern Saskatchewan began with Gary's knowledge of an expedition his father had made to the interior long before he was born. His father explored this wild country by seaplane and canoe, navigating the complex island chain of Reindeer Lake, then going west over Wollaston Lake and landing finally in a remote body of water called Waterbury. Two years later, having explored and fished every inch of Waterbury, he and his two companions returned and built a fishing camp. The fact of the camp's existence and the intriguing idea of paddling the pristine Fond du Lac River between Wollaston and Lake Athabasca pulled us north like a magnet.

Farther still, the Arctic beckoned. Sweeping through the northwestern corridor of mountain ranges is Canada's largest river system, the Mackenzie. The river empties into a frigid saltwater sea at the edge of the treeless tundra. This is the homeland of the Inuit, whose ancestors' skills and ability to adapt made survival possible in a grueling environment of punishing cold. Our deep respect for the native people of these northern climes was based solely on what we had read in books and seen in films and museums. Experiencing for ourselves the vast Barren Lands, the isolation, the wind and the cold at the top of the country would bring those stories to life.

Early in the planning stages, the route was of paramount concern. There was no question in our minds about where we wanted to begin and end; the difficulty was in determining the course in between. Once satisfied through our historical and geographical research that the waterways were there, we obtained the detailed topographic maps of our proposed route. Numbering 83 in all, these maps would be essential for navigating the country's intricate waterways. Every inch equaled four miles, every brown contour line, 50 feet. The chart symbols, once understood, are a story in themselves.

The geography of Canada made our route possible. The movement of ice-age glaciers and the resulting exposure of the ancient Precambrian Shield with its gentle topography and countless navigable waterways first enticed native people. Because they had to travel, the canoe evolved. Later the European explorers learned the skills of survival and travel from the native people, skills which served their purposes of exploration and fur trade. Together, the canoe and the beaver were instrumental in the development of Canada! So it was not surprising that over half the route which evolved from our research crossed the same waterways the North West Company fur traders plied between Montreal and Lake Athabasca.

Crawling out from beneath the avalanche of preparations and the dismal late-winter snow, we emerged one spring day filled with special anticipation. The canoe was arriving. It would be a memorable occasion because not only was this the expedition canoe, it was also the first canoe we had ever owned together. Its arrival was greeted with about as much ceremony as the arrival of a new baby. Gary had built two finely crafted pedestals on which to rest it. Nearby was placed a neat row of tools for use in outfitting the hull with the customized equipment required for the varied weather and water conditions we would be encountering.

Much to our chagrin, pressing errands called us away to Toronto for the day. On our return we glimpsed the sleek white craft peeking out from beneath the porch roof even before turning in the drive. In the same instant, we burst out with whoops of delight.

"She's beautiful!" I exclaimed.

"A magic carpet to the places of our dreams!" Gary said, his eyes glowing with pride.

Our eyes followed her flowing lines approvingly—18½ feet from bow to stern, a narrow 31 inches across and a deep 15 inches amidships. We felt confident of her ability to handle the long swells of Lake Superior and the heavy water of northern Saskatchewan's big rivers. Her straight keel line and square ends were ideal for the endless miles of flat-water travel. Her shallow arched hull promised swift passage over perilous traverses. Her depth would ensure that our packs lay well below the canoe's upper edges (gunwales), thereby allowing the tarpaulin to fasten securely and keep the equipment dry. Flipping her up over our heads, we were immediately delighted with the lightness of our load. Unoutfitted, this lengthy craft of Kevlar construction weighed only 65 pounds.

"Grand Portage, here we come!" I declared, referring to one of the longest carries we would face overland.

Within the next few days, Gary mounted her seats in very exact positions determined by our weight and height. Two cotton canvas covers padded with closed-cell foam were attached to the tractor-style seats for added comfort. A canvas tarpaulin was designed and sewn up for the purpose of keeping out engulfing waves and rain. It was fashioned in two segments which could be split on the center Velcro strip and stowed in two neat rolls beneath the bow and stern decks. It could just as easily be unrolled and attached to the canoe by way of snaps beneath the gunwales. Two holes were cut and spray skirts sewn in so that we could paddle in comfort with only our upper torsos exposed in times of cold, wet weather. The final touch was to make the canoe and expedition identifiable. Gary cut out and stuck the lettering on the left side of the hull to form the words "Trans Canada Canoe Expedition." Then for the benefit of those who spoke French we titled the right side "La traversée du Canada en canot."

In the past four months we had organized a system of lightweight and durable outdoor gear with the enthusiastic support of 12 equipment companies. For some, we would be field-testing the durability of their products under all types of weather conditions; for others, our journey was an opportunity to test the usefulness of their products for camping, canoeing and other outdoor pursuits.

The accumulated results of our months of preparation were now hung on the basement walls, covering tables and benches and carpeting the floor. Every item, down to the smallest repair parts for the stove, had been carefully considered and chosen. We needed a specialized system of equipment to suit the rigorous and varied conditions we would face on oceans, lakes, creeks and long portages. For two seasons, from ice-out to freeze-up, we would be depending upon our knowledge, our experience and, inevitably, our equipment for survival.

Space was limited to the eight feet of stowage area from the end of Gary's outstretched legs to the back of my bow seat. From the outset, we knew it was foolish to consider one person carrying the canoe. It was not the weight but the length. In a wind, the 18½ feet above one person's head would create an unwieldy sail. In the bush, it would be awkward and unmaneuverable.

Each portage would be handled in two parts. First, the four packs and two camera boxes would be distributed evenly between us and carried across. Then a return trip would be made for the canoe. We firmly believed in expending our energy in endurance over two trips rather than in one herculean effort. An accidental fall with two packs, a camera box and a canoe weighing down on our shoulders, backs, legs and ankles would very likely result in a debilitating injury. Equipment had to be waterproofed yet accessible, specialized yet multipurpose and lightweight but durable. Meeting these requirements was a challenge that taxed our ingenuity to its limits . . . and then some.

In the final week, chaos and confusion ran rampant. But then any expedition's departure would not seem complete without some last-minute panic. Prescription drugs and first-aid supplies were purchased. We would be our own medical team in emergency situations. Five food parcels, each containing a month's supply of prepackaged meals and chocolate bars, awaited posting to the various RCMP detachments and post offices along the first 3,000 miles of the route. But our film supply, which was to have been included in these boxes, had gotten waylaid. When it finally arrived, we worked feverishly, filling the boxes, checking, rechecking, wrapping and addressing them until we thankfully passed everything over the mail counter.

"Have a safe journey!" we called lovingly after one package. "See you in Marathon."

Four days before our departure, our major financial sponsor organized a press conference. The day began on the Lake Ontario waterfront near the *Toronto Star* building. A photographer and writer from *The Star* were waiting for us aboard a police harbor-patrol tugboat. Gray swells were piling up against the dockside piers while an icy wind blasted down through the towering office blocks. After donning wetsuits and the rest of our paddling attire, we hoisted up our canoe and carried it on board the police boat. We chugged out into the bay then lowered the canoe gingerly over the side. While the photographer snapped away, we paddled back and forth in the rolling swell with the gray gloom of the Toronto skyline and the CN Tower in the background.

When we arrived back at dockside, we were whisked off to the Ashbridges Bay Yacht Club where the press conference was being held. The throng of television, radio and newspaper reporters and photographers crowded into the dining room quite over-whelmed us. The Labatt's director for public relations took charge of the situation, made a little speech, then invited us to the podium. Gary nudged me forward.

I looked around at the many faces, microphones and camera lenses, imagining a multi-media vortex about to consume my every thought, emotion and aspiration. I gibbered a few words about the larger objects in our display of equipment and sum-marized the route we had chosen to paddle across Canada. Then I paused. It seemed like a dead, eternal pause. Gary stepped up beside me with confidence.

"When we set off on a wilderness expedition with a purpose, there is a great sense of personal satisfaction, a feeling of ac-complishment and of learning that we have never known in any-thing else. Joanie and I love the physical enjoyment of canoeing. But beyond all this, there is the fascination of the unknown, of discovering hidden places, and of seeing life at a very basic level by getting from place to place self-contained and self-propelled."

A barrage of questions, thrusting microphones, more inter-views, more photographs, then as quickly as the day's whirlwind had begun, it ended. We were one day closer to leaving.

We were also one day closer to another, equally important event. For over two years, we had been inseparable. Although we had long ago made our own commitment to live our lives as one, we finally decided to gather our friends and family for a public ceremony. And we decided that the most exciting time to hold the wedding would be on the eve of our departure. In bringing together these special people, we were sharing our anticipation of the voyage and the dawn of our lifelong journey together.

A traditional ceremony took place on April 30 in Bracebridge's 87-year-old St. Thomas's Anglican Church. The minister, Canon Mitchell, spoke with sensitive understanding referring to our expedition as a unique way to begin life together.

"The outdoors is a true setting for learning patience, under-standing, trust and love in being with one another." After hear-ing our vows, he looked out at the congregation and then down at us, saying, "I hope that the winds will always be at your backs and the portages will travel downhill."

# 2
# Among the Giants

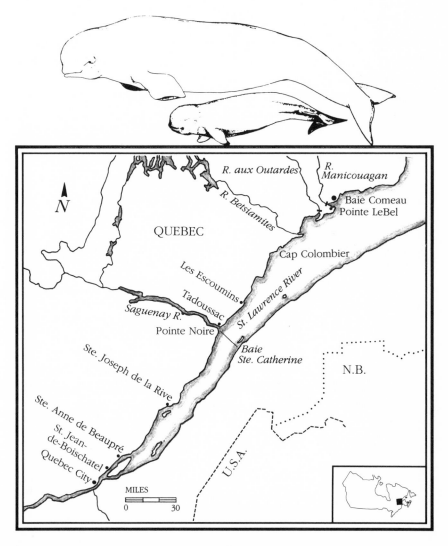

W E DEPARTED from Bracebridge heading east in a borrowed van with our precious canoe securely tied to the
roof. During most of the 700-mile journey, rain pounded against
the windshield in blinding sheets. Past Montreal we motored up
steep grades, swerved around deep potholes and narrowly
avoided a huge transport that had jackknifed and dumped its
load of timber along the soft-shouldered banks for several
hundred yards.

The downpour seemed relentless. When at last a clearing appeared, we wished fervently that we couldn't see the north shore
of the St. Lawrence River at all. It terrified us. An ominous fog
engulfed each little bay. Breakwalls of jagged rock dotted the
coastline for as far out as we could see. Although the St.
Lawrence was fairly calm close to shore, we knew that to paddle
in those bays of partially submerged boulders would be courting
disaster. Neither of us mentioned the possible consequences of
being out there. Instead we put on brave faces and discussed the
whales. Perhaps, if we had known what was in store for us, we
wouldn't have come here at all.

"Do you remember seeing that pink motel back there . . . ?" I
half asked, half suggested.

"Good idea," Gary replied, taking the cue. "This isn't too
much fun!" He wheeled the van around.

"Gisèles et Denis Comptois, Propriétaires," stated the notice
on the front desk. A friendly little woman hurried in, bubbling
away in French. Mme Comptois introduced herself and invited
us for supper. With our French dictionary in one hand and the
menu in the other, we managed to select a delicious meal. Mme
Comptois must have noticed the shiny gold ring on my left hand
for, on returning from the kitchen, she produced a bottle of
champagne from behind her back.

The following morning, we showed her the canoe. We explained that we would be paddling right past this section of the

St. Lawrence shoreline and that we would most certainly stop in on the return journey to visit her. She smiled politely, nodding her head every now and then, but we were never quite sure if she comprehended our undertaking.

"In a few weeks you'll understand when you see the canoe on your front doorstep!" said Gary, laughing and giving her a hug. She beamed at the affection.

*"Bonne chance!"* she cried. *"Bonne chance, mes amis."*

The 700 miles seemed endless. The farther we drove, the wetter and colder it got. Out of the rolling mist we swung across the mighty Manicouagan River and into the town of Baie Comeau. Huge waves crashed along the jagged embankment lining the harbor far below the town's pulp-and-paper mill. The ferry, pulling up to the pier after a stormy 40-mile crossing from Matane on the south side of the St. Lawrence, was having great difficulty navigating in the strong swell.

"This looks like a daydream gone sour!" Gary shook his head. "We'd better not look at this for too long or we'll turn around and go home!"

A statue of the town's founder, an American newspaper publisher, stood tall in the town square overlooking the bay. In stone Robert McCormick was paddling a canoe, and appeared every inch the masterful woodsman and conservationist born before his time. Yet to us it seemed the statue was sculpted in irony. Robert McCormick had established the pulp-and-paper mill at Baie Comeau to feed his newspapers in Chicago and New York. The landscape around us was depressing. A huge yellow cloud of sulfur spewing from the mill had spread far out into the bay. The sickly rotten-egg stench was overpowering, and once heavily forested hillsides were now barren.

Through the doors marked Information in the Centre Culturel, we walked into the tidy office of M. Alain Bourassa. He conversed easily in English.

"Most people do not come to Baie Comeau on holidays until the weather gets warmer, and indeed I believe that most of our lovely inland lakes are still frozen for campers."

We glanced at each other, then asked if he knew of a spot where we could launch our canoe into the St. Lawrence. M. Bourassas's eyebrows rose about an inch. He turned toward the window behind his desk and stared out at the harbor. Reverting to his native tongue, he had a little conversation with himself. Then abruptly, he faced us. The words of concern came tumbling out. "You are crazy. Look at the size of those waves. Where would you go?"

I reached into our pack and pulled out a map of Canada. Laying it on the desk, we traced the route from Baie Comeau up the St. Lawrence's north shore. There was a brief hesitation as his eyebrows lowered into a frown.

"You don't know about the whales, do you?"

Pulling out another folder, I laid it on top of the map. It contained the proposal and information about our expedition that we had prepared over the past months. As Gary pointed out, it was the 10 species of whales inhabiting the St. Lawrence that had first drawn us this far east.

M. Bourassa was still shaking his head when he said, "If you are really leaving tomorrow, I will bring the mayor with me to bid you farewell."

Impressed by our homework, but still doubtful of the wisdom of our undertaking, he kindly arranged a place for us to stay. As we departed we left him with the map and information to digest overnight.

The morning of May 5, 1983, was a marvelous one. We awoke to blinding rays of sunshine streaming out of the beautiful blue of a cloudless sky. Although not exactly beaming down with the warmth of a summer's day, the sun was, nevertheless, very heartening after four days of torrential rain.

M. Bourassa arrived with the mayor and someone from the town's local newspaper, *La Côte Nord*. He seemed cheerful and confident as he made introductions this morning. No doubt the calm seas and warm sun had a lot to do with his change of heart. The mayor stepped forward, shaking our hands and presenting official lapel pins and flags adorned with the Baie Comeau insignia. After the formalities, M. Bourassa suggested we launch the canoe from the sand beaches off Pointe Lebel southwest of town.

When we arrived at the long sand beach, the blue water of the St. Lawrence sparkled enticingly. The river was putting on a convincing disguise. A friendly farewell party had gathered on the beach. Mingling with the local well-wishers and curious onlookers were two friends who had flown in from Ontario. One was a reporter from Gary's hometown newspaper, the *London Free*

*Press;* the other was a neighbor who had agreed to return our borrowed van. A four-man film crew was bustling around with cameras and tripods capturing the moment of departure for a future documentary. Someone produced a bottle of champagne, which we decided to drink rather than break over the bow of the canoe. We could imagine the headline—"McGuffins' departure delayed when champagne bottle torpedoes canoe!"

From the moment we launched the canoe, exhilaration swept over us. Accompanying it was the lighthearted feeling of tension released after the months of preparation. We were on our way at last!

The wind was blowing stiffly from the southwest and we began to plunge through the slight chop. The sound of an accelerating motor caused us to stop and turn. Roaring along the shore toward us was an all-terrain vehicle driven by a man we remembered from the crowd of curious onlookers. Piled in the back of the vehicle and in a smaller trailer towed behind were the other members of his family, all waving goodbye enthusiastically.

At this point, the St. Lawrence was an awesome 40 miles across. It was a living thing, pulsing a regular six-hour heartbeat with its incoming and outgoing tides. We left the security of the soft brown dunes that tumbled from steep shoulders along the east side of Pointe Lebel. The shallow curling waves being tossed up on the receding tidewaters were causing us to paddle farther and farther away from shore. Imagining the map, we could picture the Manicouagan Peninsula that we were paddling around as an enormous dog's head jutting out into the St. Lawrence, its neck extending down into Baie aux Outardes upstream. The peninsula is separated from the mainland by two mighty rivers, the Manicouagan to the east and the Outardes to the west. After an hour we had passed Manicouagan Point and then we were on to Pointe Paradis, which forms the opening to the "dog's mouth."

We put 15 proud miles behind us before the sun dipped below a pink- and orange-streaked horizon. As we turned for shore, the canoe surfed momentarily on the crest of each wave. The sandy bottom raced beneath the hull, then the two surfaces collided with a sluggish skid. We hauled the packs from the canoe and proceeded to set up our first camp on a little ribbon of sand that stretched between the mighty St. Lawrence and a shallow, tranquil lagoon.

We struggled to peel off clammy wetsuits and soaked neoprene boots. For the time being we were determined that this was the way to dress while out on the river. Afterward, it felt wonderful to pull on warm woolly socks and thick cosy pile jackets. Inside the tent, space was at a premium. We made a small clearing amidst our paraphernalia for the tiny cookstove. Then I pulled out a shiny blue diary thick with empty loose-leaf pages and began writing. Gary spread out the Quebec provincial map alongside our topographic map of the area. While marking our campsite on both maps with a small dot and the date May 5, he murmured, "5,985 miles to go."

This was to become the evening ritual for the months ahead.

The tent, canoe, beach, indeed, our whole world was engulfed in a swirling white tempest the following morning. Wet snowflakes splashed against the nylon walls. We had spent many early mornings on ski expeditions contemplating the cold and listening to this familiar sound from within our cosy goose-down sleeping bags.

Groping for the tent door, I unzipped it, then squinted out at the solemn gray waters merging with an equally leaden sky. Gary appeared from the depths of his toasty-warm mummybag and peered out over my shoulder. Just then a furious gust blew a cloud of damp, cold stuff into our faces. He dove for his sleeping bag as I whipped the zipper closed again.

"What a way to be greeted first thing!"

A hurried bowl of cold cereal and orange juice did little to spur us on, but we couldn't dawdle. Clothes and equipment were hastily stuffed into the waterproof packs before we donned the cold and clammy wetsuits.

"Do we have to wear these suits?"

"Yes!" I answered. "What if we tip out there?"

"Joanie, if I thought we were going to tip, I wouldn't be heading out!"

There was a pause as we continued wrestling with the neoprene suits. Then Gary stopped and grinned at me, and asked, "Are we having fun yet, Mrs. McGuffin?"

The falling snow settled about us. We hadn't even launched the canoe, let alone capsized, but we already shivered as the chill crept through our outer layers of clothing. Setting off, we noticed the clouded sky was being slowly torn apart by an increasing west wind. Within the first two hours of paddling, an icy chill was creeping into our very bones. We headed for shore and huddled behind some boulders to share a chocolate bar. When at last we had massaged our feet and hands from a lifeless gray-blue to stinging pink with the returning circulation, we carried on.

By afternoon, we were feeling just a little despondent. The bitterly cold winds swept across Baie aux Outardes. The resulting waves were causing the canoe to wallow dangerously. Paddling this craft was like learning to ride a bicycle, Gary had told me. You have to acquire the feeling of balance. "Just relax and ride with the swell!" he instructed. Fearful of capsizing, I was filled with tension. My rotating strokes were whirling along at breakneck speed.

"Slow down," Gary pleaded. "This isn't a race!"

As we pulled ashore on a small island for lunch, we both heaved a great sigh of relief.

The tide was ebbing quickly and within moments of our landing, the canoe tilted over slightly in the mud as it lost the water's support. We surveyed our oasis in the waves. Only clumps of moss, juniper bushes and spindly spruce had taken root on this bleak chunk of granite rock. There wasn't much room for exploring, but at least it was a place which was going to stay still under our feet.

While ferreting around in a dense clump of shoreline foliage, we scared a female black duck. She bolted from her nest with such a flurry of wing beats that I stumbled over backward. Quickly Gary photographed the four greenish-buff-colored eggs. Then we hurried away, knowing that she was floating anxiously on the bay nearby waiting to return to her unhatched brood.

Deciding it was time for a tea break, I scooped up a pot of water and set it over the stove's roaring blue flame. While waiting for the tea, we lay back on the smooth rock watching the gulls and terns freewheeling in the strong winds. We were mesmerized by the marching waves waging their war against our long-resistant island. I took my first eager sip of hot tea and much to Gary's astonishment, I spat it out.

"It's salty!" I spluttered.

No amount of sugar and powdered milk was ever going to overpower the saltiness of the sea in the St. Lawrence. So we couldn't drink our tea. We had explored every inch of this tiny island, the waves were white-capped and the water was near freezing. There wasn't much left to do but to settle down and wait. The inactivity brought on thoughts of home. The more memories we conjured up, the more our feelings of depression and loneliness grew. Although neither one of us voiced our real concern, we both knew the ocean, cold, wind and tides were gnawing at our courage and revealing hidden fear. As the last glowing rays of the sun slipped below the western horizon, the wind finally let go its fury. In the lull, we quickly set out in our canoe for the forest cover three miles across the bay and made camp just before darkness fell upon us.

A distant booming echoed through the damp, cold fog of dawn. Our curiosity forced us out of the tent and on to the water. At the mouth of Rivière Betsiamites, we discovered about 20 boats fanned out across the bay. Each of them was filled with at least three shotgun-wielding hunters. Their random shooting was producing very little result. Every time an entire flock winged overhead, a bombardment of pellets sprayed the air but not one duck would fall.

Gary yelled suddenly, "Get down!" An enthusiastic hunter had his eye firmly focused on nothing else but the ducks passing swiftly across the surface between him and us. Luckily for the ducks, he was a poor shot; luckily for us, the pellets fell short, spraying the water in front of the bow like a quick burst of hail.

Our third day wore into a long one. At times my eyes would close while my arms continued their relentless reach for the water. "Keep paddling," said a little voice in my head. "Just keep paddling and it will get easier in time."

A low gray ceiling of cloud with a freshening breeze from the east foretold deteriorating weather conditions. At dusk we turned into a quiet cove, leaving the constant swell of the gulf behind. We rested our paddles across the gunwales. A few rickety cottages dotted the shore. They all seemed deserted except one. There, in the lamplit window, we clearly saw two surprised faces and binoculars being raised in our direction. A longing for the warmth behind the four walls of the white-frame cabin overcame us. The sight and smell of the woodsmoke curling from the chimney had the most alluring effect. As we came ashore, an excited couple hurried down to the beach. We were touched by the friendliness of their reception. The fact that we were total strangers was completely irrelevant; our arrival was special because they had never seen anyone paddle into the bay in an open canoe before.

Claude and Lisette Tremblay were kind and generous people. My flamboyant sign language probably had far more impact than my French gibberish but, despite my poor command of the language, they provided us with fresh water and a protected campsite next to their cabin. Claude indicated the woodpile of dry split cedar. We were welcome to make a fire any time we wished.

The overcast sky grew inky black with nightfall. The easterly blow now came in spasmodic gusts causing the tent walls to thump heavily. The strange eerie stillness of the day was giving way to our first major storm. From inside the tent, we listened intently to the rushing waves growing ever nearer and stronger with the rising tide. Then the rain came splattering against the tent in large single droplets as if beating on a drum. These drops soon merged into driving sheets as the wind increased. The squall shook our tiny tent with frightening force, as if it were trying to rip it free of its moorings. All night the storm gave no respite and we fought with nightmarish visions of being engulfed by the icy waves.

At last the tide began ebbing for its six-hour rush to the sea. The sky lightened faintly in the east as dawn came creeping in with dreary desolation. The fearsome gale had abated somewhat, but now the rain teemed down in a solid gloomy curtain. By afternoon, tent fever was running rampant. Idle ceiling-staring, reading and sleeping were replaced by rowdy wrestling matches that had the tent walls thumping from within. Lisette must have been wondering about our shaking tent, for she emerged from the cabin wrapping a large wool sweater about her shoulders. Her young and pretty face betrayed signs of motherly concern. She was worried about us living in such cramped quarters.

"Would we," she asked in slow distinct French, "like to live in their cabin for the duration of the storm?" It was not a problem, she explained, because she and her family would be returning to their home in the village of Ste. Thérèse du Colombier, two miles away. Gratefully we accepted, and settled ourselves into the tiny frame cottage. Soon our damp clothing, tentage and sleeping bags decorated the doors, furniture and floor like a brightly colored quilt. The sparse furnishings included an overstuffed couch with a view to the river, a large wood stove, a table, four chairs, two beds and a fully stocked wood box. The sweet smell of cedar lingered on the warm moist air. That night we drifted off to sleep with the hiss and crackle of burning logs filling our senses.

Now that we had a cabin in which to dry wet clothes, it was no longer necessary to stay cooped up inside. We filled the next day with exploratory hikes. Gulls, terns and great blue herons foraged on the sandy flats. Most intriguing was a lone osprey that appeared circling the bay at low tide, screeching and plunging for small silver fish.

Carefully wending our way through the bush to the edge of the point where we had paddled in two nights before, we emerged from the forest cover. We marveled at the transformation. White walls of water were rolling angrily across the coast and thundering full force against the craggy cliff. Icy sea spray spewed 60 feet into the air. The wind hurled the spray into our faces so hard it stung. It was incredibly exhilarating. The entire water surface was a contoured mass of breaking and rebounding waves in which no canoe could have remained upright for more than a few seconds. Carefully we scrambled down the cliff, avoiding the trailing streamers of slippery purple seaweed. Then, thoroughly drenched, we hurried back to the cabin.

Despite the storm, we managed to make our first enroute CBC Radio broadcast while staying at the cabin. Two weeks before at the Ashbridges Bay press conference, we had met a CBC producer, Bob Burt, who wanted us to contact the station weekly during the expedition for a series of radio broadcasts. Contacting the CBC turned out to be quite a dangerous little escapade. Surprisingly, the lonely stretch of road behind the cabin was blessed with a phone booth only a quarter of a mile away. Unknown to us, there was a decrepit old house trailer tucked back in the trees some distance away. Occupying its front step was a large, rather ferocious three-legged German shepherd who seemed to consider the land on which the phone booth sat his territory. Gary caught a glimpse of the swiftly approaching dog. He grabbed me. We ran for the booth, pushed open the door and leapt inside. I could almost feel the hot snarling breath on my ankles as Gary slammed the door behind us just in time.

We had only traveled 75 miles in our first week on the river, the weather had been terrible, and now only a thin pane of glass separated us from the frothing jaws of a crazed dog. Just as CBC Radio's host, Alan Millar, came on the air wishing us a cheerful good morning, I heard Gary whisper, "Let's make this sound like fun, Joanie!"

From Cap Colombier to Tadoussac, we felt we were becoming much more attuned to our surroundings. Paddling through this saltwater environment, we found everything new and intriguing because we had grown up near freshwater lakes and rivers in the heart of Canada. We soon came to know dozens of different shorebirds, not always by name at first, but by their behavior, flight patterns and varied songs. We felt a common bond with the loon when we heard its friendly familiar yodeling. The loons passing overhead were in larger flocks than we had ever seen in our lives. We encountered old squaw ducks with their incessant melodious chatter and pairs of beautiful eider ducks. Golden eyes, canvasbacks, mallards and black ducks were all river companions that we came to know intimately.

A strange sight had us utterly perplexed for some time one morning. There was no wind or strong current, yet the smooth gentle swell was broken by a streamer of splashing white water in the distance. Drawing closer, we identified the cause of the splash as white-winged scoters diving and feeding on mussels from the river bottom. Then, with a sudden burst, these little black ducks rose by the thousands, skimming off over the surface. Their endless movements on whistling wings fascinated us for hours.

On land every evening, we would explore the nutrient-rich tidal pools teeming with life. Skipping from one to another, we picked our way over the carpet of blue mussels and spiny sea urchins. The great blue herons nimbly stalked their way through the rich food bed, while herring gulls swooped down, feasting on the tasty morsels fresh from the receding tide.

We were paddling through one of the most naturally productive marine regions along the east coast of Canada. A deep sea trench known as the Laurentian Trough begins more than 100 miles off the Newfoundland coast, then extends into the gulf and up the north shore of the St. Lawrence River. It draws a current of cold seawater inland along its great distance. Sudden changes in the topography of the river bottom, such as those located at the head of the Trough and around the Saguenay River mouth, create dramatic upwellings and tidal rip currents. The strong tidal movements and tremendous outflow of fresh water from the Saguenay and St. Lawrence rivers add to the forces that create the nutrient-rich waters. Krill, capelin and smelt gather here in abundance to feed. In turn, they attract the great mammals of the sea, the fin, minke, beluga and even the great 90-footers, the blue whales.

Peering over the gunwale and into the dark depths, the reality of where we were dawned on me. Our canoe was suspended on the surface of a river over 1,000 feet deep. An entire realm of life was taking place at this very moment in the unknown and mysterious marine world far below us. Judging by our distance from the pale sand dunes sweeping to the water's edge near the Saguenay River mouth, we figured our position to be at least two miles from shore. As the canoe surfed on the white-capped waves chasing us up the coast and the screaming wind rushed past my ears, I barely heard Gary's awestruck exclamation: "Look at that!" I swung around just in time to witness a column of spray hanging over a smooth gray-brown back, which had broken the surface only yards away. As if in a state of suspended animation, the gigantic arch continued flowing until a small dorsal fin appeared. Terrified yet ecstatic we stared, unblinking, at the magic place where the whale had risen from the depths. The emotionally charged and frustrating 10 days of paddling through storms and penetrating cold dissolved in this one magical moment.

High upon the eastern bank of the Saguenay River mouth, the 400-year-old settlement of Tadoussac commands a panoramic view of the St. Lawrence River. The massive white Grand Hotel with its bright red roof dominated the scene as we surveyed the town from the waterfront. Exchanging rubber boots for running shoes, we left the canoe and strolled up past the hotel. It was bustling with activity in preparation for the upcoming tourist season. A thorough spring cleaning was taking place. While gardeners rode mowers up and down the sprawling lawns, the maids inside were polishing floors and setting out colorful umbrellas and deck furniture. Since the journey's beginning we had endured inclement weather and had barely covered 150 miles. The festive mood in Tadoussac, a welcome sign of summer's approach, boosted our morale immensely.

On the road overlooking the harbor, we came across the oldest surviving wooden chapel in North America. We felt a strange thrill upon reading the year, 1747. The bell in the tower was more than 100 years older again, having belonged to the original church built by the Jesuit missionaries. We were seeing some of the remnants of the earliest European settlement in Canada. When that bell first tolled, Europeans had no concept of the breadth of the land they would traverse over the next century and a half, which was the time it took before the Arctic and Pacific Oceans were reached.

At daybreak the following day, we launched the canoe at high tide in the still waters of Tadoussac's harbor. All was quiet. Even the gulls perched along the pier were quiet. There wasn't a sign of human life until a sailor appeared on the foredeck of the coast-guard ship. He waved without breaking the morning's silent spell. According to our charts, the tide was ebbing. We ignored this fact to take advantage of the calm seas. We paddled hard toward the Saguenay's western shore where Pointe Noire Coastal Station stands guard from the cliff overlooking the river mouth and the 16-mile-wide St. Lawrence.

Pointe Noire, a former lighthouse-keeper's quarters, had been converted into a whale research station. Back in 1979, I had spent a month here working with Leone Pippard, one of the foremost authorities on the St. Lawrence beluga whales. Four years before my arrival, Leone had begun a research project that involved detailed observation and the acquisition of photographs, film and written reports about this small isolated stock of white whales. The cold Labrador current flowing down past Newfoundland's Torngat Mountains and into the gulf creates a habitat similar to the whales' normal circumpolar environment more than 1,000 miles farther north. During that autumn of 1979, we were attempting to gather underwater photographs and compile behavioral and feeding-pattern data.

Looking up at those same brooding cliffs, I recognized the very promontory on which I had crouched with binoculars and tape recorder. I distinctly remembered one afternoon's observations which included a pod of belugas feeding on the tidal rips over which we now paddled. The concern for the plight of these small white whales that stirred within me then had grown stronger with the passing years and during the planning of the canoe expedition. The outflow of the Great Lakes drains through the St. Lawrence. Municipal wastes and the toxic emissions from pulp-and-paper mills, aluminum smelters, other heavy industry and waste dumps throughout eastern Canada render this river one of the most polluted of North America's waterways. Not only are the belugas and other marine life being poisoned out of existence, but their habitat is also being threatened. In the early 1960s the hydroelectric development in the Manicouagan watershed altered the ecosystem to such an extent that the belugas were forced to move to the only suitable breeding and feeding habitat remaining—the confluence of the Saguenay and St. Lawrence rivers. From several thousand whales, the population crashed to several hundred. The region simply could not sustain any more. The construction of ports and marinas, and the dynamiting and dredging of basins and bays, is eliminating the one remaining habitat on which this unique, nonmigratory beluga population depends. We felt deeply saddened and discouraged to think that in only a few hundred years, man, supposedly the most intelligent being on earth, could reduce this once abundant marine ecosystem to such a deplorable state.

Hurrying across shallow Baie Ste. Catherine near Pointe Noire, we disturbed hundreds of herring gulls feeding in the receding tide waters around Recif aux Allouettes. Over the gulls' raucous screaming, we heard a rushing noise as if we were approaching whitewater rapids. Anxiously we peered through the binoculars trying to figure out the cause of a foot-high wall of water which seemed to be advancing rapidly. Suddenly we were upon it. The choppy tidewaters had created the optical illusion of a wall. We were confused and concerned as the extraordinary movement of the currents bounced and jostled the canoe from side to side. Masses of sticks, logs and other debris entwined with fronds of brown slippery seaweed swirled around us.

From this churning maelstrom suddenly appeared the undulating rhythm of smooth white backs. "Belugas!" We were enthralled by the sight of these magnificent snow-white whales combing the tidelines in their foraging efforts. The turbulent current carried us into the path of at least a dozen advancing whales. We weren't sure what would happen next as they dove under us. I tried desperately to hold the canoe reasonably steady while Gary got out his camera with a telephoto lens.

He clicked off several frames before lowering the camera, his eyes wide with astonishment. We were on a collision course with a huge navigation buoy. Even before we could attempt to avoid its huge mass, the rip tide had whisked us by. We were on our way out to sea!

Gary slammed the lid shut on his camera box. Grabbing our paddles, we began stroking hard toward the shore, which was more than five miles away. Never before had we been in such a dangerous predicament. There was a powerful force propelling the canoe toward the vast expanse of the open river where only the huge freighters traveled. Our efforts appeared hopelessly in-adequate. We were so far from shore that we couldn't tell if we were drawing any closer to safety or not. Suddenly with grim determination, Gary swung the canoe downstream and aimed the bow toward Tadoussac.

"What are we doing?" I shouted.

"Just paddle!" was the abrupt retort.

My stomach tightened as I burned with fury. How dare we cap-size out here and drown. The thought so enraged me, it success-fully quelled my fear. The canoe plowed into steep waves and glanced off turbulent boils until we eventually crossed the tide line. The water calmed, and there was quietude again. It was as if we had just come through the eye of a storm. Some moments later we dragged the canoe up on a reef now exposed by the eb-bing tide. Collapsing on the bare rock, we held each other tightly, shaking with relief. We were safe.

The tides were a phenomenon that we had never experienced before. From now on we would try hard to live in harmony with them; we vowed to obey our charts and tables religiously. The tidal movements become particularly apparent at the confluence of the Saguenay and St. Lawrence rivers. At this place, there is not only the influence of the freshwater current from the Saguenay and the great variation in river depths, but also the St. Lawrence River narrows to a funnel shape. As the tide surges in and out from the gulf, the river varies as much as 18 feet in height along the cliffs by the time it reaches Quebec City. Some-times we would awaken very early and set off with the rising river before the sun had even made an appearance. Other times we would wait patiently until late morning or early afternoon before launching the canoe. The will of the weather and the tides ruled our daily routine and most of the time patience was a virtue we had to learn.

There was much to see and discover when we could not take paddle in hand. One morning, while huddled over a small fire sipping hot chocolate and drying wet socks, we noticed a flicker of brilliant orange in the dark somber spruce trees. It was a blackburnian warbler heralding spring. Along with this little beauty, others of the warbler clan were just returning northward after long migrations from the equatorial climes of South and Central America. Magnolia, black-and-white, and bay-breasted warblers all flirted and teased us, hopping in and out of the underbrush, singing merrily. With cameras slung around our necks, we clambered over the shoreline boulders and wandered along sand beaches at the forest edge trying, with sporadic success, to capture them on film.

At low tide one morning, we pulled into the ferry port town of St. Siméon. Downstream from the pier, a row of rambling posts with netting strung between them reached out into the river straining the current. The mesh wall ended in a circular enclosure. Inside the weir net's deepwater trap, a fisherman clad in chest waders pushed a seine net to scoop up the imprisoned fish. Several buckets full of smelts were soon lined up on the beach. We watched him empty the buckets, then throw aside the shiners, puffers and flounder. These were the discards which, for reasons of boniness or taste, were left for the greedy gulls that perched on the upper edge of the weir net. The fisherman chatted amicably, communicating more to us with his hands than he did through his speech. Then he picked up his catch and climbed to his ramshackle cabin on the hill. Trailing behind, we asked him about the conditions farther upstream. We had obviously touched upon a favorite topic as he started describing, in graphic detail, the worst storms along the coast he had ever experienced in his lifetime. His hair-raising tales of the formidable tides and hostile coastline did little to inspire our confidence for the miles ahead.

A day later, we found ourselves beating against a very strong current between the mainland port town of St. Joseph de la Rive and Ile aux Coudres. It was an uphill battle racing from eddy to eddy only inches from shore, but that night, as we pored over the map, we realized the next section would be far worse. The closely spaced contour lines revealed an impossibly sheer cliff shooting straight up from the water's edge. It would be the most exposed and least inhabited region that we had yet encountered.

Just before 5 A.M. the next morning, we lowered the canoe into the river and paddled away from the tiny community of Petite Rivière. Looking back through the dim light, we could see the silver-gray church steeple dominating the village. Its presence was typical of Quebec's north-shore towns. We knew it would be a recognizable landmark visible to us for at least the next four miles.

At first we made good time racing from one point of land to another. But then the tide started doing strange things and the waves were beginning to pound along the jagged cliff line with such ferocity that, in the face of an increasing wind, we decided we had better pull ashore immediately. This was easier said than done. It took another half hour before we saw a short sandy point. Above this, we discovered a warm protected oasis, a cubbyhole between two boulders. With the wind and spray unable to touch us, we conceded the next six hours to the river's ebbing tide.

Binoculars in hand, we spied upon the ships that were, at this point, passing within several miles of shore. A national flag flew from each ship's stern identifying its country of origin. Some, like the Japanese and Canadian ships, were spotlessly bright and tidy, while others were grim steely-gray with no sign of life on board. One Japanese freighter passed so close that we could actually see the smartly uniformed sailors swabbing down the decks with a powerful jet stream that spewed from a massive hose.

Exploring the area above our shelter, we discovered, to our surprise, an emergency helicopter landing pad and just beyond it, a sparkling creek. Below the cliff, small clumps of sunny yellow coltsfoot were blooming. This world was much softer than the harshness of life near the river's edge.

By mid-afternoon, we eagerly waited for the tide to turn and the wind to subside. The river was rising on schedule, but the wind howled just as fiercely as ever. We decided to grit our teeth and do battle with the gale. By the time we had lugged the packs and canoe over the length of two football fields of mudflats to meet the incoming tide, we were an extremely bedraggled pair.

For an hour we fought the wind. Our muscles screamed for
rest, but we pushed on. I dared not turn my eyes to shore for fear
I'd give up. But our pathetically slow progress was hardly worth
the effort.

"We're just wasting our time!" Gary said dejectedly.

Abandoning the battle, we swung the canoe toward shore. We
struggled up the beach where we huddled, cold and wet, and
once again waited for the wind to subside. It didn't, but we
pretended it had.

"Let's try and make a break for it!" Gary yelled with renewed
anger. Cursing the waves, the gale and everything else, we staggered back out, yanking the canoe over the slippery mud as we
went. The breaking surf pounded along the hull threatening to
capsize the canoe even before we had it launched. Just as we had
pushed ourselves from shore, a sudden gust of wind lifted the
waterproof map case off the thwart in front of Gary and threw it
overboard. Fuming, he grabbed the case, laying it back in the
canoe. Seconds later the same thing recurred, only this time the
case flew straight in his face with a resounding slap. Cursing
loudly, Gary grabbed the plastic case, threw it on the bottom of
the canoe, then stomped on it with a muddy boot. "Who needs a
bloody map on a day like this when I can see where we started
and where we'll end!"

It was getting dark when we finally gave in for good. For the
third time that day, we tried hauling the loaded canoe across the
mud flats toward the sheer rock embankment. The mucky plain
lying between us and the rock was particularly thick and un-
stable, much like quicksand. The quagmire, knee-deep in places,
sucked at our boots. The loaded canoe refused to budge an inch
even with our mightiest pushing and pulling.

Yanking the packs from the canoe, we trudged off with dogged
determination. But with the added pack weight, our boots sank
deeper and deeper with each step. Soon I was mired in, unable
to lift either leg forward. As I stood there contemplating my next
move, I heard a yell. I looked up just in time to see Gary topple
over, pack and all. Afraid that he had fallen face first, I pulled
frantically at each foot in an effort to go to his aid. But the
clutching mud would not release my boots. Unhesitating, I stepped out of them and slopped forward in stocking feet. Fortunately Gary had twisted sideways, landing pack first. As he

writhed around to free his arms from the straps and regain an upright position, he bore a remarkable resemblance to a marooned turtle.

I took one dismayed look at his mud-caked clothing before shifting my gaze to his windburned, mud-splattered face. He was smiling. Despair dissolved into hysterical laughter as my knees buckled. Lying in the mud, we laughed and laughed until the tears ran down our cheeks. Finally we wiped them away and struggled to our feet. Helping one another with the packs and canoe, we eventually had our camp pitched on a lumpy patch of brambles just above the high tide mark.

Looking down at my feet, Gary noticed that they were clad only in a pair of very soggy brown socks. His surprised look followed my mud-caked finger pointing toward the river. There, quite alone and barely visible, was a little pair of rubber boots. Mired down in the disappearing trail of footprints, they were already succumbing to the rising tide. By the time Gary had retrieved them, it was well and truly night. Leaving a pile of slimy garments outside, we scrambled into the tent and fell into a deep sleep.

We woke only once. It was shortly after midnight when we peered out the tent door to discover the high tide flooding the brambles and grass only inches away. Amazingly, we were perched on the only patch of dry ground. We stayed awake just long enough to assure ourselves that the tide was ebbing, then collapsed wearily for another four hours.

On waking again, we found the water's edge had retreated, as if by magic, down the cliff and far our across the alluvial plain. Sheer will power forced us from the tent and back on to the water. We moved at a snail's pace against the full-force gale. At every point of land, the waves were wildly unpredictable. The possibility of a capsize had never been more real. But we were bent upon reaching Cap Tourmente and getting off this wretched coast before we drowned. With aching backs and rubber arms, we fought to gain some ground during each lull in the wind. At last we came around the final point, and the mudflats of Cap Tourmente spread glistening brown before us.

A wonderful reminder of spring met our weary, windburned eyes. Thousands of greater snow geese covered the expansive tidal flats like a fluttering white blanket of snow. Suddenly one took to the air and the entire flock exploded simultaneously in a swirling mass. Then, with a cascade of resonant honking, they settled back to earth to continue furrowing in the muddy soil. They had arrived from the eastern seaboard in the wake of retreating winter, winging their way northward to arctic nesting grounds. Like a swinging string of pearly white beads, the snow geese undulated toward us from the distant dark hills of Ile d'Orléans. As they whistled overhead, we felt a kinship with these winged migrants in our common quest for the Arctic Ocean.

# 3
## Deeds and Devilry

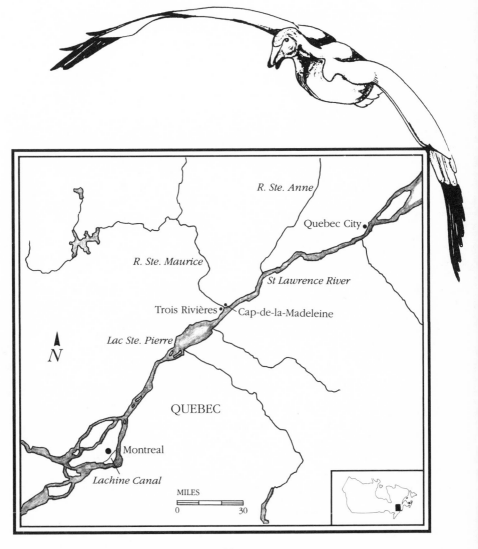

I LE D'ORLÉANS splits the St. Lawrence into two distinct channels for 25 miles below Quebec City. We chose the narrower
north passage, preferring to keep as much distance between us
and the shipping lanes as possible. The entrance to the province's industrial heartland began for us the moment we sighted
our first hydro lines swinging out across the river. Just beyond
was an arching bridge, the man-made link between Ile d'Orléans
and mainland Quebec. The dark spires of spruce on the Laurentian slopes were growing sparser as the farms, villages, cities and
harbors pressed in on the narrowing banks.

The wind had mellowed to a whisper. The whirlpools of the
ebbing tidewaters swirled quietly beneath the canoe as they were
drawn back to the sea once more. Pasted against the deepening
pink of the evening sky were the black silhouettes of the rolling
hills of Ile d'Orléans and the massive shrine of Ste. Anne de
Beaupré. With land drawing close, we were no longer exposed to
the sea, and we welcomed the protection.

A cloak of miserable, drizzling clouds hovered over us at dawn
the next day. From our tent site, we could barely make out the
water's edge, and the only hint of the snow geese's continued
presence was the incessant gabbling and honking filtering across
the Beaupré mudflats. Reluctantly, we packed our equipment
and transported it to the riverside.

The morning started out on a particularly unpleasant note,
since, along with the dampness, there was the foul stench of
sewage.

"Yuk," I snorted. "Where's that revolting smell coming from?"

"Watch it!" Gary burst out, grabbing my arm and pulling me
toward him. With no more forewarning than an echoing gurble
and a hollow gush, a huge streaming ball of pink toilet paper
came spewing through a four-inch pipe protruding from the
riverbank. Sickened, we turned away. "Wilderness canoeing,
right?!"

Then as if to mock Gary's sarcastic comment, a distinct toilet flush warned of more to come. No doubt someone would have been very surprised to learn that the contents of their toilet would end on someone else's feet. Turning red with indignation, I pronounced this to be the most disgusting, stinking, deplorable example of human ignorance I had ever witnessed.

There were more visually distressing and bad-smelling moments in store for us. Protruding from the cement wall along each small town's harbor was a row of pipe holes. Our attitude hardened as we measured—sarcastically—the hospitality bestowed upon us by the number of flushes we counted while paddling by. The whole matter troubled us deeply. Were there no laws against this? Gary quipped that they might as well have an outhouse mounted on the end of the breakwall. What was happening here? In this age of environmental concern, people were treating the St. Lawrence as a massive sewer system, the tidal action no more than a giant toilet flush to the sea.

We pulled our hoods tight and bowed our heads into the stinging rain saying hardly a word for the next few hours. As the skies were ever blackening, we decided the weather was definitely not in our favor today. Just as we were contemplating the prospect of paddling alongside 10 miles of busy highway and negotiating the Quebec harbor in the dark, a violent bolt of lightning split the sky. A crack of thunder immediately followed. A white curtain of rain moved swiftly across the surface of the water, obliterating the scene before us. We just managed to slide the canoe ashore and make a dash for the protection of the nearest porch roof when the deluge hit.

As we considered our next move, a long maroon Cadillac wheeled around the corner of the building. A friendly gray-haired man smiled from the open window. Apparently, we had landed ourselves in the community of St. Jean de Boischatel and this kindly gentlemen was its mayor. He was also the owner and chef of the restaurant where we had taken shelter. As we explained ourselves in our ever-improving French, his eyes widened with interest and he begged us to hop in for a tour of the town.

"It will be a very fast tour," he said, grinning. "I'm cooking tonight."

Off we sped down the riverside highway. The mayor was full of nervous energy. As we boomed up the steep hill to Montmorency

Park, Gary made a tactful search for the seatbelts. Halfway there, a policeman flagged us over. We felt awkward but our driver wasn't the least bit perturbed. Just as we expected the mayor to pull out his driver's license, the policeman thrust a large brown envelope through the window. After the mayor and the policeman exchanged a few friendly words, the two cars sped off in opposite directions.

He turned to us, winking. "There are advantages to being the mayor! But joking aside, this is some important information on this year's golf tournament. We're coming up to the place now."

Our tour guide was conscientious. With wild gestures, he pointed here and there to the places we were passing. His eyes were seldom on the road ahead. Moments later we arrived at the golf course he had referred to where world-class tournaments are played on its sprawling greens. Then in an instant we were transported to Montmorency Falls. Here the river takes a magnificent plunge before winding its final mile to the St. Lawrence. The whole area was steeped in reminders of the historic French-English struggle for power. The mayor pointed to a prominent stone building which commanded a startling view of the river below. This house was supposedly where the British General Wolfe resided for several days before launching his surprise attack on the Plains of Abraham above Quebec City.

Just as we were about to descend the escarpment, our tour guide braked to a sudden halt. The western sky was unfolding in unexpected splendor. Liquid golden light poured forth across the harbor, illuminating several ships that drifted gracefully toward the city. Before our tour guide could discourage us, we grabbed our cameras and headed toward the precipice. We gazed across the glistening river that lay between us and the capital. It looked inviting but we wondered and worried about paddling through our first large city harbor.

The sound of nervous drumming on the steering wheel broke our concentration. We had forgotten our friend would have tables of hungry patrons awaiting his return. The descent off the escarpment's same steep road was tackled at aggressive speed. We came to a screeching halt behind the restaurant and the mayor leapt out. His apology for the short tour was followed by a hasty invitation for supper, which was gratefully accepted.

At a very early hour the next morning, we paddled away from Boischatel, bound for Quebec City. Our plan was to work hard during the morning, reach the city and explore it, then get as far upstream from the populated area as possible before nightfall. For a long time, we had been wondering about the dangers of paddling a canoe into a major city. Now we were about to find out.

Plowing into a brisk headwind, we traversed a wide shallow bay, then approached the dockyards. The river was still in the throes of spring runoff. The current raced and boiled alongside the concrete piers. We sensed the dirty gray-brown monotony that every city seems to emit between late winter and spring. There didn't appear to be a speck of natural earth or vegetation anywhere along the shore, just piles of broken asphalt and reinforced concrete blocks.

Ahead lay a 1,000-foot freighter docked at the pier. We read the warning in large red letters on her stern, immediately above our heads—Beware of Propwash. We imagined that the prop was capable of smashing us against the pier and chewing us up into a thousand little pieces like a carrot in an oversize kitchen blender.

After passing our third ship in a row, we noticed a steep embankment of jagged boulders. It would be tricky climbing to the top of the bank, but it was now or possibly never. We feared if we didn't stop here, there wouldn't be another opportunity until we were long past Old Quebec, the part of the city we were most interested in seeing.

With much straining up precarious hand- and foot-holds, we eventually deposited the canoe and equipment within the confines of a small compound surrounded by high fencing and barbed wire. It appeared that our equipment would be very safe here. We wandered off, never looking back.

For four hours we explored the Old Quebec cobblestone streets and the massive fortress known as the Citadel. Perched 350 feet above the rolling St. Lawrence, we could look downstream toward the high point of land known as Mont Ste. Anne. We had paddled below the mountain on our way past the flocks of snow geese at Cap Tourmente. Our eyes followed the river up past Ile d'Orléans where it narrows considerably, and from which Quebec's name was derived. The Algonkian natives called this place "kebek," or "a place where the river narrows."

As we dashed up and down long flights of boardwalk stairs, Gary stopped and pointed toward the coast-guard docks on the city's waterfront. Past the guardhouse, the ships and the colorful pile of channel-marker buoys, in the center of a fenced-in compound was a slender white object, our canoe.

"Well, it sure looks safe in there," I commented happily.

A slight crease formed in Gary's brow as he said half to himself, "Too safe, I think."

The city of Quebec was a hive of industry as it was preparing for the following summer's celebrations to mark the occasion of Jacques Cartier's landing 400 years earlier. Flags were already flying, announcing the great meeting of the Tall Ships from around the world. Shop windows and street lanterns were being decorated. Gleaming new copper plating was being installed on the turrets of Quebec's picture-postcard hotel, the Château Frontenac. As we walked through the hotel's grand entrance we felt slightly out of place. There were the posh surroundings of lustrous wooden staircases and winding banisters, the elegant dining rooms and hallways with cathedral ceilings; there were the distinguished-looking patrons scrutinizing us with quizzical stares. But, we decided, our historic and hard-earned admission to Canada's oldest city far outweighed our informal attire of rugger shirts, patched pants and rubber boots.

When at last we noticed the time and felt the freshening breeze, we decided we had better get back and launch the canoe. But much to our annoyance, when we attempted to enter the coast-guard compound and dockyards, the gateman flatly refused us entry. I tried to explain the situation calmly, but either my obscure French was incomprehensible to him, or else he simply couldn't be bothered to help us.

"Our canoe is down by the shore." I motioned frantically toward the docks. "You must let us by. It's our boat, our home. It's everything we own!"

The guard was a stern, stout individual with a large double chin and thick eyebrows. The more frustrated I became, the more he tucked his square chin into the thick folds of his neck and lowered his big bushy eyebrows until they almost covered his eyes. At last, when he realized I wasn't simply a pest who would eventually go away, he contacted his superior by phone. I discussed the matter with a man who could hardly stop chuckling. I handed the phone back to the guard to finish the conversation.

We received the go-ahead but we weren't sure if anyone believed us because the stone-faced guard strutted briskly behind, hand over his holster. We were marched back through the yard of red-and-green buoys, past the freighter ships. I felt the color rising in my cheeks as we passed through the gate clearly marked, from this side, Absolutely No Trespassing Helicopter Landing Zone. We were guiltily aware of the large white concentric circles marked on the pavement stretching before us, and of our canoe and packs poised neatly some ten yards beyond.

Expressionless and immovable, the guard took up a wide-legged stance, his arms folded across his broad chest. Uttering a stream of profanities beneath our breath, we clambered, slipped and slithered back to the water's edge. We couldn't understand his suspicion toward us once he saw the canoe and realized our tale was actually true. A coast-guard station should be there to assist all watercraft, we thought. Needless to say, the guard didn't return our farewell wave.

People were more often very kind to us and we were never more grateful than through the next 200 miles of low flatlands. High spring runoff had caused considerable flooding and as a result the riverbanks on which we camped each night were drenched. And so were we. There was seldom any respite from the incessantly dirty weather. The perpetual rolling motion of the waves was beginning to take its toll on our bodies and especially our lower backs. Early that afternoon we succumbed to our aches and pains and pulled ashore at La Pérade.

As we pitched the tent on yet another sodden piece of ground, a slim-built fellow wearing a brown lumberjack shirt and well-worn jeans emerged from a nearby cabin. We gladly accepted his friendly invitation for tea. The St. Lawrence was no stranger to Jean, for he had worked it up and down on board fishing trawlers. One year he had worked on the ferry between Matane and Baie Comeau. He couldn't believe we had traveled all the way by canoe on this immense river. Jean admitted shyly that he, too, was an avid outdoorsman. His hunting and fishing stories kept us amused long into the cold, wet night, since he had to illustrate most of them on reams of logbook paper in order for us to understand.

"Did you know that this place is called the 'Chenaux Capital of the World?'" Jean had hardly given us the opportunity to ask what chenaux were before he was off on a story about the tomcod that arrive in swarming schools to spawn in the Rivière Ste. Anne every March. Later the next day, Jean drove us toward the village and the famous river. "You see all those fishing huts?" he indicated, waving an arm toward the colorful array of roof tops lining the banks. "They are part of the biggest business in town."

We didn't doubt him. There were hundreds of them, ranging from little wooden shacks thrown together with a few old plywood boards to the gaudy purple and green ones that gave the impression they were built to withstand a hurricane.

"Everyone in town sells wood and rents ice huts in the chenaux season," he explained. "People arrive from across the province in droves to catch the chenaux." He paused, then added, "Jacques Cousteau documented the chenaux season in his television program on the St. Lawrence Seaway."

With the help of our French-English dictionary and more sketches, Jean described what it was like. "When you drill your hole through the two feet of ice, the fish gush up with the water and flow out across the frozen surface. You have never seen so many little fish come from one small hole." His eyes gleamed with excitement.

Later he showed us a fine hut with a fresh coat of stain, shiny new chimney and comfortable benches inside. Quite unpretentiously he claimed that his equipment was among the best around. "And this machine," he said, pointing to the snowmobile next to the hut, "was the one I used to take Jacques Cousteau out on the ice when he came to film." As we left, we assured Jean that one winter we would return to see the spectacle for ourselves.

For several days I had been experiencing problems with my back muscles. Each paddle stroke would send a searing pain through my right shoulder and down the length of my arm. Gary suspected tendonitis, which could mean a delay of a week or more. I tried hard to hold back the tears of frustration that welled up, but when another cloudburst caught me with my raincoat off, I was so downhearted and bone-chilled that my spirits plummeted to an all-time low. Gary looked forlorn, unable to decide what to do next. It wouldn't stop raining and his Joanie was falling by the wayside. Staring gloomily at the map, he suddenly perked up.

"We're within three miles of Mme Comptois's place!"

As we talked of the woman who had so thoughtfully provided a bottle of champagne when we were heading out to Baie Comeau, our spirits "pendulumed" upward again.

Mme Comptois was the picture of surprised delight when she opened her front door and discovered a white canoe on the step. Gary gave her an affectionate squeeze.

"Come in, come in!" she burst out. "I never expected to see you again!"

After quelling our ravenous appetites, she ran a steaming hot tub which both she and Gary insisted I soak in for as long as possible. Two hours later I emerged looking like a wrinkled old prune and Gary tucked me under a pile of warm blankets.

After fortifying us with a substantial "voyageur" breakfast the following morning, Mme Comptois came down to the river's edge to see us off. So much had happened in the ten days since we first met that I was sure we were all wondering when, where and if we would ever see one another again.

My muscles felt as if they had loosened up and the jabbing pain had tempered to a dull throb. We attributed the problem to the fact that we had spent most of the time paddling on our strong sides, which we naturally favored during uncertain tidal currents and stormy seas. By good fortune our strong sides are opposite to each other, but in this instance it meant that Gary always paddled on the right while I stroked on the left. We agreed to change this habit for the sake of maintaining our most important asset for the success of the expedition—good health.

Late one afternoon, we reached Lac St. Pierre, a very shallow body of water that extends nearly 20 miles from east to west. Dredgers work constantly to maintain a shipping channel through the lake. Although the canoe draws only several inches of water instead of several feet, shallow depths are still a hazard. Once the wind's fury has been aroused, steep, choppy waves develop very quickly. From the eastern tip of Pointe du Lac, we surveyed the dead-calm lake and opted for a direct route from point to point. The first five miles were smooth sailing but then the sky grew pallid and a gentle breeze nudged us from behind. Barely 15 minutes later, capped four-foot waves snarled angrily on our stern. Their frothing peaks squeezed beneath the hull one at a time. As we perched on the balancing point of each wave, the deep

troughs beneath bow and stern caused the canoe to waver un-
steadily. Nervous energy propelled my paddle, which only left the
water momentarily to make recovery strokes. The canoe surged
forward on each wave crest, surpassed it, then rocketed down into
the icy gray-green waters. The exhilaration fueled Gary's spirit
and at each heave of a wave, a loud "Yahoo!" would fill the air as
the canoe soared forward splitting the white foam.

Gary never overshot his confidence though, and gradually, as
the heavy seas grew steely with the coming of dusk, he urged me
to paddle harder and faster. By this time, I was truly scared for
our lives. Never had I felt so helpless and alone, despite the
proximity of the highway not even two miles distant through the
flooded forest. It would have been exceedingly difficult to wedge
the canoe among the trees even if we had made for shore at that
moment.

The mouth of Rivière du Loup was a sweet sight indeed. The
sheer joy we felt upon spotting the first little cottages perched
high on stilt foundations was worth the exertions and tension of
the past hours. The river was washing against the basement windows of several flooded homes. One driveway on the river's east
bank was two-thirds under water. We turned in and paddled up
to the house. Unabashed, I knocked on the front door. The occupants were so astounded at the sight of two bedraggled but
beaming souls that they replied with a bewildered nod when we
inquired about camping on the dry pavement next to the house.

A moderate east wind and light rain the next day tailed us
down the remaining miles of Lac St. Pierre and into a delta of
low elongated islands. The muddy river had washed over the
banks and spilled back through the forest for as far as we could
see. The area was more like a mangrove swamp than the
deciduous forest of the upper St. Lawrence. As we turned into
the first quiet channel, I felt the call of Mother Nature; the need
to do my morning ritual behind some secluded tree grew so
strong that I felt as if I were going to burst. The three mugs of
hot chocolate I had gulped down at breakfast had gone through
me like water through the garden hose.

"I've simply got to go!" I exclaimed. "Right now!"

"Well go then," came the nonchalant reply from one better
outfitted with more appropriate plumbing.

"That's easy for you to say," I countered.

"I know!" Gary laughed. "How about hanging over the side, little gymnast?" he added in fun.

By some miracle, a large red-and-white boathouse hove into view at that moment. Its foundations were totally submerged but the trailer on the higher ground had been spared the wrath of the flood and appeared occupied. It wasn't the first time on this voyage that the sight of thick curling wood smoke lured us to a front door. Mooring alongside another boat on what should have been the lawn, we left the canoe and hurried up several steps to a porch. Two sodden and dejected black Labrador retrievers wagged their tails in friendly greeting as we knocked on the door.

"Er . . . bonjour," I began, not quite sure how best to put my request to this complete stranger, a plump jolly woman in a red fuzzy housecoat. I explained, with the help of my trusty dictionary, that we wished to use their bathroom since there was nowhere else to go. She beckoned us in just as a heavy rain descended with full force. Dripping and looking more than a mite embarrassed, we pulled off our rainsuits and hurriedly made for the loo.

The woman's husband watched all the commotion from the kitchen table with a twinkle in his eye. He leaned forward and looked out the window, then announced to his wife that we wouldn't be going anywhere for a while so she had better make more eggs and toast.

"Oh no," we protested feebly, "we really should be on our way."

"Are you sure?" he asked. "It's raining pretty hard."

"Well, that would be nice," I burst out quickly, in case Gary had thoughts of declining. The hot buttered toast looked awfully good and the rain-dotted river looked very cold and wet. The hospitable couple explained that this was their fishing camp and it had been one of the worst seasons they had ever experienced for flooding. They were already a month late in opening.

"By the look of things, we aren't going to open this week either," commented his wife as we watched a gaggle of fat white ducks swimming past the porch. Even the retrievers hardly gave them a second glance. Their noses sniffed the air but the poor creatures were so chilled that they simply whined and shivered miserably.

Most of the camp was under water. They were losing money every day and there was a ton of spring cleaning and maintenance to be tackled on the buildings and boats. We had to admire their optimism in the face of such difficulty.

"It can only get better," the woman chuckled.

"Yes," her husband agreed, "it can't get any worse!" A few mugs of coffee and many pieces of toast later, we parted company wishing one another a much drier and warmer June.

It was the end of May when we set off on the long and difficult day that would get us from one side of Montreal to the other. We were 15 miles from the outskirts of the city. From there, we faced another 10 miles past dockyards and busy shipping lanes. Tugboats circled around in the harbors pushing freighters into dock. No one could see our little canoe so our safety depended upon our judgment and our speed. At one point we remained in the same place for over half an hour just holding ground against the current. We felt completely out of place in our tiny craft. Paddling with all our strength, we could barely make more than three miles every hour. Our strokes were an endless, hard-fought rhythm. If we took even the shortest break, we were washed back downstream. There was nowhere to rest except in the eddies behind the docked ships where the Beware of Propwash signs had us thoroughly frightened. After nearly three hours of sprint-speed paddling kept up through fear alone, we arrived at the bottom of the Lachine Canal. This man-made waterway bypasses Montreal's Lachine Rapids.

Several fishermen standing at the riverside were curious about our journey. After explaining a little, we left our equipment under their watchful eye as we set out to explore the route to the canal. On the way back, we found a phone booth and stopped in to call a cinematographer who had been planning to meet us there. We told him our whereabouts, then returned to the river.

I heard Gary mutter, "Someone must've moved our packs." Then I too noticed the vacant spot beside the canoe. As we raced toward it, I had the sickening feeling that something was terribly wrong. We searched desperately for some sign that they were close at hand.

"It can't be!" I cried.

But it was true. All our clothing, except what we were wearing, our tent, cooking equipment, food and film, everything in the two packs had disappeared. Nearby, the fishermen were still casting and reeling quite contentedly as if nothing were amiss. They couldn't understand why we were so upset. Shaking off his initial reaction of shock and disbelief, Gary took control.

"Joanie, get the police while I try talking to these people."

I ran off, tears streaming down my face. How could this happen to us? Between sobs, I managed to convey my distressing story to a kindly gas-station attendant who summoned the police.

By the time I had returned with the officers, Gary had gathered a group of witnesses together who all had more or less the same story to tell. Apparently two people had arrived in a boat from across the river. When they picked the packs up, one fisherman asked what they were doing. Their response was prepared. Unhesitatingly, they replied that they were bringing us our equipment. The fisherman had no reason to doubt their connection with the expedition so made no attempt to stop them.

The situation was strangely calm. There was nothing we could do and the police did not think they would find anything, especially since they didn't possess a boat with which to make a shoreline search. Harbor police and no boat? It was true, we were told. Funding had been cut so severely that even with many miles of shoreline to patrol, they were expected to do their best without. One policeman told us that he and a few fellow officers had once formed a crack dive team that was capable of any type of search and rescue mission on or under the water. Their budget was cut, too, and the special force disbanded.

A short man waddled up, notepad in hand and camera slung about his neck.

"Oh, no," Gary groaned, "great time for the newspaper to arrive!"

But that wasn't all. The cinematographer Carmen Dodaro and his cheerful companion Martine also chose this moment to arrive on the scene. They were pleased to have found us. It meant we could begin filming right away. Being totally unaware of the situation, they figured it was some kind of friendly gathering. Then they noticed the police car. Once again we told our story, but this time it fell on entirely sympathetic ears.

As it was Sunday, the stores, offices and banks were all closed. There was little we could do until the following day, so we decided the best plan of action was to just keep paddling. We buttoned the tarpaulin and paddled an empty canoe, unknown to

the camera's eye, through the Lachine Canal to the mouth of the
Ottawa River. We had come through so much already that lost
equipment certainly wouldn't put an end to the journey. We
knew everything could be recouped; it was the question of how
long it would take that bothered us. The long day finally ended
when Carmen and Martine drove us and our remaining equipment to Ottawa and left us with Gary's uncle.

We had planned all along to stop in and visit Uncle Clayton
when we passed through via canoe. But now we were arriving a
little ahead of schedule and under different circumstances. He
didn't mind. He offered his home as a place to stay until we were
resupplied and on our way again.

The first morning in Ottawa was bedlam as we tried to work
out arrangements for compensation from the insurance company, contact companies involved in the expedition and work
out a new system of equipment. What had taken months to put
together would have to be replaced within as few days as possible. When we reached the point where we could do nothing for
a couple of hours, Uncle Clayton offered to take us to the
Central Experimental Research Farm where he works as an en-
tomologist. It is the only working farm within the limits of a capital city in Canada. At the entomology department, we were
shown a part of the vast collection of insects which ranged from
pinprick-size scarlet mites to large spiky beetles and brightly
colored butterflies. Drawers upon drawers of specimens con-
situted a collection on a par with that of the Smithsonian In-
stitute. We were impressed by the depth of concern and aware-
ness shown by some of the scientists regarding the complexities
of the lower part of the food chain. There are thousands of insect species left to discover. But because of the destruction of
rain forests and other wildlife habitats to satisfy man's demand
for natural resources and farmland, these insect species are disappearing before we have even had the opportunity of discovering the role they play within the web of living things.

Apart from the brief visit to the Experimental Farm, most of our
time was occupied with resupplying, reconstructing and sewing
our "system" back together again. Considering the months of or-
ganization and preparation that we had to undergo, the task at
hand was a formidable one. After taking stock of the situation, we
realized that the worst loss to us was one of the least valuable to the

thieves. Our logbook, one month of travel so faithfully recorded in words and sketches, probably lay discarded on a muddy bank. Immediately we set to work recalling the names and addresses of those people we had met. While the St. Lawrence leg of the journey was still fresh in our minds, Gary rerecorded it while I carried on with the daily diary.

Apart from the logbook, our first concern was money. Everything had been insured, but the company could hinder our progress for a considerable length of time by making us fill out forms and plow through red tape. We had only a small savings account which was by no means enough to get us going again. As we wracked our brains, a heartwarming phone call came through from London. Gary's parents were on their way up to Ottawa with our sewing machine, materials and anything else that looked useful. A group of Gary's teachers in the London Board of Education had taken up a collection on our behalf to help replace the losses. Then word was sent out through the media by the reporter from the *Montreal Journal*. Two mornings later, Alan Millar of CBC Radio made a plea for anyone knowing the whereabouts of our equipment to please turn it in to the Montreal police. It was unlikely anyone would, but we were touched by the expressions of concern and by the genuine interest in our journey. The money situation was finally solved when Labatt's came to our aid, agreeing to make the funds available until the insurance company repaid them.

One of the friends who rallied around to help was Tim Pychyl, who was in the outdoor equipment business. Since he had helped us over the winter, he knew exactly what we needed. Fortunately, all of the equipment and clothing manufacturers who had provided us with their products were keen to reequip us with what had been lost.

There was only one embarrassing note amid all the helping hands and kind hearts, and that was the media attention drawn to the journey because of the robbery. The *Montreal Journal* photographer had arrived innocently enough for a story on the expedition that fateful morning, but the resulting photo was captioned "Canoeists Delayed by Robbery." On the whole, the incident appeared to be undermining the significance of the journey. The media was not interested in all the individuals who had helped us, it seemed, nor were they interested in the whales we had encountered. We had struggled through one month of near-freezing weather and constant rain to traverse the historic St. Lawrence River in a canoe, yet these stories were being neglected in the face of the media's motto, "Bad news makes good news!"

# 4
# Whispers of the River Ghosts

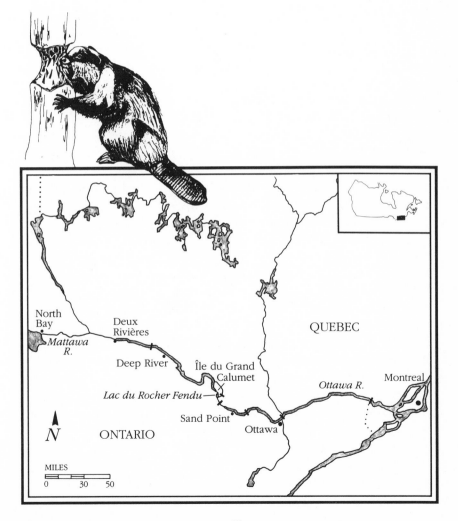

North
Bay
Deux
Rivières
QUEBEC
*Mattawa
R.*
Deep River
Île du Grand
Calumet
Montreal
*Ottawa R.*
*Lac du Rocher Fendu*
Sand Point
Ottawa
N
ONTARIO
MILES
0   30   50

A S THE CALENDAR flipped to June, the first month of summer, the barometer was rising. At the end of the unbelievably short span of four days, Gary's parents deposited us
and our fully loaded canoe back at the place where we had left
off on Lac des Deux Montagnes at the mouth of the Ottawa
River. The glorious summer weather, full of stirring life, was a
welcome change. As blue skies, sunshine and warmth brought
out large croaking bullfrogs, spring peepers and a profusion of
bursting lilac buds, we thankfully stuffed rainsuits and cold-
weather clothing to the very bottom of our packs. After waiting
so long for summer to arrive, it was pure bliss to soak up the
warm rays. However, within two days, Gary was suffering from
over indulgence. As he eased his scorched body from the canoe
and staggered stiff-legged up the bank like a cowboy with saddle
sores, I found it very hard to keep a straight face.

But the laugh was soon on me when I managed to overcook
my shoulders. Every time I picked up my 60-pound pack, the
straps rode on the blistered skin, causing my face to screw up
into a contorted expression of agony. The only consolation I
received was—"Be thankful we haven't reached Ottawa's portages yet!"—followed by a cheerful grin from the red-legged op-
timist as he waddled away.

From the moment we entered the Ottawa River at Lac des
Deux Montagnes, we were paddling on the first leg of a North
West Company fur trading route which led to the interior of the
nation. The fur trade, the oldest and longest-running industry in
Canada, was the economic backbone of European exploration. It
was born from the European demand for beaver pelts and
matured with the growing dependency of native tribes for white
men's goods. The pursuit of the beaver began in eastern North
America and worked its way up the St. Lawrence and Ottawa
River valleys. As the stocks were depleted in the face of ruthless
harvesting, fur traders moved farther and farther northwest.

By the late 1700s, the Athabasca country had become a very rich source of furs for the North West Company and it was time to organize and develop a transportation system that would move the pelts quickly to Europe. Several formidable challenges faced the Company. Access to Europe by way of Montreal and the St. Lawrence was over 3,000 miles from the fur-trapping lines. The versatile canoe, the only possible method of transportation across a land of lakes and rivers, could only travel 1,000 miles a month. With the harsh Canadian climate offering only five ice-free months, an annual return trip between Montreal and Lake Athabasca was impossible. The final challenge was the landscape which varied widely from enormous lakes to tiny streams and therefore necessitated the use of different-sized canoes.

The problems were overcome by the Montrealers when they divided the Montreal–Lake Athabasca route in two, working it with two different crews in different-sized canoes. The central depot was at Grand Portage on Superior's western shore. Here the smaller inland fur trade canoes, known as the North Canoes, carrying the winter's supply of furs met the Montrealers in their 36-foot birchbark *canots de maîtres* hauling their cargo of winter supplies and trade goods. In this way, both the cargos reached their respective destinations and the voyageurs also were able to return home, all within the span of the short ice-free season. Paddling our canoe on the Ottawa, we could not help but be reminded of this colorful era in Canadian history. Although this waterway has been drastically altered in the last hundred years by damming and habitation, there are still swift currents and the remnants of original portage paths.

Four days upstream from the Carillon Dam, we awoke to a cold, mizzly dawn in Rockcliffe Park on Ottawa's eastern fringe. We had been hoping for a day like this. Apart from giving us a respite from the burning sun, a drizzly day meant there would be few people on the riverside paths over which we would be portaging. Since the unfortunate experience in Montreal, we had developed an intense paranoia about leaving our equipment unattended around highly populated areas. Since each portage required two carries, we had to stifle our fear. The packs and the canoe were going to have to be left unguarded in order for us to get through the capital city.

Rising abruptly from the Ottawa River's placid south shore is a wall of imposing limestone cliffs. As we approached the city, we paddled by the point where the Rideau River makes its final plunge over the steep bank in a fleecy, white curtain. Far above us on a broad headland that dominates the landscape we saw the pointed towers and stone walls of the stately Parliament Buildings. We recalled reading about Queen Victoria bestowing the honor of capital city of Canada upon the rough-and-tumble lumber town of Ottawa in 1857. This appointment eliminated the rivalry between Toronto, Kingston, Montreal and Quebec, which were all vying for the position. We remembered reading a comment from that time describing Ottawa as a "sub-arctic lumber town converted into a political cockpit!"

Working our way below the cliffs as foaming whirlpools swirled beneath us, we arrived at the first of three portages. Where once the mighty Ottawa poured over the edge of a rocky formation called La Chaudière (meaning The Great Kettle), a dam now exists. It hides a thundering cataract where for centuries native tribes paid sacrificial homage to the spirits that dwelt within the mists. At the base of the Chaudière dam, we discovered an overgrown path which we followed up to a busy roadway. We waited for a break in traffic, then jumped the guardrail, bounded across the laneways, jumped the rail on the other side and breathed a sigh of relief. Trotting quickly on across a park, we arrived at the river's edge again. We dropped the packs. As we hustled back across the highway for the canoe, we were worried. All our equipment was now left unguarded. There were many people passing by, none of whom seemed to care about what we were doing. But then that was the way it had been in Montreal. All I could remember was the sickening sensation when I realized our packs were really gone. We threw the canoe over our heads and hightailed it back to the packs, arriving quite out of breath.

We had hardly launched the canoe before we were landing for the second portage. This one was longer. Half running, half walking we dashed through the riverside parks sharing the paved paths with only the occasional jogger willing to brave the rain. Taking care that no one saw us, we slipped into the shoreline foliage where we dumped our packs and camouflaged them with branches and leaves.

On the return journey with the canoe, we knew we were far more conspicuous. The drivers of cars, slowing along a very muddy section of road reconstruction, gave us long interested stares. We responded with friendly waves. The road crew stopped their work as we tiptoed our way through the chaotic rubble and weaved around orange markers with the traffic flow. Just as we were stepping around a deep pit, we heard a voice inquiring from below, "Where are you fellas going?" Peering down the hole, we looked into the grimy, smiling face of a workman.

"Across Canada!" I piped up from under the canoe. There was a pause as he digested the full meaning of my answer. "Where did you begin anyways?"

"The Gulf of St. Lawrence."

He was a little taken aback. "Where are you going then?"

"To the Beaufort Sea!"

The traffic gave him no time to reply. Impatient drivers were already honking their horns. One car wheeled by, throwing a brown wave of muddy water over us and the workman below. A stream of uncharitable comments burst from the hole. As we hurried off, we heard him yell, "Hey, good luck. Hope I read about you in the paper."

We dashed across the park and down to the riverside, feeling the anxious pangs of mistrust. Everyone we saw was a potential culprit. Even the most unlikely looking souls were on our suspect list should the packs not be there. We heaved a sigh of heart-felt relief when we lifted back the branches and there they lay.

As we lifted our packs from the canoe for the third and final portage, we surveyed the scene. A strong upriver wind was pressing the foam-capped waves into much more imposing crests than usual. It was hard to envision a canoe working its way against the strength of such a current, but the voyageurs did it just to avoid the dreaded portages. For the voyageurs, portages involved great physical hardship. To divide the load evenly, each man had to carry half a dozen 90-pound packs. Our humble effort of packing 60- to 70-pound loads was meager by comparison. The voyageur accomplished this incredible feat in three journeys over rough trails, through bog, swamp and forest. No wonder strangulated hernias were one of the highest causes of death among these men.

A loud clap of thunder urged us on to the head of the Deschênes Rapids. Docks with sailboats alongside them and several clean white buildings suggested possible shelter from the approaching storm. We weren't quite swift enough though; by the time we landed on the doorstep of the immaculate Britannia Yacht Club, we were a sogging, dripping pair. Nevertheless, the commodore made his two unannounced guests very welcome, plying us with hot tea and sandwiches from the club's cafeteria.

It was with some apprehension that we had anticipated our second visit to Ottawa. We had been forewarned that the large U.S. publication, *People Magazine*, would be flying up a writer and photographer to produce an article for one of their summer issues. When I heard that 26 million people read the magazine, I became terribly nervous. I kept wondering if I had all my historic, geographical and statistical facts about the trip right.

"This isn't a test," Gary chided. "They aren't going to give two hoots about when Mackenzie reached the Arctic Ocean or whether our canoe is 10 or 20 feet long."

The journalist spent an entire day filling notebooks with answers to questions on our personal lives and the experiences and feelings that we had developed about our country paddling this far. The photographer confirmed the direction the story was to take when she arrived with a clearcut assignment—to attain a photograph depicting a romantic moment in the canoe. Twenty rolls of film later, she felt she had the shot.

The photographer had flown straight in from New York City. She was utterly amazed at the beautiful rugged wilderness. We shrugged. This was a crowded community park with over half a million people on its doorstep. I informed her that once we were farther north there would be periods on our journey when we wouldn't see people for two weeks or more.

"No people?" she asked incredulously. "Won't you be scared? What if your canoe sinks? What if you get appendicitis or something?"

It seemed strange to tell someone whose home was in New York City that the large populated areas were far more frightening to us. At least in the wild places we just had each other to watch out for and to rely upon.

She looked us up and down. "How do you ever keep so clean?"

"Well, we love to swim," I answered, "and it wasn't the snow on the St. Lawrence that stopped us from going in! Some days we went to bed with smelly feet and greasy-feeling hair but those were the days when we were too thankful to be in a dry tent to care much about it. On nice days, I wash our clothes in the cooking pot and lay them out on the canoe packs to dry."

This photographer was as inquisitive as the writer had been. "But you must get tired and lonely?" she queried.

"We do, but we love it!" Gary replied. We tried to explain in a roundabout way that, yes, the expedition did entail plenty of discomfort at times, but it also offered a very comforting simplicity that is lacking in everyday life.

"Close your eyes for a minute," I instructed. "Imagine the cold rain driving in your face, trickling down your neck. Feel your feet going numb in soggy neoprene boots and your stomach growling because you have paddled 40 miles and the last meal you ate was eight hours ago. Now imagine a nice dry tent, a warm sleeping bag, a pair of wool socks and a mug of hot chocolate. It's not too difficult to appreciate the simple things in life under such circumstances."

The rest of the world with all its artificial problems all vanish in the concentration on our day-to-day efforts. There is a great sense of physical achievement that accompanies periods of grinding effort. As we paddle, we become part of the world around us and everything that happens has a direct effect on our day, our moods and our entire sense of being. Nothing is just visual since our senses become very perceptive to the smells, tastes, sounds and textures of our surroundings. We have time to talk, look, listen and dream.

We weren't sure if she gathered the full meaning of our message, but it certainly seemed to end the volley of questions. If the article in *People Magazine* would include something about the whales in the St. Lawrence and might encourage readers to appreciate the natural environment and their own physical well-being a little more, then we felt the two days spent in Ottawa would have been worthwhile.

It was hot, hazy and absolutely calm as we rounded the final bend before Chats Falls. Although the enormous dam structure placed our journey firmly in the twentieth century, it wasn't hard to imagine approaching this same place 200 years earlier. There wasn't a single soul around as we glided into the deep northeast bay below the dam and sought out the portage. As always when we discovered an "original path," we became very excited. An unmistakable trail had been etched in the ancient bedrock by hundreds of thousands of load-bearing footsteps. Through eyes that squinted against the salty sweat trickling from overheated brows, we envisaged ahead of us on that trail ghostly images of short, stocky voyageurs hunched and straining beneath bulky loads. Slowly and steadily we completed the portage, then forged against the icy spring-fed current.

Hot, hungry, thirsty and tired, we had lost most of our pep by the time we paddled past Arnprior and Braeside. We were just about to look for a campsite when the most delicious aroma of charbroiled steak wafted by our sensitive noses. We followed the smell with the eagerness of a hound on the scent of a deer. Then at Sand Point, quite unexpectedly a voice hailed us with a friendly welcome, "How about a cold beer?"

As if on cue, we both put on the brakes and swung our canoe around. There was no denying our enthusiasm for the offer. We quelled our feelings of greed and guilt and pulled up to the dock. Who was this wonderful person calling us in out of the blue?

It was a couple, Art and Betty Appleby, who had been on the lookout for us since our last radio broadcast from Ottawa. Once we began chatting and the maps were spread on the floor, we were there for the evening. Mr. Appleby explained that our journey was of special interest to him partly because of its adventureousness, but also because he was familiar with the northern system of lakes and rivers that we would be following. As an RCAF pilot in the geodesic survey detachment of the Department of Mines and Surveyors, he had flown surveyors all across the Canadian Arctic. North of The Pas from Reindeer Lake to the Boothia Peninsula and Victoria Island, he only had rough explorer maps to follow. Most often he navigated simply by the color and clarity of the water—the still waters of the lake being clear and the moving current of rivers disturbing the sediments into a muddy brown. Art flew ground surveyors into regions through the Mackenzie valley, and set up the physical radio sites in the region north of Yellowknife from which aerial mapping and surveying were verified. Gary and I studied the detailed topographic maps on the floor with growing appreciation for the years and the skills it had taken to create them.

Walking around their property on Sand Point the following morning, the Applebys discussed the local region's history. Before the water levels were raised in the early thirties with the building of hydroelectric dams, Sand Point had been a lengthy spit. Samuel de Champlain had supposedly camped here with his party while traveling up and down the Ottawa River in the early 1600s. Champlain, known in Canadian history as the Father of New France, established the first continuously occupied white settlement north of Florida in 1608—where Quebec City now stands.

Pointing at a large white house gracing the point, Art informed us that this was the Appleby homestead.

"The superintendant of the Brockville and Ottawa Railway lived there in the 1870s before the CNR was constructed. The railway came chugging up from the logging town of Arnprior. It turned around in the engine house situated right here." He strolled over to their stone barbecue and indicated the very spot. "From here, the freight loads were transferred to the steamship which docked at the pier upstream from Sand Point."

As we waved goodbye to more new friends, we viewed Sand Point in a different light. We no longer had just a present-day impression; the Applebys had peeled away layers of history to reveal a much broader perspective on this small piece of the Ottawa Valley.

The flocks of nesting gulls and terns on the tiny islands and shoals of the Ottawa River provided much entertainment as we paddled. They would rise in great swirling flocks screeching in indignation at our presence. They expressed their fright in copious droppings. We dared not look up. The first well-aimed bomb splattered across the map and Gary's outstretched legs. Several more landed on the packs where freshly washed socks had been laid out to dry. Just when we thought the bombardment had ended, a large herring gull rolled in out of the sun on broad angular wings. It dropped low, diving straight for the canoe. A volley of plops strafed the surface before spraying the bow deck and my lap with slimy whitewash. As it swept up toward the sky, I could have sworn there was a wicked look in those beady eyes.

Paddling among a few stray pulp logs, with the smell of wet wood hanging in the air, we were sent off into another world by the steady rhythm of strokes. We imagined the Ottawa Valley as it must have been 300 years ago, wall-to-wall trees. Towering far above them all would have been the majestic white pine extending thick feathery branches upward as if holding up the sky. But the vast forests of durable, arrow-straight pine were doomed when the Napoleonic Wars cut off Britain's supply of shipbuilding timber from Europe. The British turned to Canada's vast forests, and lumbering became British North America's number one industry during the 1800s. The log drive would begin during spring breakup. Millions of logs were moved on the swollen spring currents of the smaller rivers from which they eventually swept into the Ottawa. After the timber had been squared, sorted and assembled into great log booms, they were guided down rapids and towed across lakes until they reached Quebec City. From there, entire forests were shipped across the ocean.

In our mind's eye, we recreated the atmosphere of the legendary log drives. We "heard" old fiddle tunes as we belted out the words to frolicking songs like "Big Joe Mufferaw paddling up the Ottawa . . . ." The life of a lumberman a century ago was fraught with danger and hardship. He could drown pulling the last of the logs from the bush onto soft spring ice. Even more dangerous was the job of wrestling log jams in the frigid waters of swollen rapids. Too little speed, a misplaced foot or a careless slip took the life of many an unfortunate "white-water man" as he tried to scramble to safety across the seething jumble of wood.

Halfway between Montreal and Mattawa, the Ottawa splits into two main channels around Ile du Grand Calumet. The western route was shorter by miles, but because of the tremendous spring runoff, the rapids would be high and the current strong. For the most part the Ottawa River's power has been harnessed for hydroelectricity, but this six-mile passage has retained its wildness. On Lac du Rocher-Fendu, we made our decision. We would follow the voyageurs' example and take the eastern Quebec-side route which involved one long carry past the major drop, then smooth sailing for 20 miles. The two-mile Grand Calumet portage would be the longest we faced east of the nine-mile Grand Portage out of Lake Superior. Heading toward the dam, we passed through a bay peppered with deadheads and floating pulp logs. It saddened us to know that these bays were once productive spawning beds for sturgeon and pickerel. But these beds have long since disappeared beneath piles of waterlogged and rotting timber.

Scaling the steep bank with canoe and packs, we emerged onto a dusty gravel road. The sun was already very intense for mid-morning. During the first two-mile trudge with the packs, we grew very thirsty. On the return journey for the canoe, we were considering having a drink at the next farmhouse's garden hose when Gary spotted a brand new .22-caliber rifle in the long grass at the roadside. Since it had only a few surface scratches, we figured it must have fallen from someone's truck. Half a mile farther on we turned into a laneway and knocked on the door.

A little French woman answered. Gary had said hardly two words about the gun when she burst out ecstatically, "You've made my boy's day!" Relief mixed with joy was written all across her face.

In return for our good deed, she brought us a large pitcher of orange juice jangling with ice cubes. Her husband offered to truck our canoe around the dam, but we declined, explaining that we wished to make the journey as best we could under our own steam.

Back on the trail, plodding along with the canoe weighing heavily on our shoulders, I thought we must be absolutely mad. "It's over a hundred degrees," I grumbled. "My neck's bruised, the sweat's stinging my eyes and my feet are sore from walking in wet boots." Gary didn't say a word. But after dropping the canoe at the end of the portage, he whisked me off my feet and ran into the coolness of the river.

Gary certainly knew how to respond to my emotional swings. When I was scared for my life on the St. Lawrence, he channeled my anxiety into anger. That anger, no matter who or what it was directed against, made me a stronger, more aggressive paddler and got us to safety that much faster. When I was bored with a tedious section of the river, my senses would suddenly awaken when prodded by a few of Gary's comments about sights, sounds or smells around us. The flood of observations that ensued kept me enthralled for hours on end.

The steep-walled corridor and the east-west lie of the Ottawa River makes the area prone to strong westerly winds. However, the weather since leaving the St. Lawrence had been unusually calm and scorching hot. The only force to slow us was the current, and even it was much subdued by the hydro dams.

Late one afternoon, after some heavy stroking up a long stretch of swift water, we agreed to push on as far as the little village of Westmeath and then call it a day. In the shade of a big old basswood tree, we pitched our tent. Leaving me to finish making camp, Gary set off for Westmeath with his camera. As well as taking some photographs, he was planning to bring us back some thirst-quenching treats for supper. While pulling out sleeping bags and pads and laying out the food and cooking equipment, I chattered and sang to myself in a nonsensical manner. Suddenly I stopped, feeling that a pair of eyes were on me. Turning toward one of the rear openings in the tent, I spied a little face topped with a mop of red hair which then disappeared. I unzipped the door and hopped out, coming face to face with the surprised expressions of an entire family. They were clad in swim suits and had fishing rods in hand. The little redheaded "peeping Tom" tugged on his mother's arm and asked forthrightly, "Why does that girl have such a funny face?"

Some might have been a bit taken aback but I knew he was quite right. To greet them, I had removed my mirrored sunglasses, unintentionally revealing my strange "owl" eyes. The sun had branded my cheeks and nose, leaving large pale circles where my glasses had been.

We quickly made friends and they soon invited us for breakfast the following morning. When I declined, explaining that the cool, early dawn comprised our most cherished paddling hours, Pat, the father, replied, "No problem, we're early birds too! You name the time and we'll be up. Just look for the oldest, shabbiest house on Main Street and you'll have found us."

"Shabby" seemed an unkind way to describe one's own house, but they weren't kidding. The two-storey house with its sagging porch, peeling white paint and overgrown bramble hedges created in us a strong sense of melancholy. But the first feelings of emptiness as we traipsed up the dew-soaked path fell away as we opened the creaking kitchen door. The kitchen, with its high ceiling and pale green walls, was graced by an old wood cookstove. The stove was the centerpiece and source of heat for the home. On its smooth surface lay a pan of sizzling bacon and a plate of delicious-smelling toast. Pat looked up from his cooking.

"Good morning, c'mon in. Another fine day for canoeing." He grinned. "You thought we were joking about our house, didn't you? Well, she may look decrepit now, but underneath it all, she has fine character."

He explained that he had recently moved his family into this small town, only 15 miles from his parents' farm, after the hectic pace of southern Ontario life had become unbearable. The two children enjoyed school in a one-room schoolhouse with a teacher who genuinely cared for teaching. They had planted a vegetable garden as soon as they arrived and the fresh produce, combined with eggs and milk from the family farm, helped their budget enormously. Pat's latest bit of economizing involved the drivebelt on the waterpump. He used corn syrup from the kitchen in place of expensive belt dressing.

Pat's wife, also named Pat, explained that they had arrived in the spring to find the rooms piled high with junk left by a long list of previous owners. "But," said her husband proudly, "this is the oldest house in Westmeath, and we have wonderful plans for it!"

As we watched the foursome wave goodbye from the porch an hour later, we agreed that there was a family that would not go hungry for food or happiness.

Bounded by the placid Ontario farmlands to the south and the dark, mysterious Laurentian hills to the north, the broad Ottawa River drains a great wilderness dappled with gleaming lakes and lively streams. At Lac des Alumettes, we saw the granite of the Precambrian Shield touch the river's edge for the first time since we had paddled by the great buttress on which Quebec City stands. Steep cliffs plunged from hundreds of feet above us to submarine depths far below. As we left the populated south behind, we welcomed the wild ruggedness of the landscape that was now drawing in around us.

Each week since the start of the trip, Gary had been jokingly hinting to our friends at CBC Radio that they should join us along a stretch of the Ottawa River. This section was as close as we would come to Toronto. One Thursday morning, the producer Bob Burt expressed his keenness to accompany us. The only problems were his lack of a canoe, equipment and a partner. For most the idea would have been dropped right there, but Gary had a solution tucked away in the back of his mind.

"I know! There's Phil Chester!"

Gary had met Phil the previous year. He was a teacher in Deep River where he lived with his wife and three small children. Since his home was right on our route, he had encouraged us to stop in for a visit on our way through the Ottawa Valley. He was a well-built fellow with a fiery character and a heart of gold. Phil always seemed to be heading off in a dozen different directions. Besides teaching school and spending time with his family, he managed to squeeze in playing with the local leagues in the hockey and baseball seasons. His love of the outdoors and of canoeing led us to believe that there might be an outside chance he could organize some way for Bob to paddle with us.

On Friday evening, we pulled ashore at the prearranged rendezvous at Deux Rivières. We made camp on a warm sandy beach where masses of tiger swallowtail butterflies had congregated. There we waited for Bob and his unwitting partner, Steve Starchev. Steve was a CBC Radio technician and musician and, as far as we knew from Phil, had only paddled a canoe once in his life. Bob had planned a fairly lengthy route—30 miles from Deux Rivières to the Mattawa River and 10 miles up the Mattawa to Samuel de Champlain Provincial Park.

"I hope they know what they're getting into," I remarked, somewhat dubiously.

"No problem," said Gary. "It'll be fun!"

Shortly thereafter, a baby-blue Cadillac wheeled smoothly down the laneway from the highway, its convertible top rolled back, and two familiar faces hailed us from behind the windscreen. The classy spectacle was closely followed by a rather dingy yellow vehicle sporting a well-loved cedar-strip canoe on top. Phil Chester's "old yellar" was stuffed full of paddles, life jackets and other canoe-tripping paraphernalia. Bob leapt out excitedly, not knowing whether to shake Gary's hand or hug me first, so he did both at once.

"Gee, you're lookin' great! It sure is good to see you guys!" Bob was bursting with vigorous energy as usual.

Quiet, smiling Steve joked about his ability to travel so far by canoe. "Bob says we can make it, no problem! But pencil-pushing is not exactly guaranteed to build the physical stamina needed for a 40-mile canoe trip."

While Steve agreed to stay behind with the equipment and set up camp, we roared off up the highway with Bob leading and Phil in hot pursuit. The tentative plan was to leave Bob's car at the provincial park, then have Phil drive the three of us back to Deux Rivières. Bob and Steve would accompany us to the park via canoe on the Saturday, then pick up their car and return to Toronto. On Sunday morning, Phil would drive from Deep River with his children and paddle partway up the Mattawa River with us.

It was pitch black by the time we returned to Deux Rivières where poor Steve was being eaten alive by the mosquitoes. "There seem to be a few holes in your screen, Bob," grumbled Steve, with some annoyance.

It occured to us that neither of them appeared to have any food with them. We offered what we had, but Bob waved our offer aside. He bustled up to the general store and returned moments later with a small brown paper bag containing no more than a bottle of cola and a bag of chips.

"Oh, for heaven's sake, Bob," Steve lamented. "Couldn't you do better than that?"

A little later, when we were all tucked in our tents, we could hear a lot of wild slapping.

"Close the door, c'mon close it! We're getting eaten alive!" Then came the crinkling sound of the chip bag being opened and the fizz of soda pop. Nylon walls are thin, inadequate sound barriers. We could even hear Steve's quiet voice: "Chips and pop?! I can just imagine what breakfast is going to be!"

"Canoeing's fun. You'll love it!" said the cheerful Bob before they finally settled down for the night.

Gary leaned over and whispered, "Tomorrow is going to be a day neither of them will ever forget!"

It was 5 A.M. Bob was jogging back and forth in front of the tents wailing out some tune off-key. He stopped near our door. "A little cold," he shouted, folding his arms and doing a little jig on the spot. Meanwhile, Steve was left to battle the mosquitoes that slipped in through the open door.   In a minute Bob returned to his tent, opening the zipper and letting in more mosquitoes.

"Close the door, Bob!"

Still lying in our sleeping bags, we heard the valves on their air mattresses being released and their one garbage-bag pack being stuffed.

"Hey, would you guys like some oatmeal?" Gary called out.
"No, that's OK," answered Bob. "We'll get a snack later."
"Yeah, right Bob," commented Steve. "How about some coffee?"
"C'mon Steve, let's get this show on the road!" declared Bob as he pulled the tent apart. "We've got a long way to go."
"You're not kidding!"

For the first five miles they were a chipper pair setting a stern pace. We were impressed. But during the next five, the scorching sun burned through dawn's cool protective mist and the upstream current grew stronger. Their tireless pace slowed considerably. The water was quite calm and, with little effort, we were pulling ahead. Every now and then we stopped to listen to their comments echoing over the water.

"What beats me," said Bob, "is how they keep getting so far ahead when we're practically dying."

"Dying! Who cares about that? I just don't think my fingers will ever pluck a twelve-string guitar again!"

We felt a bit like the carrot in front of the donkey—keeping just far enough ahead so that they could keep paddling by concentrating on us instead of on the endless river. We looked back in time to see Steve slither down the back side of the bow seat like a lump of jelly. We paddled back to him and I produced bandages from the first aid kit and applied them to his swelling blisters.

At Mattawa, they collapsed on the riverbank. The thought of 10 more miles did not rate overwhelming applause . . . but lunch did.

On the final leg of our marathon, we turned west off the Ottawa and directed our canoe into the outflowing Mattawa River. This thin ribbon of river winds its way down from Trout Lake on the east side of the watershed divide at North Bay, Ontario. It was an important link in the fur trade route and, for the most part, remains pristine.

Little Plain Champ Dam is the first of 11 historic carrying places. With slouching shoulders and squelching sneakers, Bob and Steve heaved their canoe, bags and bicycle pump across the trail. Later on, while meandering through a steep cut of granite rock which was ablaze with evening's orange glow, Steve delved into his duffle bag and withdrew a tin flute. Pushing back his floppy denim hat, he began to play. Clear sweet notes trickled forth, then grew in crescendo from a soft pitch to a frolicking tune of Irish origin. Darkness stealing across the eastern horizon ended the music and a 16-hour day on the river.

"Lord, we must've walked 20 miles to get this baby," Bob lamented, referring to the Cadillac by the river's edge. Steve and I looked at one another. Gary and Bob had gone to fetch the car from the park entrance only 15 minutes before.

"You guys must've wondered what happened to us," Bob sounded concerned.

"Paddle 40 miles, feel like you have walked 20, then drive 300—all in one day," joked Gary.

Sunburned, blistered and sore, they thanked us with sincere appreciation. We found their gratitude especially touching after the rigorous day they had endured!

Phil Chester was at the park bright and early the next morning with his young son and daughter. Together we fished, swam, roasted hot dogs and even managed to paddle a few miles and cross a few portages.

Each portage had been named by the voyageurs for some event or characteristic of the trail. Portage des Rochers was a path of scrambled boulders and Portage de la Cave passed through a short dark woodland. Rapide des Perches was so named because it was the final section of upriver paddling for the Montrealers after which they threw away their perches, or setting poles. (Saplings of approximately 10 feet in length were cut and shod with metal to form the setting poles that the voyageurs sometimes used in ascending rapids. The technique of poling, still very much in existence, required timing and balance on the part of the poler who stood in the canoe's stern.)

Phil and his little team helped carry our equipment around Paresseux Falls before turning back.

"It sure has been fun," said Phil in a rather serious tone. He stuffed a piece of homemade friendship cake into our hands along with a copy of *Pilgrims of the Wild* by Grey Owl. Phil deeply respected and admired this famous author and conservationist. Through his books and powerful lectures, Grey Owl had battled for the rights of wildlife and native people. After his death, it was discovered that, although he had lived his life in the Canadian wilderness as an Indian, he was born an Englishman and was named Archie Belaney.

After reaching North Bay near the end of June, we would both return home to visit with our families for a few days. Gary's parents picked him up and drove north to Temagami, while I caught the bus and headed south to Bracebridge. Seeing my family was both a joyful and a sad occasion. I was excited to see everyone and bursting with stories to tell, but my grandmother's health had taken a final downward turn.

My grandmother had always played a special role in my childhood and adolescence. The fact that she lived in England, 3,000 miles away in a different world, made the desire to see her all that much more intense. Every three years, I managed to fill my bank account with enough funds to purchase a ticket overseas. The excitement was in the planning and dreaming of an adventure in a far-off land. During my grandmother's life, she had loved traveling and living in different parts of the world with her husband, a soldier, and her only child, my mother. Hearing her stories and looking at her albums of black-and-white photos undoubtedly contributed to the development of my love for adventuring. When at age 81 she left England to come and live with us in Canada, it seemed perfectly natural. She spent two very happy years in Bracebridge with my parents. She had taken great delight and interest in our trek through the Appalachians in 1981 and drove to Maine with my mother to meet us at the trail's end. It pleased her immensely to take part in the canoe expedition plans and the wedding preparations of her first grandchild.

It was distressing to find someone I loved so crippled. When I saw Nana for the first time in nearly two months, I found her pale and withered. Stifling the tears, I sat on the edge of her bed as I had been doing since I was a little girl.

"I've come home to tell you of our adventures on the St. Lawrence!" I smiled, taking her thin hand in mine. How many countless times had she told me stories sitting at my bedside in England? I launched into hair-raising accounts of being swept from shore by the ebbing tides. I could feel her grip tightening. I told her of the snow geese and the whales and her pale blue eyes sparkled. I even managed to make her laugh out loud, something she had not done for days. Two days after I had arrived home, Nana passed away in her sleep. We held a quiet memorial service in the church where we had gathered for a much happier occasion only eight weeks before.

Since we first began planning the canoe voyage, my parents had hoped to accompany us on the French River west of North Bay and Lake Nipissing. Nana's death did not deter them, for despite the deep sense of grief and loss, there was above all a feeling of heartfelt relief that the suffering had ended. We thought the canoe trip would be wonderfully therapeutic for them. So the prospect of this venture, and our consolation in knowing Nana would be with us all in spirit, left us with light and happy hearts as the visit home drew to an end.

# 5
# Nu-tache-
# wan-asee

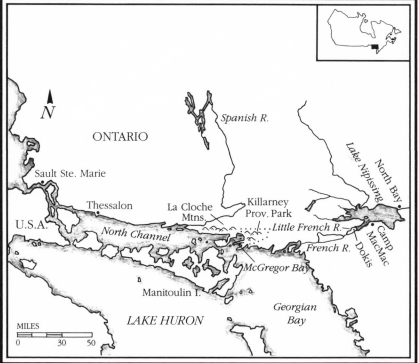

L AKE NIPISSING IS an expansive body of shallow water found in the depressed corridor of land between the Ottawa Valley to the east and the Great Lakes to the west. When the glaciers retreated, they left this elongated puddle that splashes out in all directions. Its northern shoreline is scalloped like the edge of a puffy cloud. The southeastern corner is drawn into deep elongated bays sprinkled with dozens of shoals and islands. The western end is fringed with the watery tendrils of the Sturgeon River, Veuve River, Macpherson Creek, Amateewakea River and the French River. All of these drain into Lake Nipissing except the French. As it leaves Lake Nipissing, the French River splits into two channels, the French and the Little French, which flow around Okikendawt Island. The channels converge, then split again into the North and Main Channels around Eighteen Mile Island before bearing straight west for Georgian Bay.

It was June 27 when we entered Lake Nipissing by way of a tributary called La Vase River. The air hung heavy with humidity. Far to the west the horizon could barely be distinguished from the oily smooth waters. Although the heat tended to lull us into a state of lethargy, a persistent whisper in the corner of my mind wouldn't let me forget how vulnerable we were to the stiff winds and steep, choppy waters that could arise so quickly on this lake. Nipissing was deceptive, and therefore dangerous. We heeded the advice of our "little whispers" for they were born of experience and our respect for the lake brought on by the stories Gary's parents had told.

*Lake Nipissing: July, 1949*

*The gleaming lines of a freshly varnished fishing craft split the oncoming swell with remarkable agility. The navigator was cleverly maneuvering through the choppy seas on a course where the wind deflected the spray away from the boat's interior. His one excited passenger perched on the*

*edge of the seat clutching the painter, or bowline, in one hand, the gun-*
*wale in the other. Her brown wavy hair was neatly tucked under a red*
*peaked cap. She wore a smart wool lumberman's jacket and red rubber*
*boots turned down at the top. Every now and then she would swing*
*around, beaming at her husband in the stern. The irrepressible warmth*
*of her smile revealed her love of being out with him in the brisk weather.*

*Half a mile from shore and just ahead, the* Chief Commanda, *Lake*
*Nipissing's supply ship and ferry boat, had slowed. Her heavy steel hull*
*was gently pitching to and fro in the choppy swell. The couple nuzzled*
*their small fishing boat under her great cargo doors. These were im-*
*mediately thrust open by a couple of sturdy deckhands. From the hold,*
*there appeared hefty crates of supplies which were lowered into the waiting*
*boat. As the cargo descended, the man at the fishing boat's helm con-*
*tinued skillfully to readjust their position in relation to the huge ferry.*
*When their weekly cargo had all been stashed safely on board, the couple*
*backed away from the* Chief Commanda. *A 45-gallon drum of fuel was*
*rolled from the cargo doors into the lake. The fishing craft circled in on*
*the floating drum, then secured it to the stern with a length of rope.*
*Slowly the boat turned and chugged off toward the fledgling camp on the*
*southern shore of Lake Nipissing. The name* Camp MacMac *was*
*emblazoned proudly under the gunwales along each side of the craft.*
*Mervin and Loreen were putting down the McGuffin family roots in*
*northeastern Ontario.*

We swept by Callander Bay, then out beyond Deepwater Point,
traversed South Bay and snuck by the famed Cross Point where
the winds come hurtling in from all directions. The afternoon
passed quickly. Our arms were paddling but our minds were on a
certain Camp MacMac that once stood on these shores all those
years ago. Gary's parents had sold their camp in 1951. They then
built themselves a wooden cabin cruiser and set out to explore
the intricate coast of Georgian Bay. They had no idea what became of Camp MacMac after they left. We had marked the
camp's location on our topographic map with a tiny red X. What,
we wondered, would we find there now? Even if the camp were
still in existence, it would probably not resemble the place we
knew from a few faded photographs.

Noticing a Powassan cedarstrip boat trolling along the shore,
Gary snatched up the binoculars. I could sense his excitement as
his lips mouthed the words. "MacMac. It says Camp MacMac!" His

voice rose. As we stepped up our pace, the canoe skimmed across the surface. We gained on the craft as it passed around the point into the curved sandy bay. We stopped paddling and let the canoe drift forward until it came to rest against the beach. Looking about us, we had a strange sensation that we had been here before. I wriggled my toes in the coarse, granular sand, remembering Loreen's words, "The sand feels just like brown sugar."

We roamed among the utility buildings and cedar cabins. It was nearly all the familiar handiwork of Gary's parents. It appeared that subsequent owners had simply made additions rather than alterations. There were the outhouses where Loreen had dug, as instructed by Merv, "until your head disappears from sight." Down by the shore, there were the blueberry bushes thick with this year's crop of ripening berries.

The fishermen had come in off the lake for the evening and most of them had gathered around our canoe. One man, quite a bit older than his two companions, was very inquisitive about our journey. After talking for a while, we learned that he had been coming to this place on and off for years.

"Hey, did you know a McGuffin built this place?"

Gary decided to have some fun and find out a little family history. "Is that right?" he asked innocently. "Was he much of a fisherman?"

"I've never seen anyone then or since who could catch fish like that guy! Biggest muskie I ever saw came in on the end of his line. Yes sir, if you wanted to catch fish, you came to Camp Mac-Mac!"

"You could learn a lot from somebody like that."

"Darn right! He's probably forgotten as much as anyone will ever know about the bush or this lake."

Gary smiled. "Yeah, I might just know who you're talking about."

By now the wind had kicked up a brisk chop on the bay. It was time to go. We still had some distance to cover before reaching the Dokis Marina. It was there that my parents, John and Jennifer Wood, were to meet and accompany us for our descent of the French River. The semicircle of fishermen pressed in closer as we launched the canoe and struck out for the point. Our last view of MacMac before rounding the point was of the friendly gathering on the sandy beach that felt like brown sugar.

Slipping through some islands and rounding a final jut of land before reaching the Dokis Indian Reserve, we spied a red canoe resting on its side next to the landbound hull of the *Chief Commanda*. Our pace quickened as we caught sight of my parents waving from the pier. I was very excited indeed. They were so well organized, having followed our instructions right down to the point of attaching their waterproof sacks to the canoe thwarts. I could see by the number of plastic shopping bags being tucked into various pockets and packs that we were going to eat well for the next few days.

Just as we were about to take off, a large broad-chested man dressed in coveralls patched at the knees and elbows ambled down to the water's edge. Topping off his round, jolly face was a blue and white cap stencilled with the words *St. Clair Dokis & Sons*. He wrapped his great bear paw hand around my own and squeezed it warmly.

"Hello, my name is St. Clair Dokis, chief of the Dokis Indian band."

Chief Dokis was proud of the marina operation he ran here on the reserve with his wife and seven sons. St. Clair explained that the island we were on was called *Okikendawt*, which was Ojibwa for "Dokis." He had lived here his entire life. In fact, his father had been the local mail carrier for years, driving a dogsled team between North Bay and Georgian Bay in winter. In summer, he had done it all by canoe. Chief Dokis informed us that the decrepit old ferry boat pulled ashore was the first generation of the *Chief Commanda*s. This was in fact the same ferry that had delivered supplies to Camp MacMac in the early days. Now a much larger, more modern *Chief Commanda II* plies the waters of Lake Nipissing.

Before we left, he presented each of us with a cap exactly like his own. We all removed the hats we were wearing, tucked them away and donned these new ones. Chief Dokis beamed with pleasure and pride as we all paddled away wearing our brand new headgear.

Within the hour we had made camp with my parents, overlooking a narrow deep water channel splitting two islands. On the smooth granite ledge, Jenny laid out the silverware, tea cups and saucers, and papertowel napkins. Gary cooked hamburgers, I tossed a salad and John picked blueberries. We gathered around the campfire to eat supper and study the maps. The flickering light illuminated the paper as Gary's forefinger traced out the route to the north. The Little French River twisted around the perimeter of Okikendawt Island. Its varying course revealed narrow constrictions which would undoubtedly be cascades and rapids. We hoped these would prove navigable. Then, at precisely 9:30 P.M., the mosquitoes appeared in droves chasing us into the tents for the night.

As I lay in my sleeping bag half-awake, straining to catch the distant hooting of a barred owl, I drifted off into a troubling dream. I was lunging for a strong brace on the current that poured beneath the bow of the canoe. I was anxiously searching for the downstream route yet I could find none. In every direction the river only poured toward us, over us, under us but never with us. The following morning, I related this dream to the others as we approached the first set of rapids known as Free Flowing Channel. Gary suggested that what was just ahead would quickly put to rest my anxious subconscious.

Free Flowing Channel is actually a small gorge where the river empties through a cut barely 10 feet across and bound by sheer 20-foot granite walls on either side. Leaving the canoes at the upper end of the portage path, we picked our way along the trail which was strewn with glossy-leaved poison ivy. From the top edge of the gorge's walls, we reconnoitered the rapid. It would be a short, tight run. Apart from simply staying upright, responding immediately to the waves rebounding off the walls by bracing and drawing would be the challenge. From either side, my parents had a terrific vantage point from which to watch us descend.

Riding on the smooth dark V, we were swept through the opening, committed. In such a constricted channel, the rebounding waves between the walls created some very forceful surges. The bow submerged then reappeared as a wave went rolling along the deck and pouring off the sides. Then to the sound of cheers from above, we emerged safely in the pool below.

After my parents had portaged their equipment around the little gorge, we all donned life jackets and hurled ourselves into the wider rapids at the bottom for a cool swim. Floating on our backs and traveling the river roller coaster feet first, we frolicked there for nearly an hour before striking out again.

The midday sun, clear and dazzlingly bright, shone out of a deep blue sky. Boils, swirls and ripples across the surface caused its reflection to shatter into a trillion fragments that glittered and sparkled on the flowing river. Our canoes slid past ancient granite walls that lined the riverbanks. Along these rocks, we examined the strange graffiti. During spring, yellow pollen drifting from the pines settled on the water. At the river's edge, it melded to the rough granite, forming perfectly parallel bands, highly visible when the summer river level was two feet lower.

Later we discovered another sign of fluctuating water levels. The beaver lodges in the area were enormous, sometimes measuring more than the length of our canoe and the height of a man. Fresh leafy twigs protruding from the jumbled mat of branches forming the structure hinted at the beaver's presence. Before winter, these industrious rodents collect an abundance of branches, mostly poplar and birch, and store them on the lake bottom near the lodge's underwater entrance. Throughout the months when the lakes and rivers freeze solid, the beavers dive from their lodge's hidden entrance beneath the ice and feed from their underwater larder.

On an inside river bend where at one time the water had raced far higher and faster there were two circular bowls of rock as large as round as bathtubs. Kettles, as they are known, are formed when a small rock finds its way into an indentation in the bedrock. The current swirls it around in the same place. As the pocket grows deeper, other pebbles called grinders join the first stone and they swirl with one another. Over thousands of years, this natural tumbling machine creates marble-smooth rocks and conversely, the stones create ultra-polished basins. While paddling to James Bay on the Missinaibi River three years earlier, we had discovered many kettles at Thunder House Falls. Some were enormous while others were only several inches in diameter yet so deep that when we threaded a six-foot fishing pole into them, we could not touch bottom.

At Five Finger Rapids, the French River splits, sluicing through a series of channels none of which we dared to run. At the portage's lower end, a wall of high rock overhanging a deep-water channel provided us with a wonderful spot to dive and swim. At Little Pine Rapids, we plunged through a very narrow and deep chute to avoid the shallow staircase of rocks that fans out across the rapid. Farther downstream on Big Pine Rapids, we plunged through the steepest standing waves with a whoop of delight. In a moment, the river was filling the canoe, and the packs, still attached by a length of webbing and a climbing carabiner, bobbed around in the floating bathtub. Struggling to balance the wallowing craft, we managed to keep it upright and paddle out of the current. On shore, the water was quickly dumped and the waterproof packs laid back in the hull.

I saw my parents trotting down the shore toward us. Soaked and grinning sheepishly, I admitted, "We were showing off a bit!"

The following morning in the small bay above Blue Chute, we sighted a lone pine. Having been struck by lightning, it was now just a skeleton of its former self. The long, straight limbs encircling the trunk were decorated with the hunched figures of roosting turkey vultures. We stared up at them and they down at us, until we drifted around the next river bend.

The current picked up speed carrying us smoothly on its back toward the entrance to Blue Chute. As the bow slipped over the lip, there was no turning back. But this time we had attached the tarpaulin to keep out the water. Rushing headlong into the bouncing waves, our canoe split the white foam flinging it away to the sides.

As the waves diminished and the river settled into a steady flow, we angled for shore in time to photograph my parents paddling down. First the tip of Jenny's red hat appeared above the lip of the rapid; then Jenny, the canoe and John taking up the stern. Through the telephoto lens on the camera, I watched their expressions of intense concentration as the canoe slid swiftly toward the bucking waves. Although they had studied the river from the bank before proceeding down, their view from water level was entirely different.

John angled the canoe a little too far left.

"Go right!" I burst out. But the warning was swept away in the rapid's roar.

The wave curling in off the left side of the big V caught the bow on an angle. The canoe lifted smoothly on the crest and rolled. While Jenny's paddle whirled around like a windmill gone wild, John grabbed for the gunwales. With no paddle support on the water, over they went.

In an instant, Gary was throwing John and Jenny a line and pulling them and their canoe to shore. Jenny's sodden hat completely covered her eyes, but I glimpsed a beaming smile.

John was laughing heartily. "I guess I need a bit more practice!"

"Well, get ready! There's Parisienne Rapids and Crooked Rapids coming up!" Gary winked at me knowingly. They wouldn't tip again today.

Two afternoons later, we were bound for the highway crossing the French River. Thick storm clouds had spread across the sky. Pink streaks of forked lightning darted earthward followed closely by a volley of thunder. We hurried on with three more miles to go. The rising wind carried the smell of rain. A dark curtain unfurled, spilling its contents across the land from the Great Lakes eastward. Just as the first droplets splattered around us, we ducked under the shelter of the marina's covered docking facilities. Quietly we all assisted in the unpacking of my parents' canoe. Gary and John returned to the Dokis Marina for the car while my mother and I readied our last supper. This was the end of our voyage together. A lot of water would pass beneath our canoe before we saw one another again. Later, we exchanged big hugs and kisses, then we struck out for the river mouth and Georgian Bay.

Fingers of smooth granite rock jutted out from the mouth of the French River. Scarred and scoured by the immense weight of the ice-age glaciers 10,000 years ago, the eastern shore of Georgian Bay is sprinkled with hundreds of shoals and islands. Shoulder to shoulder we hunched over the map determining a route through the natural maze. The scale of our map was small so that a lot of topographic detail was lost. In behind the islands bunched close to shore, the view to the horizon was completely obscured. Once in the canoe, the difficulty would lie in navigating among a bed of shoals and small islands where the landforms appeared to meld into one another creating solid barriers. Weaving through the pink and black shoals gave us a sensation almost like flying as we stared into the clear water. Our attentiveness to the obstacles that lurked below us was far more acute than would normally be necessary on a glassy smooth lake. Mountains of rock would rise to the surface. Their summits were black and almost invisible. I would shudder whenever the canoe would come within inches of striking one. Traveling over the unrippled bays, we were more tense than when paddling in white water. All of a sudden, a hair's breadth from the bow, a big shape would lunge upward. Quickly I would pry the hull away, then another would rise on the other side. I constantly pried and drew on my paddle while Gary steered our long-term course through the islands.

In the 40 miles between the mouth of the French River and the fishing village of Killarney, we slipped through the maze as much as possible in order to avoid the full force of the afternoon westerlies across this water body known as the sixth Great Lake. The snow-white hills of the La Cloche Range appeared above the northern horizon as we rolled across the last open stretch of water before reaching the protection of the islands once again. Killarney Provincial Park occupies part of this magnificent quartzite range. We had never visited the area before now, but we knew the region was becoming increasingly well known for one thing. Sadly, it is that all the park's lakes can no longer support fish and other aquatic life because of the fallout of acid rain. People have referred to them as the Windex lakes; a dubious distinction bestowed to describe their swimming-pool-blue clarity.

Acid rain, one of the worst environmental problems facing North America today, is a by-product of sulfur emissions from power generating plants, smelters, petroleum refineries and pulp and paper mills. When sulfur dioxide and nitrogen oxide are emitted during the burning of fossil fuels, a chemical reaction with water vapor in the air produces corrosive nitric and sulfuric acid that falls as rain or snow. These pollutants can be carried in the atmosphere thousands of miles from their source. Apart from the most obvious and devastating effect of killing our lakes, acid rain damages forests, crops, soils; it corrodes metal and damages throat and lung tissues. This destruction has been going on for decades. Within our lifetime alone, the effects have become alarmingly apparent. In Killarney, this is especially so because the geology is quartzite based. Because there is little limestone in quartzite- and granite-based areas, all of Canada's Precambrian Shield has very little neutralizing capability against the acid rain. Thousands of lakes in Ontario alone are susceptible to eventual annihilation if our industries and our neighboring country's industries do not make progress toward eliminating sulfur emissions.

This "silent killer" is only the beginning. It crumbles the very foundations upon which entire food chains are built. Every horrific news broadcast of terrorism and war ever heard pales in significance by comparison. Mankind has forgotten the most important and basic level of existence. That existence depends solely upon conscientious stewardship of the natural world. If we paddle by these snow-white mountains in 10 to 20 years what will we hear? Will gulls be shrieking, fish leaping, cattails rustling, loons yodeling? Or will it be a silent shore?

Skimming through a narrow passage with the wind to our backs and up through a tunnel beneath the road at McGregor Bay, we discovered the old voyageur channel. By way of this route, we could sneak by the exposed traverse to Manitoulin Island. We also had another reason for choosing this route. We had heard tell of a very special rock. At the end of the passage, just as the grassy bank began widening to a small lake, we laid eyes on a suspicious-looking large hunk of black basalt. This had to be La Cloche. When I threw a rock at it, the boulder emitted a hollow sound. This was no insignificant discovery considering that apart from La Cloche Mountains and South La Cloche Range, there are two lakes, a peninsula, a channel, a creek and two islands in the region all named La Cloche in honor of one bell-ringing rock!

Once into the Bay of Islands, we had officially reached the North Channel of Lake Huron. While slipping through the screen of islands on our way to the village of Algoma Mills, we paddled by the mouth of the Spanish River. For Gary, this passage brought back fond memories of a summer canoe trip several years back. He remembered long stretches of white water linking pretty little lakes lined with cliffs, beaches and a widely varied woodland of birch, pine, spruce and ash trees. The clear whiskey-colored waters flowed over a river bottom of dark granite rocks and boulders. Gary spoke as if describing an old friend. "It has a little bit of everything."

While among the islands, we hardly realized that we were paddling on one of Canada's largest freshwater lakes. But from Blind River to Thessalon, there was a mere scattering of islands to protect us. The lake was in constant motion, swaying us to and fro. Even if the wind had died, the swells would still rebound off the shore and ricochet against one another. We wallowed, surfed and bobbed on the awkward surface while an annoying wind blew at a constant angle across our bow. It required a continuous effort to maintain a straight course when the canoe reacted by turning toward the open water. The air felt warm and thick. An aura of fishy smells surrounded the outlying shoals where the gulls raised their offspring. The hours dragged into more hours. If ever on the expedition we felt woozy and seasick, it was right here.

Ever since we had begun traveling directly westward and into the sun on the Ottawa River, Gary had been developing a very blistered lower lip. He applied vaseline, zinc oxide ointment and various creams we carried in the first aid kit, but none of them worked. Finally, in desperation, he resorted to a bandana. With his sun hat pulled down to his dark glasses and the bandana pulled up to his nose, he looked like a western outlaw.

In Thessalon, we were shocked to learn about a disastrous chemical spill that had occured on the Spanish River the very day we had paddled by its mouth. The pulp and paper mill in Espanola, E.B. Eddy Forest Products Company, accidentally allowed several thousand gallons of potassium salt to spill into the river. The reddish-brown soapy substance wiped out the pike, pickerel, largemouth and smallmouth bass, sucker and sturgeon. Now many thousands of fish carcasses polluted a waterway that had, only days before, been an angler's paradise. Sport fishing businesses and the people of the Serpent and Spanish River Indian reserves had part of their livelihoods obliterated. Not only this, but the terrestrial wildlife dependant on the food source was forced to move elsewhere. Both the immediate and long-term environmental effects of pollution that we had seen while paddling along the Georgian Bay - Lake Huron coast had a very powerful impact on us. During our time on the St. Lawrence, our reaction to the horror of pollution spewing from every village was dulled by the ubiquity of it all. But in this beautifully clean, wild place, the effects were so blatant.

On a quiet Sunday morning in early July, we approached the Sault Ste. Marie locks. Small power boats buzzed around the harbor like bees rushing between the garden and the hive. They paid us little heed as they swung wide and flew off around the bay. There were a few colorful windsurfers tacking upwind against a gentle breeze. Closer to shore, a two-man rowing shell sliced through the uneven surface, the paddlers raising their oars like a water boatman beetle on a beaver pond. A huge freighter bound for the lower Great Lakes rumbled along the American side after having negotiated the locks. In the channel on the Canadian side, we met the tourist boat, *Soo Locks Boat Tours*. It was loaded to capacity with curious visitors who had been through the Canadian locks to visit Lake Superior and the Algoma Steel mill. They returned our waves eagerly, some pressing binoculars and cameras with telephoto lenses to their eyes to decipher the words along our hull.

The St. Mary's River connects Superior and Huron. Four hundred years ago, when an Ojibwa settlement flourished at the present-day site of Sault Ste. Marie, the natives harvested an abundance of whitefish from the St. Mary's Rapids. But not long after the white man arrived, the river was harnessed at its upper reaches to form canals, then locks, to provide easy passage between the two lakes. Today the American locks, on the river's south shore, handle the large freighter vessels. The smaller Canadian locks, operated by Parks Canada, are primarily reserved for recreational craft.

From our water-level view, the hefty 100-ton lock doors, built of Douglas fir, loomed like the impenetrable entrance to some great castle. Stealthily we crept along beneath the concrete pier to a bright yellow ladder. A sign above instructed us to call the lock master from the phone provided.

"Hello," I said, "we have a small craft waiting to come through."

"Wait below, well clear of the doors," came the reply.

I returned to the canoe. Water was already boiling from beneath the gates as gravity drew the level to the height of Huron. Seconds later, the formidable doors swung wide and boats of every description poured forth—houseboats, powerboats and another tour boat, all of which were at least twice the length of our canoe. Once the way was clear, we darted forward, our eyes glued to the end of the 900-foot passage.

From below, we could see someone peering downstream over the edge of the lock. It was as if he were searching for something. Then it occurred to us that he might be looking for the "small craft waiting to come through." Our canoe, being small and silent, could easily have passed through unnoticed. We guessed right, for after we shouted and waved our paddles, the man turned and came jogging back along the platform.

There was an excited shout above. Gary looked up in time to see a great length of rope uncoiling toward us. At the same time as we grasped it, the gates began to close. "Hey, you guys must have a motor on board," the voice yelled down, referring to the speed with which we had entered the locks. Gary and I pointed to each other and shouted in unison, "Yeah, we sure do!"

We chatted away the 10 minutes while rising on the incoming waters quite alone in the lock. Then the opposite set of gates rumbled open and we pressed forward to a chorus of "good luck." We scurried by the flotilla of large craft waiting on the Superior side of the locks, out past the Algoma Steel mill and into Lake Superior . . . the largest freshwater lake in the world.

# 6
# Lake of Legend

THIS MAGNIFICENT expanse of clear water covers 31,700 square miles. Its average depth is nearly 500 feet. Even if all the water from Michigan and Huron, the second and third largest Great Lakes, were poured together, the result still would not exceed the volume of Superior. It is fitting that this body of fresh water, second to none in size in the world, should lap against the edge of the oldest land mass, the Precambrian Shield. Together they offer breathtaking colors, an infinite variety of rock, sand beaches and enormous great skies mirroring the tantalizing blue waters.

In our minds, Lake Superior was already a forbidding power. We had heard many stories of canoeists attempting to paddle its coastline. None belittled it. Our maps revealed several lengthy sections of coast where it could be difficult, if not impossible, to get ashore in a storm. There were the long traverses across deep bays that seemed to stretch to the horizon. The icy cold waters were stirred by winds of awesome proportions, long feared and respected by Superior mariners. Many well-seasoned seamen who pilot the ships between Sault Ste. Marie and Thunder Bay consider the lake more dangerous than the open sea. We were swept away by our own preconceived notions of Superior. Deep down we both wanted very much to spend a long time exploring the islands and bays yet we knew that we could not. This lake was the measure by which we determined whether or not we could make it to The Pas, Manitoba, before freeze-up. It was already mid-July, which meant we would have to take advantage of every minute of fine weather for paddling.

Steep waves were hurtling themselves full force against the immovable ancient wall of granite rock at the sheer face of Gros Cap, the doorway to Whitefish Bay and Lake Superior. These mighty waves had grown from the distant expanse of open water on the western horizon. For what seemed like ages we bobbed around on the backwash, still paddling within the protection of

the cliff. Then we rounded the headland and struck out for
Goulais Point more than 10 miles away. The depth created long
swells, while the westerly wind blew at right angles to our intended direction. Gradually we found ourselves easing the bow in a
northeasterly direction so that the canoe rushed along with a
tailing wind. It was thrilling. If this was a foretaste of paddling on
Superior, we looked forward to it eagerly.

The distant shore was low and in the morning light appeared
deceptively close. For nearly an hour, we cruised along gaily
swinging our paddles to the lilting beat of voyageur songs. We
barely noticed the changing conditions, the slightly cresting
waves, and the added push of the wind to our side. At least, not
until I commented innocently about the whitecaps on the western horizon.

"That looks like a reef out there."

White spray was pawing its way across the aquamarine surface.
Cumulous clouds were cutting a scalloped pattern against the
blue sky. I swiveled around in my seat just in time to catch the
look of concern on Gary's face as he lowered the binoculars and
stared at the map. A slight furrow formed between his eyebrows
and his lips tightened into a grimace. "That's not a reef!" he said
with urgency. "There's a squall moving in very fast. Paddle,
Joanie!"

We swung the canoe toward shore which was by now some two
miles away. Terra firma was suddenly very distant indeed! The
adrenalin rushed through our veins and a strength born of fear
put extra power behind our strokes. It was not long before the
wind was tearing the tops off the waves around us. We fought to
keep the canoe from wallowing sideways. Atop the cresting
waves, we couldn't afford to go at right angles for fear of being
swamped and rolling over. The thought of swimming in those icy
waters gave us cause for grave concern. We would not survive for
very long. Quite literally our lives were in each other's hands.

It seemed forever before the land drew close enough for us to
distinguish the details of the shore. In the shallow bay, great
foamy waves boomed down on half-submerged pinnacles of
boulders and the passage through them was clearly going to be
touch and go. The timing would have to be perfect yet we could
not take a second to discuss it. I took a quick glance back over
my shoulder to see if any large waves were coming. The idea was

to catch the crest and ride in on the surf avoiding the boulders as they became submerged. It would take but a split second to rip a gash in our tender thin-skinned hull.

Whoosh, we were on top, hurtling at the stony shore. The pillow of water on which we rode was like a magic carpet speeding us over the dangerous black boulders that loomed just below the surface. At that moment all fear was replaced by a sudden burst of excitement. Our canoeing skills were being pitted against Superior's waves and one tiny error on our part would cause us to lose dismally. In a moment, we were through. A grinding crunch reverberated along the underside of the canoe as we made impact with the pebble beach. We leapt out, dragging the canoe in behind us just as the next breaking roller came crashing down on the stern. For a moment Gary was completely immersed in the chilly water. Then, with a herculean effort, we heaved the entire 200 pounds of canoe and equipment and scrambled forward to the safety of higher ground.

Our immediate concern was for the condition of the hull, especially the bow, which had struck shore with exceptional force. We stared hard at the smooth white surface from all angles. Unbelieving, we ran our hands down her length. Amazingly, there wasn't even a fresh scratch. The smooth, well-worn, age-old stones had rolled beneath us like a bed of ball bearings, taking the brunt of the impact. We dropped onto the warm sand next to the canoe. Our fear gradually changed to admiration. Far away the clear blue waters decorated in tumbling streamers came galloping across the endless horizon. As the waves moved closer, we appreciated their size. The black pinnacles of rock appeared and disappeared as the immense waves passed through, some unscathed but most shredded into a turmoil of angry white foam, all ending their long journey in a thunderous explosion of spray. Each wave collapsed, rushing back to the lake through the sand and the variegated display of marble-smooth stones. That afternoon, our respect for Superior grew ten-fold. We felt we had learned a valuable lesson that would stand us in good stead in the weeks to come. Nevertheless, despite this brush with danger, we never felt we had to crawl within inches of the shoreline all the time.

We learned quickly that the best times to paddle were between the quiet dawn and mid-morning, and then from early evening until dark. As the morning wore on, the warm sun gradually heated the granite rock surrounding this immense frigid body of water. Cool air drifting in across the lake warmed while passing over the rock and ascended into great mushrooming cumulous clouds. These turbulent air currents gave rise to the huge swells. One moment the powerful, wild beauty of waves battering precipitous cliffs filled us with awe; the next moment we were touched by the sight of delicate purple bell flowers flourishing in the meager cracks on some exposed shoal. Even the temperatures were extremely varied. On arriving one hot, sunny afternoon at Pancake Bay where the blond beach stretches for half a mile in either direction, we leapt from the canoe anticipating the exhilarating tingle of the icy lake. What we didn't anticipate was jumping from the icebox onto the scorching hot sand of a sunbaked beach.

The Ojibwa Indians' Inscription Rock at Agawa Bay is a 100-foot wall of rock rimmed by a smooth ledge at its base. A slight backwash reverberated off the wall as we skimmed alongside it. Lake Superior was in a very serene mood this particular morning. As we drew in close to the ledge and gazed up at the design of red ochre lines, shapes and creatures, we sensed the mystical spirit of this ancient place. For more than a thousand years, Inscription Rock has been adorned with this deeply meaningful artistry. Here is where many native rituals took place—the coming of manhood, the appeasement of the gods of the lake with gifts, and the inscription of legendary stories and mythological images.

Just beyond Inscription Rock, we slipped the canoe alongside a jumbled pile of boulders and climbed out. With practiced ease, we hoisted the canoe and packs to a place far from the reach of pawing waves. Gingerly, we crept along the narrow ledge which curved toward the lake. It was smooth, almost slippery, gradually worn that way by the constant pounding of waves and the great clinging weight of winter ice. There were faint lines at the east end of the rock, barely recognizable as drawings had we not been searching for them. But the most captivating group of figures dominated the middle piece of rock just at eye level. This group consisted of the most respected manitou in Ojibwa legend, a spiny-backed horned creature named Missipeshu, two undulating sea serpents and a canoe with two paddlers. I was struck by the realization of how long ago these had been painted. Yet we claimed a kinship with the artist. We knew he had arrived by canoe. He probably pulled his birchbark craft high onto the same boulders where ours was now lying. As he painted, he would have been conscious of the formidable presence of the great water body at his back. He touched the same rock, felt the same wind and was rocked on the same waves hundreds of years ago.

The spell was broken by a uniformed provincial park warden striding into view from the path above. He was guiding a group of chattering tourists who had arrived from the highway via a rough trail. Unfortunately, the trail should have been much rougher to discourage all but the most interested. When one tourist complained about the condition of the path and someone else said, "Yeah, these better be good!" I wondered why these people bothered to come at all.

Below the boulders and back on the lake, we were alone again.

"Look at that!" Gary pointed toward the southwest where an unusual cirrostratus cloud formation was building on the horizon. A sweeping white plume had developed a jagged edge on one side. Its resemblance to the spiny back and tail of Missipeshu was uncanny. In Ojibwa legend, a few swipes of Missipeshu's giant tail stirs up the wind and waves. Riffling waves skittered across the surface and splashed gently against the hull. We felt the soft brush of a breeze backing from west to south signifying the approach of a warm front and a change in weather.

From Michipicoten Harbour, we paddled directly westward toward Pukaskwa National Park. One third of the park's circumference follows the Lake Superior shoreline between the Pic River and the Pukaskwa River. A rugged 40-mile trail meanders between the deep boreal forest of white spruce, balsam fir, aspens and birches, crossing sandy bays and wooded cliff tops. On a fine July afternoon, it seemed like a friendly coast when you stood on shore and looked out upon the lake. The view we saw was one which hasn't changed in centuries. Even more inviting was the view from lake to shore from our canoe. We could tuck ourselves behind screens of islands, hug the coast or slip into bays with such names as English Fishery Harbour, Gids Harbour and Shot Watch Cove. Pukaskwa is, apart from its other attributes, a sanctuary for any number of plants and animals. The area has the distinction of being the southernmost breeding ground for woodland caribou in Canada.

During our next windy afternoon on Superior, we were forced off the lake into the protection of a serene little bay. It was rimmed with hills of granite, and a smooth, sandy beach extended a long distance from shore. Soft green grasses swayed beneath the evergreens. Had it not been for the feathery spruce trees bowing in the relentless wind along the edge of the bay, we would never have guessed that the lake was rolling so violently. Much to our excitement, we spied the distinguished stance of a bull moose pausing for a moment in a clearing. Slowly and majestically, he turned, disappearing into the woodland. While examining and following his hoofprints in the sand, we also discovered the splayed prints of caribou. Growing near these tracks were several sprawling vines of purple beach peas. We bent down to examine them and then spent the rest of the afternoon on our knees, with cameras and tripods in hand. We crawled through a tangle of long grasses where stately orange wood lilies stood guard. Deeper in the woods, we beheld tiny pink twinflowers and thick carpets of verdant sphagnum moss, red soldiers and wispy trails of goats' beard caught on branches like the hair of some animal in molt. Superior has to be appreciated on the grand scale, but there is much beauty to be found in examining the minute details as well.

The next day, as we slipped quietly through a group of isolated coastal islands, we spotted large, bulky clumps of sticks adorning several treetops. A well-established heron rookery had made this lonely shoal its perfect home. The shoal's location made it vulnerable to violent winter storms when high winds pummel the islands and heavy ice clings to the vegetation. Under this harsh treatment, the growth of the trees is permanently stunted. Poplars, birch and spruce stand bent, crippled and barely a tenth of the size of their full-grown species farther inland. It is in the nature of the blue heron to nest in the very top branches of these trees, which would normally send them towering 60 or 70 feet overhead. The stunted tree size enabled us to observe the birds nesting. I played decoy, paddling the canoe just offshore, distracting the herons' attention while Gary wiggled up the smooth rock on his belly, camera in hand. Some nests were crowded with as many as four young herons. They looked especially peculiar stretching their skinny necks straight up. Surprised, bulging eyes were riveted on our every move. Their heads were crowned with a funny little cap of fuzzy pinquill feathers. Some were exercising their fledgling wings. One was perched on a long spindly branch which bounced up and down each time the heron bent his knobby-kneed, matchstick legs. The adults hunched their necks into the typical S-curve and watched us cautiously. Several rolls of film later, Gary eased himself back into the canoe.

We had been taking the crystalline clarity of Superior's waters for granted over the past few days. It was wonderful to dive in head first, and glide silently across a lake so transparent you felt as if you were flying. But we had expected this of Superior. So one afternoon, while paddling near the Pic River on Pukaskwa's northern boundary, we were especially dismayed to see that the water was turning a heavy, dark color. Far in the distance, at the corner of the lake where the gigantic arch of blue sky fell below the hills, a tall smokestack was visible. The deadly finger pointed skyward and trailing from its tip was a ghastly stream of dark vapor, hydrogen-sulfide gas, one of the waste products of the pulp-and-paper industry.

From high upon Marathon's shores, we overlooked a bay carpeted in yellow foam stretching several miles out. Some distance away, a tugboat maneuvered an enormous log boom. On the edge of town, behind the Everest Hotel, twin mountains of logs had grown from the thousands of eight-foot lengths piled there. From a distance, they resembled mounds of gray and brown matchsticks. We were told that this was the town's three-year supply of wood needed to keep the ancient mill in operation. The mill had been there long enough that it was now employing a third generation of residents. In a one-industry town, hard choices develop between the need for jobs and the need to protect the environment.

The morning we awoke outside Marathon, one of Superior's famous thick white fogs had rolled in, smothering the town and its bay. This fog was not the heavy damp blanket fresh with the coolness of the lake. It reeked with a powerful, sickening stench. The pollution spewing from the pulp-and-paper mill filled our lungs with noxious fumes reminiscent of rotting eggs. Each breath was drawn in hurried little gasps.

Shortly after setting off in the canoe, we were horrified to discover the source of the yellow slick across the bay. A poisonous stream of effluent came spilling down from the mill, through the forest and over the rock, and tumbled into Lake Superior. Day after day, month after month and year after year, the insidious little river flows unchecked. With other mills at Terrace Bay, Nipigon-Red Rock and Thunder Bay contributing their own share of pollutants, there is a level of mercury contamination in the lake's fish population. Even Superior's great depth of fresh, cold water cannot continue diluting the toxins forever.

Every paddle stroke we took was a delicate maneuver. As the purple droplets fanned across the surface on the return sweep of the paddle, we thought of them as an acid that could corrode our clothes and skin. We wanted to get out of there as quickly as possible. Gary scrutinized the map, then took a compass bearing across the bay. The distance was no more than a couple of miles, but the visibility was barely 40 feet. After several minutes of traveling blind, we detected a throbbing boat motor. Without saying a word, we veered back toward shore. On lengthy traverses, the early travelers had faced the danger of getting caught in a sudden squall. Not only did we take a calculated risk with the weather, but we were also in danger of being run over by another boat!

After what seemed like hours, we made a recognizable bearing on land. As the wind was gradually shredding away the fog in long ragged fingers, railway tracks appeared mysteriously 30 feet above us. Here, near the Caldwell Peninsula, the railway made a tight swing toward the lake. During November, when storms lash the coast, the spray from crashing waves whips the passing trains, icing them before they disappear back into a tunnel in the rockface.

West of the peninsula, the shoreline curves around a shallow sandy bay, now part of Neys Provincial Park. This place has had a rather wretched past. During the Second World War, it was a prisoner-of-war camp for German soldiers. At that time the only access to the area was by way of the railroad and the lake. With the impenetrable forests riddled with bogs and mosquitoes on one side, and an icy-cold freshwater ocean on the other, the prisoners were confronted with far more intimidating barriers than guards and fencing.

The Pigeon River Lumber Company's pointer boats have lain rotting on the Caldwell Peninsula for so many years that they are as gray and weathered as the granite rock itself. In the heyday of Superior's logging industry, Nipigon Bay and Black Bay were used as holding areas for the log booms. The grinding of logs against logs caused an enormous buildup of bark on the natural sandy lake bottom. This buildup had a profound effect on the productive sturgeon and pickerel spawning beds in these bays. Unable to dig through the bark to the sand, these fish abandoned the site and the population declined dramatically. Here the wasted logs are hidden from view, but not so on the cobblestone beaches, where they have been tossed like matchsticks far up on shore.

Beachcombing Superior's cobblestone banks was an endless source of enjoyment. When my pockets were stuffed with colorful, marble-smooth pebbles, I would empty them, select a few to keep, toss the rest and begin again. The orderly arrangement of the beaches fascinated us. From one end to the other, the lake has sorted and neatly organized the rocks according to size, from the largest boulders to the smallest stones. Not only did we see a pattern in the cobbles, but the beaches themselves were neatly tiered. As we left the canoe and climbed up toward the forest, we were passing through an evolution of different shorelines. Since the retreat of the mile-thick Wisconsin Glacier 10,000 years ago, the land has been rebounding back from the tremendous weight of ice that squashed it down. The shoreline is still being reclaimed at a little less than a quarter of an inch every year.

Geological history is fascinating, but its concepts are vast and difficult to grasp. The time frame encompasses more than our minds can accommodate. Human history seems more immediate and relevant. So it was when we discovered one of the ancient cobblestone structures known as a Pukaskwa Pit. We knew instinctively what we had found. Gary pointed silently, his finger outlining the shape. We drew a little closer. Long ago someone had removed the rocks and left a depression forming this pit. Some pits are quite small; this one was large enough for a man to sit inside. There are a number of theories put forward as to the reason for the pits' existence—maybe the theories all apply depending on the size and location of each pit. Possibly they were shelters. This one certainly could have been, with the added protection of a makeshift skin roof. Perhaps the pits were food caches or smoking pits to preserve meat and fish. The little pits located in the more exposed beaches were possibly places where young Ojibwa boys came to seek visions to guide them through life.

Although our canoe was tiny and vulnerable to the elements, we felt the lake was far less menacing to us than if we had been traveling in a larger craft. We discovered refuges from storms that even our map did not indicate. We could slip quite easily into tiny bays and through carved archways or surf up onto some minute patch of sand and tuck ourselves in between rocky crevices. We practiced our escape routes in fun while docile Superior swayed languidly in the abnormal calm. The cycle of wind was not playing itself out as usual, and this was having interesting effects upon the lake. The cliffs, beaches and shoals could all be explored very easily. There weren't the usual ricocheting waves bounding around nor the pounding surf on each beach landing. Many local people informed us that they had never seen Superior in such a placid mood for so long before.

Black Bay Peninsula is like a large foot separating Nipigon and Black Bay. On the tip of its toe are two sizable round humps that have been likened to part of a woman's anatomy. The Paps rise some 600 feet above the lake providing travelers with a reliable landmark. The day had been one of long traverses across the Magnet, Montreal and Middleburn Channels of the Black Bay entrance. These were now behind us. Our longest, most exposed traverse lay straight ahead.

Sheer blue-gray cliffs soared 800 feet from the water's edge to the plateau of Sibley Peninsula at Thunder Bay. From a distance, the end of this great elongated landform resembles its name, the Sleeping Giant. Indeed, the Sleeping Giant expressed nicely our experience of the entire lake. Just to the east of its base is a little village called Silver Islet. Brightly painted cottages, pink, yellow, green and blue, lined the shores of the snug little harbor, where once the richest silver mine in North America operated. In a nutshell, a local sailor described the legend of Silver Islet's short-lived fame.

"You see that tiny island out there," he said. "That's the one where three million in silver was mined 'til the foreman got drunk and forgot to keep the coal-fired pump stoked. The mine flooded and everyone just moved away. It was quite a procession, they say, houses on the move across the ice to Port Arthur and Fort William in the dead of winter."

Silver Islet survives now as a summer retreat with no phones and no stores.

From Thunder Cape at the very tip of the peninsula, we confronted a seven-mile traverse to the round hump of Pie Island. Just as we were leaving the mainland behind, Gary noticed a freighter appearing over the southern horizon bound for the Thunder Bay port. We stopped, undecided as to whether or not we should go on. As farfetched as it might seem, our paths could conceivably cross at the same time. Ever since our experiences in the Quebec and Montreal harbors, my mind had played out scenes of being run over by a ship.

"Let's wait," I suggested.

So we returned to shore. Ironically we had expected everything except ships to slow our progress on Superior. We followed the movement of the vessel as it approached the channel between us and the island. It passed quietly by, en route to the harbor which was ringed with granaries. Millions of tons of wheat, oats, barley and rapeseed are transported annually by railroad or ship out of Thunder Bay (once known as Port Arthur and Fort William), making it the largest grain-handling port in the world. For the ships traveling in from foreign lands, Thunder Bay ends a long journey through the St. Lawrence–Great Lakes Waterway.

In the early evening light, Pie Island was only a flat lopsided shape in the purple-blue haze. Uneasily we gazed across the calm oily surface. Every now and again, a light southwest wind would raise riffles. By the time three ships and another hour had passed, we could wait no longer and risk losing this window of calm. We struck out for Pie Island. At times, the weather is a formidable adversary, but on this fine summer evening, we raced hard without trepidation. Ahead, the sun had just dipped below the steep escarpment of the Nor'Westers, and behind us the precipitous cliffs of the Sleeping Giant were bathed in the salmon-pink afterglow. Twelve days paddling and two days windbound had seen us safely within reach of Grand Portage and Pigeon River. We felt triumphant! It was July 25 and all our fear of getting iced in before reaching The Pas simply melted away!

# 7
# The Last
# Nor'Wester

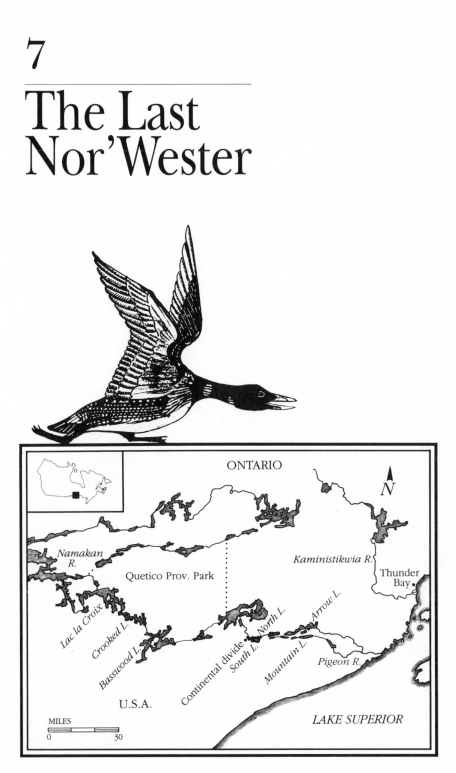

O UT GO THE PICKLES. Hot dogs for supper tonight to finish up the ketchup! Here! Have a banana!" I was hurling the heavy luxury food from the pack with gusto. Eight or nine miles was a long way to carry the load over Grand Portage to Partridge Falls and every portage after that. For the next leg of our journey, between Lake Superior and Lake of the Woods, we would be following a system of small lakes and rivers along the Canada–United States border. It begins just south of the Ontario–Minnesota border near the mouth of Pigeon River. For the first 50 miles, we would be constantly portaging, paddling and pulling the canoe upstream until we reached the continental divide between the Atlantic and Hudson Bay watersheds, nearly a thousand feet above Lake Superior. This 50 miles constituted the steepest section of our entire expedition.

In the last 650 miles, we had grown accustomed to paddling over vast expanses of water. The hardship of portaging heavy packs was almost forgotten. Along the way we had accumulated a variety of bulky foods that filled our packs to ponderous proportions—large pots of peanut butter and honey to spread on several kinds of crackers and buns, extra powdered milk, two kinds of fruit drinks, cobs of corn and fruit.

"Yuk!" I exclaimed, picking the slimy, dripping remains of a squished plum from the bottom of Gary's pack. One tiny plum could sure spread itself around. Despite our ruthless pruning, we were still obliged to carry two weeks' supplies to see us through to Fort Frances.

It was a hot, windy morning when we turned our backs on the long swells of the freshwater sea and hoisted up our heavy loads. The first lap of the voyage inland was a nine-mile carry christened Grand Portage in the heyday of the North West Company fur trade. The portage route bypasses the lower reaches of the Pigeon River's impassable limestone gorges and steep waterfalls. We had developed a leapfrog system for wilderness portages over a mile in length. It consisted of carrying the packs for a while, then dropping them and returning for the canoe. That was the part we enjoyed. Without being burdened with a load tugging on our shoulders, we often ran back to the canoe thereby covering the whole distance relatively quickly.

In the steps of Pierre de La Vérendrye, one of the first white explorers to travel west of the Great Lakes, we set off to retrace this fur-trade highway. Most of La Vérendrye's men mutinied on this trail in the autumn of 1731. I sympathized with them as the irritable mosquitoes and horseflies buzzed and whined around our heads. Trudging along the dirt road under the hot sun, the packs weighed heavily on our shoulders. To buoy our spirits, we kept thinking how light our loads were in comparison to those of the voyageurs. Imagine a 180-pound load straining on the tumpline around your forehead!

"Now that would be super brain drain," Gary joked.

We had coined the pun "brain drain" on the Appalachian Trail to describe the feeling we had on particularly hot days when the pack straps bit into our neck muscles until our heads throbbed.

"Worse than that, think of the menu!" commented Gary. "I can't imagine you living on Indian corn boiled in lye and fried in bacon grease."

"You're a fine one to talk," I retorted. "You don't even like cabbage rolls!"

"I'm just saving them all for you because you like them so much." Gary winked. "Besides, why are you complaining? I'm carrying them."

Just as we were getting ready to set off again after a short break, a very old pickup truck with running boards and fat fenders came rumbling up. It stopped and the driver got out.

"You're almost there!" he said.

We were astonished by his formal attire, a suit and highly polished black cowboy boots. His black hair was slicked back from a clean-shaven face. But the most striking part of his costume was a chrome-plated revolver tucked into a black leather holster hanging from his side. He resembled one of those high-priced gunfighters right out of a spaghetti western. I was taken aback to see him walking around with a handgun so blatantly displayed. Then I remembered we were in the United States where the gun laws were very different. We talked briefly before he climbed back into his vehicle. Waving, he called out, "I'll see you at the river!"

When we met again at Partridge Falls, the stranger revealed that he came from Chicago and spent the summers as a chef in a restaurant up here in the Boundary Waters. He struck us as being entirely out of his element in the northern bush. On the trail leading down to Partridge Falls, Gary hurried on ahead with his camera. The friendly stranger and I followed him through the bush. Before descending the slope, I stooped to inspect a patch of yellow mushrooms. His genuine interest in our journey had me chattering away about this and that. Then he turned to the subject of guns.

"Have you ever seen one of these?" he purred softly, extracting his bright silver pistol from the leather holster. I froze, wide-eyed. I had never seen a real handgun brandished about in this manner before. Wild thoughts began racing through my mind. Shall I make a break for it? I know I could outrun him! A little voice in my head screamed, "Run, run!" But still I stared in horrified fascination as he twirled the pistol around his finger and stroked it lovingly.

"It's a .38 Special."

"Is that so?" I croaked. This was becoming like one of those terrible nightmares where you want to move but your legs have turned to rubber.

"Yes," he said, pulling something from his pocket, "it takes these silver bullets. Like to shoot it?"

"Oh no . . . nnn . . . o thanks!" I stuttered, thinking all the while, "You fool, take it then he can't shoot you." Where, oh where, was Gary?

He slid a couple of bullets neatly into two of the chambers, then glanced around. Just as I was taking a determined step to escape, he pointed the gun skyward and said, "See that crooked tree branch up there?" and fired. The sharp blast made me put my hands to my ears. But for all the commotion, the branch was still intact.

"Umphh!" he muttered disappointedly. "You want to try?" he asked me again.

"No really, that's OK!" I answered steadily, my nervousness having been somewhat quelled.

Just then I looked beyond the cowboy, whose back was turned to the Partridge Falls trail, in time to see Gary appear. He came charging up the path like a bull moose, brandishing an enormous stick. The expression on his face was too much. I burst into helpless giggles, then laughed outright until the tears streamed down my cheeks. Before the man could turn around and find out what had caused my outburst of laughter, Gary dropped the stick and slowed to a casual jog.

"Your wife won't shoot my .38," he said, throwing a bewildered glance in my direction. "But maybe you would like to?" he asked, handing Gary the pistol.

"What are you shooting at?" Gary asked.

"Oh, how about that old crooked branch?" He pointed at the same one that had been the target of his first shot.

In one motion, Gary raised the gun, fired, shot the limb clear off, then handed the gun back before the branch had hit the ground.

"You didn't even aim!"

Gary shrugged. "You just have to move."

Startled by the comment, I glanced at Gary. Behind the mask of seriousness, the corners of his mouth were definitely twitching. I distinctly remembered hearing that line in an exchange between two outlaws in a western movie we had seen not too long ago.

Our cowboy was staring, mouth agape, at the crooked branch lying on the ground. Then gathering himself together, he shook our hands and insisted it was time he was on his way. As he pulled away down the dirt road, I turned to Gary. "How did you do that?"

"The same way I met you—through a giant stroke of luck!"

The Pigeon River foamed and gurgled past boulder-laden shores and flowed over the gravel bottom, only ankle- to knee-deep in most places. For the rest of the day our clothes were wringing wet; pulling, poling and paddling on an upstream trek through dense woodlands of cedar and spruce. In the marshy areas, swaying walls of vivid green grasses filled the air with a lovely rushing sound. From the protective covering, several anxious teal hens bolted upstream, feigning injury to draw us away from their ducklings. The day came to a close on Fowl Lake after we had found and struggled our way over two very overgrown portages. Bitten, itchy and grubby, we scrambled into the tent, which we had pitched on a muddy patch of grass at the lake edge. Neither of us felt ambitious enough to make supper tonight. Thoroughly exhausted, we pulled out the sleeping bags and lay there listening to the changed evening chorus. Instead of waves washing against the rolling cobbles, our senses were filled with the haunting wail of a loon and the drone of mosquitoes. Hundreds of the bloodthirsty pests were caught in the airspace between the nylon tentfly and the tent. They were so numerous that they made a sound like the pitter-patter of raindrops. Then aerial divebombers, the dragonflies, appeared, darting to and fro snatching up a gala feast.

Apart from the physical effort of the portages and the nuisance of mosquitoes, we faced another challenge having paddled inland. On the Great Lakes, navigation had been very simple. With the shore on one side and the lake on the other, we had only to watch out for weather and possible places to take shelter. Now Gary had to be very diligent about map reading. The waterways squiggled and squirmed through islands and around peninsulas. The portages and the route were seldom obvious, often hidden from the view.

One evening, camped on Mountain Lake, we studied the following day's route carefully. The drainage pattern of the waterways makes a peculiar twist here which must have been very confusing for early travelers. Even though we were still three lakes and four portages east of the true height of land, Mountain Lake is actually the highest water body along the international boundary of the Pigeon River system. It drains from both the eastern and western ends. Unsuspecting early travelers would have been fooled into thinking they were returning to Lake Superior. In the westerly direction, the flow ends up in Rose Lake, which, in turn, drains toward Arrow Lake. (Arrow Lake runs parallel with Mountain Lake and the rest of the Pigeon River system and eventually rejoins it further east. The path of water makes almost a complete circle.) At Rose Lake, we would be following an "uphill" portage for the last time. It would end in South Lake, one side of the true continental divide.

Just before we made the continental divide portage, Gary spied a cow moose chest-deep in a little reed-filled pocket of water. We steered in quite carefully, remembering she was in her element and far faster than we were. Then we noticed the curious mule ears of a calf poking above the grass like radar. The calf waded into view on long spindly legs. Now we were even more cautious. The cow was a powerful, protective mother. We were no match for such an adversary in the event that she charged. We backed off quietly. In the middle of the portage path, there was a substantial looking boundary marker constructed from a washtub filled with cement then overturned. A cone, resembling a traffic pylon, had been placed on top. On one side it was marked Canada, with United States of America on the other. It was such an unobtrusive device to mark the boundary between two great nations. The Boundary Waters Canoe Area Wilderness stretches along 150 miles of the international boundary and encompasses a million acres of protected wilderness inside Minnesota's Superior National Forest. On the Canadian side, Ontario also has a million acres in the provincial park called Quetico. The portage between South and North Lakes marked a break in flowing water, a continental divide between two vast watersheds—the St. Lawrence–Great Lakes and Hudson Bay. Crossing the smooth trail, which was little more than half a mile long, we reached a significant point in the journey. From now until we reached the mouth of the Saskatchewan River at the northern end of Lake Winnipeg, it was all downhill.

Ever since we left Lake Superior, the weather had been wildly changeable, with afternoon breezes so brisk that we struggled against the headwinds on even the smallest lakes. Now a strong northeast wind was sending black thunderclouds scudding across the sky. A solid gray curtain was slowly enveloping the distant hills. We just had the tarpaulin snaps fastened when fat droplets splashed across the deck. A cold drenching rain passed quickly. Several more squalls struck over the course of the morning before which we just barely had time to pull up our spray skirts and throw our raincoats on.

After bucking the waves, wind and rain well into the afternoon, our stomachs began growling in protest. A small bowl of granola and powdered milk just wasn't enough to fuel us for six hours of paddling. We were on the verge of stopping when another cloud burst overhead like a water balloon. After we shouted and yelled at the sky, the rain finally surrendered and the sun returned. We dashed for shore, hauled out the lunch pack and spread ourselves out on the rocks, equipped with peanut butter, cheese, crackers, juice and chocolate bars. Gary leaned back on his life jacket. As he tilted his head toward the treetops, I thought I heard him say, "Oh, oh, we're in for it!"

The warm sun was swallowed up in yet another cloud. The downpour unleashed upon us felt as though someone had wrung out a heavy wet sponge. We didn't have time to move. The crackers were instant mush. Slowly, the peanut-butter jar filled with water. We were past caring. Gary went on calmly unwrapping his chocolate bar, rain streaming off the edges of his hat brim. What a forlorn, soggy, goose-pimpled pair we were.

"Let's camp!"

"Best idea I've heard all day!"

Before we even had the packs on shore and the canoe turned over, the rain stopped. We stripped off our soggy clothes and strung them on a line. We were concerned about soaking our last set of dry clothes so we made camp without a stitch on. Then, like Eve, I dove into bushes thick with fat ripe blueberries. I picked and picked and picked. When it comes to berry picking, my obsession gets worse the more I find. Gary often lost me on the Appalachian Trail among the raspberry bushes and the wild cherry trees. "Just a few more" always turned into lots more. In the end, it was always worth it. There would be enough blueberries for supper, and breakfast and lunch the next day.

The storm clouds passed quietly, and before sundown warm rays filtered through the tree branches, highlighting the sparkling beads of moisture. Somewhere a veery's drainpipe whistle heralded evening. A few grackles and warblers joined the chorus, singing and chirping merrily. They were glad the storm was over, too.

Tracing a Z-shaped route along the Boundary Waters, we wound our way through tiny blue lakes with such wonderful names as Saganaga, Basswood and Crooked Lake. Linking these are rivers, twisting and turning between banks thickly clustered with spruce, jack pine, birch and poplar.

Dawdling along the shoreline of Basswood one evening, we heard a loon's stirring infectious laugh. Another answered. Then another. Soon a whole raft of black-headed divers became wildly excited. Some lifted their bodies in a vertical position throwing spray with feet and wings. Others performed a sort of butterfly stroke leaping across the surface. All told I counted three dozen. But despite the number, their very presence intensified our feeling of remoteness and solitude in this wild place.

After getting an early start one morning, the smell of sizzling bacon wafting on the breeze greeted us at the head of the Basswood Falls portage trail. Farther up the trail at a place that overlooked the rapids, we found a group of canoeists sitting around their breakfast fire. They had pulled ashore the night before and were now contemplating whether or not they should shoot the rapids coursing through the channel. All eyes were wide, therefore, as we swung around the point of land and leapt forward with the dancing river. From wave crest to wave crest we bounded, then swung into an eddy just above a growling sousehole. To the canoeists, it appeared that we were in great peril. Swinging wide, the canoe arched above the hole, turned downstream and shot off like an arrow, narrowly skirting the obstacle. A chorus of cheers sprang up from the ledge and echoed down the short gorge until we disappeared from sight.

Beyond Basswood and Wheelbarrow Falls, we stopped to share experiences with a group of canoeists at the end of the Lower Basswood portage trail. Holding the canoe away from shore, I stood knee-deep in the cedar-stained river. The muddy bottom and cool water felt good on my hot, blistered feet. Moments after paddling away from shore, I glanced down at my boots. Through the transparency of my wet nylon pants, I glimpsed hundreds of tiny black wriggling things. Trying to keep calm, I began slipping off the pants. Then a fat, black tail oozed down between my boot tongue and laces. Choking back a scream, I removed my boot ever so slowly, wincing with horror. Nothing! The bloodsucker was only on the boot. Sighing with relief, I casually pulled off the other one. Every moose, loon and human within a mile of our canoe must have heard the blood-curdling shriek. Squeezing my eyes shut, I flung my foot out to the side of the canoe for Gary to see. I couldn't speak. My foot was black with two-inch-long wiggling leeches. They squirmed between my toes while thick clumps of tiny ones clung to the blisters like petals on a chrysanthemum. I couldn't feel a thing, but the ghastly sight was soon made worse when I swiped my boot across them. I had forgotten that leeches cling to skin with a suction-cup mouth; my foot was now streaked in blood. Gary angled the canoe toward shore and landed.

"We don't have any salt, do we?" Gary asked hauling out the food pack.

"No! Just do something!"

"I know, soup mix!" Gary exclaimed, rifling through the pack's contents.

"Soup mix?!"

"Tomato or chicken?" Gary asked, holding up two different packages.

"I don't care!" I shrieked. "Just get them off me!"

Gary sprinkled the powdered soup liberally over my foot. The salty mixture worked like magic. The leeches curled up into little balls and dropped onto the rock in a seething pile.

"I don't suppose you'd like soup for lunch?" he asked wickedly.

Somehow we had managed to get through the winding waterway of Crooked Lake without getting lost in Thursday, Friday, Saturday and Sunday Bays, as some hapless surveyors once did. In this region, glacier-carved granite of long skinny basins has created an intricate and confusing shoreline. On our small-scale map, the bays appeared very narrow. Occasionally, one of the innumerable islands spattered on the twisting channels was unmarked on our charts, thereby further confusing us. Beyond the thundering cataracts of Curtain and Rebecca Falls, we rounded the point into Lac la Croix with sharp, crisp strokes.

Pam Epps, a close friend and the foreman at Quetico's Junior Ranger camp, had managed to make contact with us before we left Lake Superior. She encouraged us to visit Joe and Vera Meany, the rangers of the Lac la Croix station, on our way through the park. To ensure that we would indeed stop in, she had said, "I'll send them a letter right away so you won't be strangers arriving. And I'm sending you guys a letter and parcel, so you better stop and pick it up. Maybe I'll be there, too! You never know."

Pam was one of those friends whom we wouldn't see for months, even years. Then all of a sudden, quite out of the blue, the paths of our varied lives would merge in the most extraordinary ways.

We were approaching the spot Gary had marked on the map after getting instructions from Pam. The first sighting of

Quetico's western ranger station included the long wooden dock, the sand beach and the provincial and national flags fluttering amid the poplar- and pine-treed shore. And then we saw a uniformed park ranger bent over a motor, his tool box open next to him. We assumed it must be Joe Meany. The slicing rhythm of paddle blades across the water broke his concentration. He straightened up, ran a hand through his hair and yelled out a greeting.

"It's Gary and Joanie, isn't it?"

We nodded.

"How did you get here?" he asked incredulously. Our gaze crept from our paddles to the canoe beneath us.

"I mean," Joe reiterated, "how did you get here so quickly? We heard you had entered the park but that was only four days ago!"

Grinning sheepishly, we glanced at each other. After three months on the water, we had acquired the endurance to put in exceptionally long days. We did not travel with blinkers on nor were we sprinters unless the situation demanded it. But arising early, setting up camp late and having an efficient packing, portaging and camping system helped put the miles quickly behind us.

Our gliding momentum had carried us past the end of the dock. Joe hurried over to the beach, smiling heartily. Grabbing the bow with surprising strength, he sent us toppling back onto our seats as he lifted us half the canoe's length onto the dry sand.

"Hi, I'm Joe. C'mon up and meet my wife, Vera." He led the way up to their cabin through an immaculate campground. Joe was obviously a man who had a place for everything and everything was in that place. No sooner had we passed through the doorway than we spied two of the most beautifully sculptured paddles we had ever seen. Reflections played on the blond surface of the paddle blades which were emblazoned with the words XY Company. Joe caught our look of interest but waved us into the kitchen.

Vera was not surprised to see us at all. She gave us a thorough good welcome and said to Joe, "Don't you remember Pam's letter said August third?"

Vera handed us the letter. Unbelievably, Pam had predicted our arrival to the day. How could she have known? There was even mention of a parcel and letter arriving on the August third ranger-camp supply run. What timing! While we waited for the plane to arrive, Vera served up the most delicious fish chowder and the last of their fresh fruit, vegetables and milk. As we ate, Joe sat back to tell us a story.

In 1967, the provinces were putting together teams of 10 men to participate in the 3,280-mile Centennial Canoe Pageant from Rocky Mountain House, Alberta, to the Expo site in Montreal. Joe and his brother Don were natural participants, in view of their national and international canoe racing experience. But while Don waited for the Ontario team to organize themselves, Joe and two friends decided to do it alone in the fastest time possible. A three-man kayak was designed and built with a nonstop journey in mind. The craft was 25 feet long. It was rigged with a sail for more propulsion, and foot pedals so that it could be steered by any one of the three men. A specially designed cart was constructed for running the boat through 80 miles of portages. The men paddled, portaged, ate and slept moving day and night. Fatigue wracked them. Then disaster struck.

On the Kaminstiquia River near Thunder Bay (the alternative route to the Pigeon River system that we paddled), the kayak capsized in the rapids. Joe's spray skirt failed to release. Still attached to the boat, which went careening over the rocky bottom, Joe was badly injured. His two friends paddled him out to the nearest hospital. Despite a broken nose and jaw, he rested only one day before setting off again. Lack of sleep rendered all three men delirious by the time they set off around Lake Superior's southern shore. Joe was battered and broken, one man couldn't swim and the other almost abandoned the journey near its completion. Amazingly, they made it intact to Montreal in 40 days, although they barely remembered the actual arrival. Later, their kayak was put on display in the Kanawa Canoe Museum in Minden, Ontario.

Joe told the story with such excitement and fire in his eyes that it seemed it had happened to him only yesterday. Dramatic events like these often take on far more importance as the years pass, especially if they are told and retold with the kind of passion Joe had just shown.

A drone of engines overhead cut short our questions and we headed down to the dock to meet the supply seaplane. On our way, our eyes drifted once again toward the beautiful XY Company paddles hanging on the wall.

"Just a minute," Joe said as he picked them up. "Have a look at these." He thrust the paddles into our hands.

"Like 'em? They're yours. My brother Don made them by hand. He would be proud for you to use them."

They were feather light and the finish was so smooth. He could tell by the way we fondled them, running our hands up and down the shafts, admiring the mitered seams and beautiful cedar grain, that we truly appreciated them. There was no hesitation in our acceptance. No need to say, "Oh no, we shouldn't." We knew the meaning of a well-thought-out gift and the pleasure of seeing it received.

The pilot had no mail or parcels for us. Apparently, there had been a watermelon, marked "from Pam" on board but it was delivered to a group of fire rangers at the last stop. The thought behind the watermelon was more important than the melon itself. We wrote a short note and asked the pilot to deliver it to the Junior Ranger camp where she worked.

*Dear Pam,*

> *The watermelon was appreciated by a very hot and thirsty crew.*
> *Love from Gary and Joanie*
> *P.S. See you at Christmas...maybe???*

Joe dashed back and forth along the dock with his wheelbarrow, unloading the supply plane, until he saw we were ready to go. He strode over to shore and gave us a final push into the lake. We kept the new paddles well clear of the gunwales, cracking the strokes sharply through the water in perfect unison. Half a mile out, we stopped and waved goodbye. Joe was still standing on shore, hand over his forehead shading his eyes from the glare of the setting sun. We knew he wanted to be with us gliding to unknown places, but he had sent the paddles in his place.

# 8
# River of Sorrow

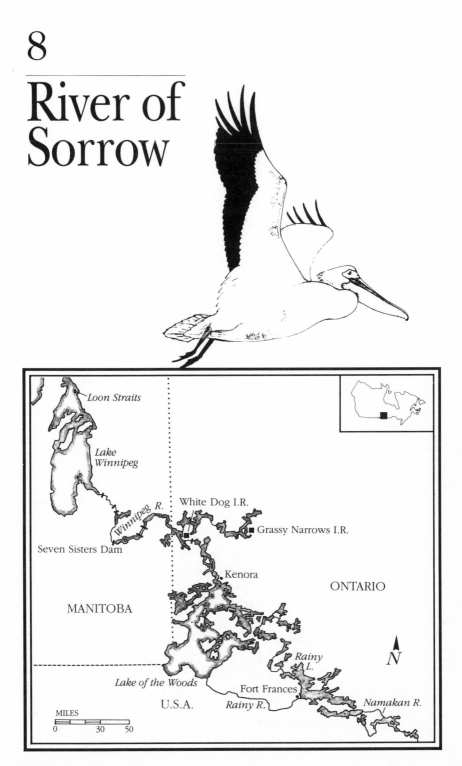

I T WAS 7:37 A.M. when we pulled ashore at the Neguaguon Lake Indian Reserve. We had less than 10 minutes to locate a phone to do our weekly CBC Radio interview with Alan Millar. I knocked at the door of a little ramshackle cottage. Murmurings from within penetrated the paper-thin walls. Then the door swung slowly open. A thin brown hand clutched the knob, fingers bent and crippled with arthritis.

"Hello," wheezed a creaky voice.

I felt ridiculous explaining our problem at this early hour.

"Come in then," he offered with a spluttering cough. We pushed the door back further and stepped inside, into what was the largest of the cabin's two rooms. A bed took up most of the floor space and, to our astonishment, the blanketed figure of an old man occupied it.

"Phone's down there," he smiled feebly, pointing a gnarled finger at the foot of the bed. We returned the smile, feeling affection for this fellow whose gracious hospitality knew no limits. Who else would allow complete strangers into their bedroom first thing in the morning to use the telephone? After much searching, we discovered the phone underneath a pile of old jeans on a little shelf. Gary dialed CBC. I pressed my ear to the back side of the receiver to listen in on the conversation.

"Well, our two intrepid canoeists have managed to plug themselves into a pine tree somewhere in the northern bush again," Alan was saying over the air. "Good morning!"

As he answered, Gary lifted his hand, directing a little wave toward the bed. I looked up—peering out from under the rumpled bedspread was a row of bright, smiling eyes. I counted six pairs before they popped back out of sight—the grandchildren of this old couple, we presumed. Soon the bed was alive with a squirming bundle of giggling laughter.

After Gary described our surroundings to the chuckling Alan, he handed the phone to me. We could picture the listening audience around the breakfast table as I launched into a graphic account of the bloodsucker episode.

The Namakan River's first rapid is a curling sluiceway that can lure an unwary traveler into its grasp. The riffles are long, easy and fun. Then all of a sudden, the river drops, snaking around boulders in a turmoil of white water and foam. The doorway to the river was more than a little disconcerting to the early white travelers, traders and voyageurs. It was no wonder the longer alternative Loon River route was used by the voyageurs for so many seasons. In 1829, one ambitious man, the Governor General George Simpson, mounted the Namakan River current to determine its true nature and feasibility as a route to the west. The following spring, he descended it with his teenage bride, Frances, who recorded in her diary that it was a practicable and safe route at any time for boats or canoes.

The Namakan forms the western boundary of Quetico Provincial Park. It is quiet and very wild. Below Ivy Falls, we had our first magnificent sighting of a bald eagle plunging for pickerel in the current. Huge sturgeon surged to the surface in shallow bays. In every little marsh, great blue herons would come flapping up from the protective covering of the reeds. There was Ivy Rapids, Quetico Rapids, High Falls and Lady Rapids, some of which could be run while others had to be portaged. As we swept around an island in the rapids below thundering High Falls, we were greeted with a chorus of cheers. Only hours before our arrival, an aluminum canoe had capsized upstream. Its occupants floated through the white water unharmed but the loaded canoe banged against a boulder and crumpled before continuing downstream. The people on shore had rescued it and the frightened couple.

Before descending the rapids, we had stopped to admire the magnitude of the water plunging over the ledges of High Falls. It was awesome compared to the gurgling streamlets near the height of land where we had paddled several days back. We recalled the duck-puddle lakes maturing into feeder streams, these in turn forming larger lakes. Even the Namakan had swelled noticeably from its beginnings in Lac la Croix to this final plunge before Namakan Lake. I suddenly had a very vivid three-dimensional vision of Canada, imagining the country's contours and basins

directing and collecting the flow of fresh water. Gradually gathering, growing and maturing, waterways play out their lives like
people, with almost as many characters and moods.

Between Namakan and Rainy Lakes, we discovered an oasis on
this hot August evening. At the end of a long shady lane lay the
rambling white Kettle Falls Hotel. The hotel had opened its
doors in 1913, in the heyday of lumbering in the Quetico wilderness. It became the stopover and watering hole for loggers
traveling between their homes in Fort Frances and International
Falls and the northern bush. This evening it was going to be our
watering hole. The aroma of freshly baked bread drew us to the
big screened porch where guests were enjoying meals made on a
wood cookstove. We slipped through into the bar where lively
tunes were spilling out of an old juke box. The hotel's wooden
floors were still pockmarked with the spikes of loggers' boots. In
the middle of the floor, a couple of fishermen wearing peaked
caps covered in crests, pins and buttons were playing a game of
snooker. Gary nudged me, pointing at the pool-table legs closest
to us. They were noticeably longer than the other two. This was
to compensate for the sloping floors. In fact, as I looked around,
I realized that everything in the room had been adapted to make
it level. Pasted discreetly on the walls amid the menagerie of
stuffed animals, pheasants and fish were old-fashioned pictures
of scantily clad women.

The Kettle Falls patrons were as colorful as the unusual decor.
Four very fat women perched on barstools behind us. They bab-
bled continuously, suffering somewhat from an excess of alcohol.
A delightful fellow from Minnesota and his booming brother-in-
law were launching into a debate with the bartender over the
best lure for pickerel when we sidled up to the bar. They both
had sunburned faces. Their necks and arms, below the edges of
short-sleeved T-shirts, were scarlet. It was obviously their first day
of holidays and they had whiled it away in a fishing boat under
the glare of the burning sun.

When they noticed us, they turned and grinned. "You two look
like you've had about as much sun as we have."

The untanned circles around our eyes, usually covered by our
glasses, emphasized our rosy cheeks and noses.

"Say, where have you fellas come from?" piped up the bartender. After we explained that we had paddled in, the Minnesota

sportsman noted that he had read the inscription on the side of our canoe.

"If you really are paddling across Canada, then the drinks are on me," he declared.

"You know, I remember hearing you fellas on the radio one morning," the bartender added.

Then the pool players contributed that they too had heard us on the radio. The questions prompted stories and the more we told, the more questions they asked. Every now and then, someone would yell out, "Drinks for everybody! It's on me!"

An hour later, the pool players called out in a slurred tone, "Another round!" By this time we had downed half a dozen cans of pop. We tipped our hats to the bartender and slipped out completely unnoticed.

We left the hotel, and we left Canada, well fortified to paddle the length of Rainy Lake to Fort Frances along the southern side of the international boundary. From the canoeists' paradise of Quetico, we emerged into a maelstrom of late-twentieth-century cottagers enjoying their idea of "wilderness." From enormous houseboats to family craft, everything was motorized. The whine of the outboard successfully drowned out all the natural sounds of the northern landscape. It felt like we were on a stormy sea as we pitched to and fro on the dozens of colliding boat wakes. After a cottager's surly rebuff to our request for a place to camp in this lakeland suburbia, we struck out for the lake's northern side. It was a frightening few miles. With nightfall fast approaching and our flashlight's battery power waning, we were very vulnerable. Not only was the bay alive with the red, green and white running lights of powered vessels, but the seaplane base was also active. Aircraft returning with the onset of darkness were landing on this stretch of water with disturbing frequency. Getting hit by a plane while paddling our canoe really would be the ultimate collision with the twentieth century!

We appeared out of the inky blackness, landing on the shores of another unsuspecting cottager whose only suggestion was to camp on "their island." Groping blindly across the bay, we almost paddled straight into it. The "island" turned out to be a mere hunk of rock sloping on all sides. By the time the tent was pitched on the arched back of rock, a million hungry mosquitoes had found their way inside. The noise of their buzzing and the irritation of their needling nearly drove us wild before the last one was finally smeared across the ceiling.

The French voyageurs called it Rivière de la Reine, Queen of Rivers, because the low placid countryside felt so much like the lower Ottawa Valley. To those not yet accustomed to the rugged spruce bush and granite rock of the Canadian Shield, this reference to home alleviated some of their homesickness. The beautiful name was shortened to Rivière Reine, and then altered by the English to Rainy River.

The broad brown Rainy River forms a corridor flanked on both sides by tall stands of lush green reeds and bullrushes. This region was once submerged and formed part of the ancient Lake Agassiz. Beyond the greenery, muddy banks descend from productive farmland where hay, barley, oats and corn are sown. In the small woodlands separating the fields, lethargic cows peered out from between the trees at our passing canoe. The longtime habitation of this hospitable country was evident in the century-old homesteads.

But one thing was marring our enjoyment of this 80-mile stretch of our journey to Lake of the Woods—Gary's blistered lip, now deeply infected. Despite all the tender loving care I gave with the aid of ointments and sunscreen, nothing had helped. Gary needed an antibiotic, which meant a doctor's prescription. His entire jaw was throbbing with pain and his lower lip was ballooning with inflammation. Feverish and constantly thirsty, Gary ate nothing for two days. He longed for the relief a bag of ice cubes or even a cool drink could bring. Clean water was not usually a problem, but on this river, affected by both the pulp-and-paper mills at its headwaters and the runoff from agricultural land, we had to carry all of it. There was never enough. To make matters worse, a persistent hot dry wind slowed our progress to a crawl.

When we finally arrived at the village of Rainy River, it was all we could do to pull our canoe ashore and struggle into town. I had never seen Gary so utterly despondent and miserable. His broad shoulders slumped and a permanent furrow had formed across his brow. He hadn't joked or laughed properly in several days. As we entered the health clinic, a wave of cool, sterile air swept over us. A doctor with a kind smile led Gary into a small examination room. When they reappeared, he assured me Gary would be his old self in a day or two. He prescribed an ointment and tetracycline pills to eliminate the infection. At the prescription counter, the druggist dispensed the ointment and pills with sympathetic understanding. Then, just as we were leaving, she tucked a small brown jar containing cortisone cream into Gary's hand.

"This'll do the trick next time. When your lips get blistered just smear some of it on." I reached for our wallet.

"No, no," she said, "no charge. Happy and safe paddling to The Pas!"

A group of pelicans glided across the windblown lake on powerful sweeping wings, just barely keeping their wingtips dry. The entire V formation moved in a continuous undulating wave as the pelicans picked up the wing beat from the leader and passed it along from front to rear. Entranced, we handed the binoculars back and forth. It was strange to see these birds at such a northern latitude. In our minds, pelicans would be more at home in a tropical climate such as the Florida Everglades.

Lake of the Woods grows out of the long sinuous root of the Rainy River. It develops into the smooth bulb-shaped Traverse Bay from which a profusion of watery tendrils weave northward through an intricate maze of islands. We were proceeding northward from the mouth of the Rainy River. Our route, which would take us straight up the center of the lake, now slipped among the low-lying slivers of land known as the Sable Islands. The sandbars extending far from the land were awash in ankle-deep water. We sloshed along, dragging the barely floating canoe behind. Scores of gulls and terns wheeling above squealed in agitation at our presence.

Just as we approached the northern end of the islands the extraordinary bulky figure of a white pelican surprised us as it came gliding around the point. Its curious, round-eyed expression was followed by a casual about-face and it sailed back toward the open lake with its ponderous bill tucked stoutly under its chin. Resting our paddles across the gunwales, we savored the special moment of discovery. White pelicans were a bird we had never seen in the wild before today. Living out their lives in peaceful undisturbed harmony with their surroundings and their neighbors, the gulls, terns and cormorants, pelicans dislike being harrassed so much that they will abandon their nesting sites if encroached upon. Being fully aware of their nature, we remained unmoving—respectful of the distance it was putting between us.

Traveling directly northward, with the Aulneau Peninsula to the east and Falcon Island to the west, we sliced through the very heart of Lake of the Woods. On today's maps this narrow strip of water begins as the Tug Channel. It is squeezed into a bottleneck at the French Portage Narrows and emerges among hundreds of islands in the north end of Lake of the Woods. In the days of the fur trade, this channel was actually an isthmus of land over which the voyageurs portaged. However, even though they had to unpack and haul the loads and canoes across the land bridge, it was still considered the fastest, most efficient route. North of the channel, it was a navigational challenge to determine where we were all the time. Throughout this area, the islands roll in behind one another in a complex backdrop that defies one's depth perception.

Just west of Ontario's mining and pulp-and-paper town of Kenora, we located one of the three outlets from Lake of the Woods to the Winnipeg River. From Portage Bay in Keewatin, we made a short, easy carry into the river, unbothered by the log booms that filled the other two. This waterway was once wild and masterful, dropping in a series of spectacular rapids and falls over 270 feet in the 275-mile journey from Lake of the Woods to Lake Winnipeg. As a free-flowing river, the Winnipeg thundered through gorges and wound northward in a wide silver stream. The voyageurs who traveled the route between Fort Chipewyan and Grand Portage annually undoubtedly felt that this was the grandest segment of their long voyage. Then, in the name of progress and to meet the growing power needs of Manitoba, the river was swallowed up by seven hydroelectric projects. It was changed into a staircase of lakes and condemned to a life of labor for man. Not more than 100 miles away, the sprawling metropolis of Winnipeg, capital of Manitoba, is the major consumer.

The presence of dams and the pulp-and-paper industry on a waterway can have serious unforeseen effects on those who live nearby and depend on harvesting its resources. As we neared the Indian reserve of Whitedog on the English River below the first of the Winnipeg River dams, we were seeing a town forgotten and maligned by both these industries. When the Winnipeg's natural flow stopped because of the construction of hydroelectric dams, much of the river's ecology was drastically altered and ruined. The Indians at the Whitedog reserve were dependent on their harvest of wild rice for both diet and cash income. In 1958 when this particular dam was completed, Ontario Hydro flooded the area without any forewarning to the people living on the reserve upstream. They moved, posthaste, with all their belongings to the Whitedog reserve downstream. Here, the Whitedog people were building earthen dams to divert Hydro's spring release of water, which was backing up into Whitedog Lake and flooding the wild rice crop. Even after this there were years when the Hydro releases were greater than normal and the entire crop was wiped out—no help to rebuild the Whitedog control dam and no compensation for lost income was forthcoming.

As we paddled by the Whitedog reserve, we saw fishermen and their Indian guides trolling back and forth across the river amid the bloated, belly-up carcasses of whitefish. It appeared that the river was still being contaminated by the pulp-and-paper industry, namely the mill owned by the Reed Paper Company in Dryden, Ontario, even after years of controversy. The main chemical culprit is mercury.

Mercury, a fluid, silvery metal utilized in the pulp-and-paper mill industry, has affected the life and health of every living thing in the English-Wabigoon River system, which runs into the Winnipeg River at the Whitedog and Grassy Narrow reserves. Heavier than lead, the metal sinks to the bottom of rivers and lakes where microscopic organisms convert it into highly toxic methyl mercury. The organisms are consumed by the bottom-feeding fish and eventually the mercury, with its dangerous, deadly side effects, is passed through the food chain to fish-consuming birds and mammals.

At the reserves, where the mainstay of the diet is fish, the unsuspecting native population ingested high levels of mercury. In the years to follow, the people were afflicted with the painful, paralyzing, blinding effects of a terrible nervous disorder known as Minamata disease, named after a Japanese fishing village where the effects were first tied to the consumption of methyl mercury.

During the greatest outbreak of public debate over the issue, the Ontario government supplied a freezer holding several thousand pounds of mercury-free whitefish to the Grassy Narrows band. The freezer didn't work and despite the Indians complaint it was never repaired, so all the fish rotted. The minister of natural resources waved aside complaints of the incident by claiming that the freezer's malfunction was caused by an act of deliberate sabotage.

The story of the mercury poisoning in the Whitedog and Grassy Narrows reserves is a horrifying, complex and politically embarrassing one. It involves federal and provincial cover-ups to protect the well-being of the polluter and the sport-fishing industry. It is an issue that involved a one-industry town dependent upon the jobs provided by the polluting culprit, the Reed Paper Company. (The company itself, a huge multinational conglomerate has financial and political relationships which override concern for the environment.) Then there was the influence of the independant and biased government scientific communities, and the stories produced by the media. The sportfishing industry became involved, since its success impinged on the dollars brought in by the fishermen. No one wants to eat mercury-contaminated fish! Finally, there is the Whitedog and Grassy Narrows native population itself, which has endured physical, emotional, social and economic destruction. The Whitedog–Grassy Narrows story is not an isolated case by any stretch of the imagination. Such incidents are played out time and again in Canada and all around the world. Just because we don't live downstream from a pulp-and-paper mill doesn't mean the water coming from our faucet is thoroughly safe to drink. Maybe the most frightening part of all this is the realization that chemical poisoning can happen in anyone's backyard irrespective of color, race or religion.

When we had passed the Whitedog reserve, the megalithic gray structure of Seven Sisters dam loomed ominously on the horizon like some enormous penitentiary. To contain the headpond created by the dam in this flat country, concrete arms extended from each side of the dam and embraced 10 miles of shoreline around Natalie Lake. Under a heavy ceiling of cloud, with the rumbling of the turbines filling the still air, we approached very cautiously. Gary peered through the binoculars

*A mat of white waterlilies speckled the surface of Lindstrom Lake south of Frog Portage, the divide separating the Saskatchewan and Churchill River watersheds.*

*On the southern edge of Pukaskwa National Park, the Cascade River pours over a ledge into Lake Superior. The plummeting waters provided an invigorating shower.*

*July 1983 was a month of unusual calm on Lake Superior, the world's largest freshwater lake. Undisturbed by wind, the icy-cold bays gradually warmed and swimming behind granite shoals became a daily pleasure.*

*Slipping over shallow waters close to shore, we experienced unusual geological formations, such as this natural archway south of Simpson Island on the north shore of Lake Superior.*

*Despite the stunted tree growth on Lake Superior's harshly weathered shoals, great blue herons have established a nesting colony amongst the low-level crowns of birch and spruce.*

*Stormbound or windbound days provided time to focus on the plant life of the woodlands and shores. The florid brilliance of wood lilies brightened and softened a harsh landscape of rock, trees and water.*

*Soaring on wings spanning nine feet, a straggling wave of white pelicans glides between the golden layers of cloud over Lake Winnipeg.*

*A frothy white curtain spills dreamily over a smooth ledge at Manitou Falls, on the Fond du Lac River. In contrast, the river's right-hand current storms into a buttress of limestone and plummets through a needle's-eye channel with foaming fury.*

*Halfway through one of the nine waterlogged, mosquito-breeding portage trails linking the meandering Blondeau River with Wollaston Lake.*

*With fascination, we watched massive sheets of rain obliterate the landscape during one of many isolated storm cells that swept along Lake Athabasca's north shore.*

*Lucy Adams, a native of the Mackenzie delta, continues an age-old, late-summer tradition of netting and smoking whitefish.*

*Smoked whitefish is hung upon outdoor drying racks, then packed in bales and stored as a staple food for the winter diet of the delta people.*

*Droplets splashing from the return sweep of a paddle stroke reflect a fiery Mackenzie River sunset near the Arctic Circle.*

several times, trying to determine on which side we should portage. If we chose the wrong side, we would have to pass right
across the face of the dam. I could picture us getting too close—
being swept into the yawning intake, then the smooth sleigh ride
down a gigantic penstock into the swirling turbines. I shuddered.
My imagination was forever running wild.

The sight of a vehicle on the east side prompted us to head in
that direction. After portaging down the road, we arrived back
on the river. From our canoe-level view, we could gaze over the
banks of swaying grasses and scrubby bushes to small stands of
poplar and the occasional field of prairie grain. Near Seven Sisters dam, billowing smoke was further blackening the already
stormy sky. As we drew closer, an acrid smell filled our lungs and
made our eyes brim with tears. Orange flames were licking
through the dry turf and the low scrubby spruce. A number of
explosive lightning storms over the past few evenings had played
havoc with the tinderbox-dry bush. We had had very little rain
for weeks and the fire rangers were being kept extremely busy
across northwestern Ontario and into Manitoba.

From Pointe du Bois dam to Powerview, high-voltage towers
spanned the river and looped across the flat country, carrying
the power of the river's tumbling waters to cities and towns. For
the most part, we couldn't experience the true nature of the
river as it was hidden beneath headponds and held back by man-
made structures, but one evening the original current made a
partial resurgence at Sturgeon Falls. The wispy mare's-tail clouds
were streaked pink, mauve and gold as they curled across the sky
in the face of a strong westerly blow. The wind tore upstream,
ripping the frothy white caps from the enormous standing waves.
As we were sneaking into a large eddy on the west shore, an exceptionally strong gust took us by surprise. The canoe had drifted up the eddy and was forced back into the current before we
knew what was happening. Immediately, we abandoned all hope
of hugging the shore and running the safe channel. The canoe
was poised on the brink of an angry souse-hole that sucked and
growled. In a split-second unspoken agreement, we lunged
across the current and swung the canoe downstream into the
engulfing turbulence. Narrowly skirting the recirculating hole,
which was big enough to cartwheel the canoe end over end, we
plunged into the long, deep wave troughs. The horizon kept ap-

pearing and disappearing until the wave train of Sturgeon Falls rapids finally petered out.

Autumn was dotting the landscape with rustling golden birch leaves. The poison ivy woven through the rocks and crevices around the dams was turning scarlet. Ducks were congregating, the blacks and mergansers being especially prevalent. Throughout the river's upper stretch from Lake of the Woods to Lac du Bonnet, we made frequent sightings of blue herons and bald eagles. When nightfall came and man-made structures, like the spiderweb of power lines, became invisible, the Winnipeg River was transformed into a lonely thin lake haunted with the beauty of summer evening voices—the repetitious chant of whip-poor-wills and the hooting of the barred owl.

Near the mouth of the Winnipeg River, we climbed the bank to the pulp-and-paper town of Pine Falls. Our view of the landscape was an endless sea of piled logs surging toward the mill. The familiar sickly sweetness wafted down to the river on the hot afternoon breeze. Our final parcel of food and film was awaiting us at the post office. The supplies we picked up here would have to last us through 300 miles up the length of Lake Winnipeg and another 150 miles up the Saskatchewan River to our destination.

We entered the figure-eight-shaped Lake Winnipeg with as much apprehension as we had felt approaching Superior. Few lakes rival Winnipeg in its capacity to create totally unnavigable conditions for small craft within a matter of minutes. The almost complete lack of island cover along much of the southeastern and northwestern shores allows prairie winds to whistle unchecked across the 9,500 square miles of extremely shallow water. In many places the lake is only 10 to 12 feet deep. Adding to our anxiety was the fact that the lake has piled an invincible barrier of pewter-smooth driftwood against the coastline for a number of miles north of the mouth of the Winnipeg River. Occasionally, the wall is broken with tiny sandspits, river mouths and shoreline indentations. But in places where the pounding waves have undercut the shore, entire banks of trees have tumbled into the lake.

Long strands of slimy green algae draped over our paddles as we lifted them from the water. The heavy stench of the iridescent green mat of vegetation was made even more potent by the fishy smell of tern and gull droppings fouling the water and whitewashing the rocks. On the southern horizon, cumulous clouds were billowing into black thunderheads. The atmosphere was thick with humidity. A storm was brewing. The surface of Lake Winnipeg was deathly calm. Then the wind began to blow, rising in strength with frightening speed. Within minutes, the whole surface of the lake seemed to be breaking in a two-foot chop. Battered again and again by large waves, we were finding it more and more difficult to stay upright. "Growlers" washed over shallow boulders. We cringed when we felt the canoe hull brush against these immovable dangers lying just below the surface. In the gathering gloom, pink sheet lightning wavered in eerie formations behind the wall of cloud. The setting sun left a blaze of magenta along the edge of the horizon. Thunder rumbled ominously, pressing us on to find a safe haven for the night.

We squinted into the darkness, barely making out a patch of sand with tall swaying grasses behind it. By the time we pulled our boat ashore, the lake was wild with white foaming crests that crashed along the shore. Struggling with our billowing tent that threatened to take flight any moment, we finally had it pitched behind an upturned tree's root system. We anchored the tent to that and secured it even more by dragging in some heavy driftwood stumps. Just as the first rain came driving across the open water, a flock of snow geese winged their way past our tiny campsite. We were not the only ones seeking shelter from the storm.

Entirely unlike Superior, Lake Winnipeg's shoreline is constantly rearranging itself. The little beach on which we began the night was almost 10 feet across and three times as long. By dawn, the lake was foaming up against our doorstep and spraying the walls. Bleary-eyed, we quickly hauled everything onto the higher ground in a field of thick grasses. It was a decidedly lumpy floor but nice and dry.

For two days we found ourselves weatherbound on an inhospitable stretch of Lake Winnipeg's southeastern shore. The clearing was hemmed in by a dense forest of spruce, decaying birch trees, stinging nettle and prickly thistles. From a photographer's standpoint, there was a lot of subject matter. September's flowers were in bloom. Among the purple asters were

feathery clusters of goldenrod and orange jewelweed whose delicate little seedpods give it its other name, touch-me-not. A light
prod coaxes the casings to explode in a shower of minute seeds. I
was intrigued by a pattern of cobwebs in which ambitious en-
gineers quickly threaded lines back and forth. Little brown sacs
hung throughout this delicate dewdrop lace. As I examined
them more closely, I realized that one sac was speckled with tiny
offspring that skittered around each time I touched the web.

Gary was just as intrigued by the wild coastline, so completely
changed from the previous evening. Entire shoals, once visible,
were lost to view in the roiling brown surf. Eyeing the smooth silvery driftwood pummeled by countless storms, he saw weird and
wonderful creatures. From the starkness of wood, Gary's camera
eye roamed over the brown waves and far up into the cerulean
blue sky dotted with cotton-wool clouds.

"Come here, Joanie!" he called urgently. "The pelicans are
coming."

I slipped through the bush and ducked down behind the
canoe with him. Large flocks of white pelicans appeared in wave
after wave over the horizon, heading north into the strong
headwind. They ferried across the sky, using the wind as a
canoeist uses the river current to his advantage when traveling
upstream. Pelicans normally do a lot of gliding. It is no wonder,
on wings spanning eight feet! But today the rhythm of wing beats
was constant.

White pelicans are sociable birds, preferring to eat, nest, breed
and fly in groups. What they need in order to survive is fairly
simple—large areas of marshy, low-lying lakes in which to nest
and an abundant source of fish. Looking at our map, we could
see several protected bays and a speckling of islands 15 miles farther north. No doubt this was their destination. Once the wind
subsided and let us paddle on again, we would find out for sure.

The high winds had churned the lake into a brown silty soup
garnished with bits of green algae, sticks and diluted gull guano.
This fishy, smelly liquid was our only source of drinking water.
Consequently, we had to go through a long and tedious process
of water gathering. Armed with yards of toilet paper and a
couple of T-shirts, we constructed a filtering system through
which we poured this revolting mixture. After several filtrations,
finely ground silt still hung suspended in the water so we took

the brown liquid and proceeded to boil it thoroughly. We poured off the liquid, careful not to disturb the sediment settled on the bottom of the pot. Now came the final stage—four large sweet spoonfuls of purple grape-juice powder were poured into every bottle of drinking water to mask the color and taste. The rest was left for cooking.

For nearly a week after, our bodies ached for no apparent reason. We felt feverish and listless and meals were a really picky affair. It took three days to eat what we would usually have eaten in one. The only thing to which we could attribute our debilitated condition was the foul water. When the winds finally subsided, we traveled north toward Loon Straits. Along the way, at the Manigotagan and Wanipigow river mouths, we discovered upward of a hundred white pelicans gliding majestically among the protective band of tiny islands.

Through the uppermost branches of the trees on a point of land south of Loon Straits, we caught sight of a Canadian flag flapping wildly in the ever-strengthening breeze. The thought of human habitation was a welcome one, for it appeared the wind was about to force us off the lake again. As we paddled by the point, a meadow covered with wild flowers and long grasses came into view on the far shore. In the middle of the field were swings, a slide and monkeybars. Not far away was a building that looked like a schoolhouse. Its windows were boarded and the walls feathered with peeling yellow paint. Nothing moved. There is something melancholy about an empty playground, where the grass is long and untrampled by little feet and the joyful exuberance of children at play is missing.

We traversed the bay toward a partially complete frame house and a dock where two people stood, waving in welcome.

"Hello," called out a smiling blond-haired woman. Beside her stood a solemn little girl with long black pigtails. Her chin was pressed against her chest and her large brown eyes peered out from beneath a fringe of hair. Her expression was a mixture of curiosity and suspicion. Anne Monkman introduced herself and her daughter, Linda. We soon discovered that the paling yellow building had, indeed, once been a one-room schoolhouse. This friendly woman had been its last teacher.

The pounding of nails in the empty frame structure ceased and a tall dark man with a strong handsome face of native origin appeared in the doorway, hammer in hand. Carl Monkman was born and raised at Loon Straits. In fact, the island just off the point was called Monkman Island. Carl was an architect and builder by trade, although he could turn his hand to any number of things. He brought chunks of sprucewood to life in his carvings of animals and birds. He was also a mechanic and pilot, and owned his own aircraft, a two-man Pipercub float plane. With a broad, welcoming smile, he helped Gary heave the canoe onto the dock. Then another girl appeared. Quiet, tall and willowy, she was Sharon, Linda's older sister.

"Now you've met the whole family except our boy. He's working in Riverton," said Anne. Riverton was the name of the village almost due south on the west side of Lake Winnipeg near the tip of Hecla Island. "Won't you share some lunch with us?"

During the meal, Carl filled us in on the history of Loon Straits. Commercial fishing had once supported a community of 140 residents. When the fish stock in Lake Winnipeg was so depleted that it no longer provided a decent living, people left for the western shore. There are only a few commercial fishing operations left along the eastern shoreline in the native villages of Black River, Manigotagan and Wanipigow. Hundreds of fishing nets hang unused in the back of old woodsheds. Carl remembered with sadness the days when netloads of pickerel and sauger were dragged ashore both summer and winter.

There were more cottages up behind the Monkman's small house. Carl pointed them out and gave us a short history of each one.

"This is where my grandmother lived. Tom Monkman, a distant cousin, lives up on the hill. Further down the road, I have another distant cousin, Gladys."

"Can I take them to see Gladys, Dad?" Linda burst out excitedly.

"You better ask Gary and Joanie," Carl answered.

No sooner had we said yes than she was dashing off around the house. We heard a motor kicking in. Moments later she reappeared on a three-wheeled all-terrain vehicle. Our pint-sized driver skidded to a halt. We piled on the back and took off to meet Gladys.

A sign on the front of Gladys Oddleifson's home identified it as the Loon Straits Post Office. Beside the front door stood a bright red phone booth. The Oddleifsons had the only two out-going phones in the community. Linda herded us inside. Intro-ductions had barely been made when Linda scurried back out to hunt for frogs in the long grass with Gladys's young grandson.

"Oddleifson is an Icelandic name," Gladys was telling us as she pulled back the kitchen chairs. "Do have a seat! I'm just making up a batch of pickles for Bob." The gigantic jars of dill pickles lined up along the counter were the largest we had ever seen. In addition to being the postmaster for this tiny community of five, Gladys's husband Bob sets his nets in the spring and fall fishing seasons. He also maintained the diesel-powered generator and cared for the navigation buoys on this part of Lake Winnipeg.

"In fact, Bob's out on the lake right now checking buoys," Gladys said.

We had another stop to make at the home of Gladys's brother, Tom. His delight at having unexpected visitors was obvious. Before we knew it, we were sharing in our third round of tea and toast. Everyone's hospitality was filling us to the brim. Tom talked of the early days and the fishing. But his tone was most nostalgic when he talked about the children. "The school was full. Children were everywhere. I loved their laughter and their fun when they came to visit. Loon Straits is too quiet now."

Just then a little dark-haired girl went flying past the window on her motorized tricycle. Our taxi had arrived to take us home. We bade Tom farewell, then the three of us wheeled off down the lane.

Out beyond the point, a rolling sea of whitecaps made it impos-sible for the Monkmans to travel home to Riverton that Sunday evening. Carl's suggestion that we take the boat around the more protected Loon Bay was greeted with delight. We all bundled into the cabin cruiser. With its seasoned pilot at the helm, the boat weathered the rough waters well. On the far side of the bay there was sand and granite rock, a far more amicable shoreline than the one we had been following farther south. Our tracks along the beach crisscrossed those of black bear, lynx and wolf.

When Gary pointed out a large white goose swimming near shore, Linda let out a shriek of joy. "It's David," she cried rushing forward. "Oh David, David, where have you been?"

"He's Linda's favorite pet," Anne explained quickly in response to our astonished faces. "Last weekend he disappeared just before we left to go home, much to Linda's distress. She's been worried about him all week."

Linda tried to grab David but succeeded only in pulling out a handful of tail feathers from the indignant goose. Gary was right behind, ready to capture him should Linda miss. He placed the startled goose into her outstretched arms. She squeezed him with affection and buried her face in his wing. Once back at the cabin, we found David a cardboard box where he could spend the night before returning to Riverton.

Later on that evening, we brought out the maps of our journey and the logbook stuffed full of notes and sketches. After some time, the conversation around the kitchen table drifted toward the subject of adventure and risk-taking. Spending time on Lake Winnipeg had brought the Monkmans their fair share of risk. Carl had flown his plane and piloted his boat through some pretty forbidding weather conditions over the years. He recounted one particularly memorable experience. His motor had conked out and he had spent one very long night sailing his boat home through a storm powered by a jury-rigged blanket. From then on, he always carried an extra motor whenever he went out on the lake.

We felt that Carl and his family were kindred spirits in that they had chosen to live in an environment that brought with it a certain amount of risk. But none of us rushed into risky situations without considering the dangers involved. With forethought, we made preparations and devised backup systems in case the anticipated dangers became reality. We shared an attitude about what constituted a sensible approach. It involves having sound judgment and the skills to handle the task at hand. It means having the right equipment, knowing how to use it, and being aware of the limits to which your skills and equipment can be stretched.

There are different kinds of adventure. Many people can tell exciting stories of near disaster where ignorance and foolhardiness created the situation and sheer luck got them home alive. But then there is the calculated risk, where danger goes hand in hand with the experiential know-how to determine one's destiny.

As the first light was stealing across the eastern horizon the next morning, Carl and Anne were packing their cruiser for the trip home to Riverton. The wind had calmed just enough for them to consider the crossing safe. We stood waving goodbye from the end of their dock. Carl was leaving his future home for the moment, but the following week he would be back to further his dream of living on this isolated peninsula once again. The boat plunged heavily into the deep wave troughs, sending spray cascading over the bow. Carl stood at the helm, his hands wrapped firmly about the wheel, his family tucked safely below deck. Yes, there was danger, sure, there was risk; but he was in his element and he was free!

# 9
# Haunted Passage

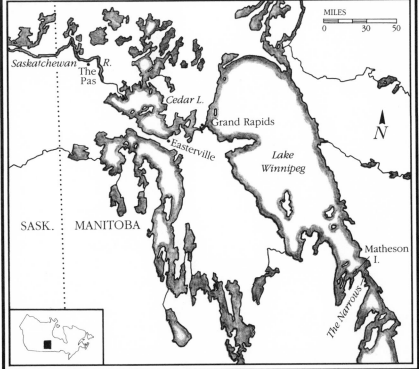

F ROM LAKE WINNIPEG'S two-mile-wide narrows, the water
body swells northward like a large inflated balloon. As we
moved from the eastern to the western side of the lake, we
noticed a remarkable change in the geology of the land. On the
eastern side, we had traveled past driftwood-covered beaches and
smooth sand coves embraced by granite rock. This was the
Canadian Shield. It had become a familiar sight to us, as it was
the landmass we had followed for a good part of our journey. At
The Narrows, the Shield tilts downward and disappears under
the successive layers of post-Cambrian rock that runs along the
western shore. It was here that we discovered and explored the
flowerpot formations of sculptured dolomite. In one spot, we
scrambled down a long square tunnel which was created when
the flat, overhanging slabs of rock collapsed. The tunnel was
narrow enough that we could wedge our backs and feet against
opposite walls and inch our way up to the ceiling.

We paddled beyond Matheson Island's cable ferry crossing and
Canoe Pass Island, then struck out for the tip of Moose Island,
which was more than five miles away across open water. It was to be
the first of a number of very exposed traverses. Had we felt it
necessary to stick close to shore, paddling around Fisher Bay, Kin-
wow Bay and Sturgeon Bay would have taken a great deal of time.
Fisher Bay, for example, is 25 miles long, which would have meant
an extra 50 miles of paddling. We decided instead to head out
directly across their gaping mouths. Nevertheless, as we skirted the
curvature of Lynx Bay, we became once again keenly aware of our
extremely vulnerable position. Paddling beneath cliffs rising
straight up from the water's edge, we couldn't help thinking that a
rising wind could easily capsize us and dash our canoe to pieces
against the cliff face. Lake Winnipeg had already given us a pretty
fair demonstration of its capabilities in that department.

But there is always wild beauty in treacherous places. In the
precipitous cliffs reflecting the warm orange hues of the setting

sun, we saw a particularly fascinating formation. Since the lake was calm, we paddled in closer. Resembling a gnarled bony finger, a column of white dolomite over 30 feet high supported a solid table of rock on which grew a tangled mat of spruce trees. The column was the thickness of an aged white pine's trunk and formed from several hundred layers of dolomite rock imprinted with billions of fossils. Centuries of storms battering the cliff had caused the rock to crumble leaving only the column. It, too, will collapse one day. What the powerful movement of water is capable of achieving never failed to leave us in awe.

Lake Winnipeg is a mere remnant of the former Lake Agassiz, which was a product of the last glaciers. Within recent geological history, Agassiz was the largest freshwater lake in existence, measuring 700 miles long and 250 miles wide during its greatest period. The glacier barricaded the northern flow of rivers, thereby acting as a dam and backing the water into an enormous headpond, namely Agassiz. The Red River (which was actually part of the lake at this time) overflowed its southern end. The water, trickling southward, finally ended up in the Missouri-Mississippi watershed.

The particular glacier which gave rise to Lake Agassiz also shaped the present central North American plain. When the lake finally drained as the glacier receded 10,000 years ago, Lake Manitoba, Lake Winnipegosis, Lake Winnipeg, the Winnipeg River, Lake of the Woods, the Red River and the Rainy River to Rainy Lake as well as a maze of tiny lakes and mosquito-breeding sloughs, were left on the western Shield. The glacier that squashed Manitoba flat was well over one mile thick. It pushed across the Shield in a northeast to southwest direction, which explains the lay of the inland lakes and the extensive elongated bays on Winnipeg's western shores.

The essentially straight northwestern shore is made up a series of shallow bays. Here we discovered sweeping stretches of white beach. We christened them the "Canadian Bahamas," although there were no palm trees and no people! The water was nowhere near the color of the Caribbean's crystalline turquoise, but it had taken on cool, translucent qualities that made it much more refreshing than the water at the southern end of the lake. The shining white sand was fine, hard packed and extremely alluring. At every spit, we leapt from the canoe. Enormous flocks of shrieking, dive-bombing terns would rise in an agitated wave as we scampered through the shallow waters, then dove in like porpoises. To dry off, we would walk back along the upper edges of the beach where thick clumps of sedge grew beneath overhanging willow fronds. Beach pea plants crawled in a tangle through the sand. Still farther back from the lake we came across a bog, a familiar feature of the landscape of eastern Manitoba. Here we found plump juicy blueberries growing in profusion. We picked and picked until our fingers and tongues were stained purple.

Each indentation of sandy beach on the northwestern shore of Lake Winnipeg ends in a rocky promontory or a cobble beach where we could have wandered for hours, even days, probing the fossil remains of billions and billions of tiny creatures. On one such occasion we discovered an abandoned fishing camp high upon a cobble mound where commercial fishermen had once carried on their activities. There were aluminum-lined storage houses and a bunch of smaller cabins now in a dilapidated state of repair. They formed a straggling row in front of the spruce bush. During the winter, the fishermen would fill the storage houses with ice blocks cut from the frozen lake. After unloading their catch, during the fishing season, the men would dress and pack and store the fish in these cold insulated storage houses. Every three days a boat would pass the camps picking up the fish for delivery to Winnipeg.

Although Lake Winnipeg lacks the spectacular beauty of Superior or the variety of the boundary waters, there is an abundance of life such as we had not seen since leaving the lower St. Lawrence. Each day we observed bald eagles, their white fantails blinking in the warm summer sky. There were huge flocks of terns, little white gulls and cormorants. Pelicans were everywhere.

One evening we found ourselves in the midst of a swarming hatch of tiny white mayflies. They didn't bite, but their delicate wings became entangled in our hair and clothes. That same evening we watched a comic spectacle—a blue heron being harassed. Terns flew out from a nearby colony to investigate the passing intruder. Before the heron knew what was happening, it was surrounded by a squadron of swooping terns zooming in from all directions. The heron's great wide wings were no match for the aerial acrobatics of these wily birds. They forced the heron to land in the lake far from shore. We could just imagine its storklike legs dangling in the deep waters below. Somehow, it managed to half beat those huge wings and lift itself from the surface again. The terns were merciless. The heron expended a great deal of energy taking off and landing several times before the terns finally allowed it to depart in peace.

Sheltered in the lee of Morass Point, we made camp under the heavenly brightness of a full moon. The beach was littered with a variety of animal footprints. The wide paw tracks with five clearly defined toes and claws identified one set as belonging to a black bear. The neat little row of dog-like tracks was the mark of a coyote. There were the splayed hoof prints of moose and the tiny pattern created by inquisitive weasels. Over the past months, we had had plenty of nocturnal visitors. But we seldom saw the creatures, only their "stories in the sand" left for us to read the following day. This night, however, would be different.

At two o'clock, I awoke to find Gary peering out the screen of the tent. A clicking and clanking of rocks rolling against one another heralded the approach of a nighttime prowler. The full moon lit up the beach as well as any streetlight. From around the back of the tent, the little creature waddled into view. He sniffed the air with curiosity. We sniffed back. There was no mistaking the long white racing stripe extending from the tip of that weaselly nose to the end of a black bushy tail. Now this was a very precarious situation. We hissed loudly. The skunk wasn't even mildly impressed, let alone threatened. It came closer, pressing its nose against the screen. Fearing that the skunk would claw its way through the screen into the tent, Gary gave it a swat dead on its nose with the back of his hand. Surprised at the rebuff, the skunk leapt backward, its tail springing to attention.

"Oh no." I covered my face, fully anticipating the sickening spray!

But surprisingly nothing happened. Gary quietly unzipped the screen door and reached out to collect a few rocks. He chucked these at the retreating plume. Half an hour later, however, the skunk's curiosity got the better of it and it was back snuffling at the door. Another biff on the nose and a barrage of rocks sent it fleeing once again. But it was persistent. Before long it was back. This time we decided it was time for us to go.

"You win. We're leaving!" Gary exclaimed with exasperation.

Although the skunk didn't know it, the night developed into one of the most magical nights of the voyage. The bow of the canoe sliced through a moonlit path of sparkling silver, while overhead the Northern Lights glowed and glimmered in undulating curtains of viridescent waves. For three tireless hours, we swept through this dreamland. Then the sky began to melt from deep velvet blue through purple to soft pink until finally a fiery orange sun burst over the horizon. The moon faded quickly with the brightening sky. It was daytime again on Lake Winnipeg.

A light breeze arising from the north allowed us to make an undetected downwind approach to a colony of cormorants. Several of them were hunched up on a large boulder, their wings held stiffly away from their bodies, trying to catch the first warm rays of the dawning sun. They held their strange statuesque position as we paddled quietly by. It felt good to see the birds accept our presence without taking to flight in fear.

A short while later we had another encounter with the terns. This time they were picking on a hapless yellow warbler. The tiny thing burst out from the willows, flew straight across our path and plummeted headfirst into the lake. It fluttered frantically on soggy wet wings while the obnoxious, knife-winged terns swooped in like screaming maniacs. I yelled at them angrily while Gary plucked the bedraggled bird out, saving it from drowning. Its tiny size was emphasized as it nestled in the palm of Gary's large strong hand. He transported it carefully to shore and found a safe tree branch where it could recuperate.

The sleepy morning and windy afternoon slipped by with countless paddle strokes. Then came the harbinger of evening, the magical yodeling of the loon. I waited expectantly for the moment. Gary drew a breath, lifted his head and answered their call. This was the call of home and it never failed to send a thrill of excitement down my spine. Gary's yodeling triggered a reverberating response from several distant pairs. Soon they had rafted together and the joyful sound filled the air around us. I felt as if they were welcoming us to the end of our year's travel by encouraging us home to Rabbit Lake.

Many people grow up with sounds that are then associated with home or the places they love best. Whether it is the foghorn to the mariner or the blast of a train whistle to the prairie farmer, the roar of ocean tides to someone who has lived by the sea or the honking of returning snow geese to a native northerner, these sounds and the feelings they evoke become ingrained in our souls.

The sun had settled comfortably below the rim of the prairie as hundreds of teals skittered off across the surface and a flock of sandhill cranes piled into their roosts on an inland pond, their guttural notes rising on the cool air. It was also time for us to settle in for the night. Tired and satisfied, we realized we had been traveling for over 19 hours, and had put an unbelievable 95 miles behind us.

The Saskatchewan River has the distinction of being Canada's fourth largest river system. Draining 150,000 square miles, its 1,200-mile course across the three prairie provinces begins in the Alberta foothills as an enormous winding Y. The twin branches eventually merge east of Prince Albert, Saskatchewan, and flow into Lake Winnipeg's northern end at Grand Rapids. It is a shallow river meandering around a jigsaw of teardrop islands and constantly shifting shoals. The light brown water, thick with sediment, travels its sluggish course through bush and vast plains, seldom displaying any dramatic surges of power until it reaches Grand Rapids. Here the Saskatchewan River once plunged to its journey's end through a limestone gorge descending almost 60 feet in one three-mile section.

Thirty feet below us lay the Grand Rapids riverbed; the turbulent rapids reduced to a mere trickle and the thunder of white water silenced forever. In the early 1960s Manitoba Hydro harnessed Grand Rapids for hydroelectric power. The power dam was constructed to receive the water flow through turbine generators while a control dam was built to stop the water flow through the original gorge. The headpond formed behind the dam is one of the 10 largest man-made lakes in the world.

Before striking out across the enormous forebay area of Cross and Cedar Lakes, we decided to have a closer look at the operation of the Grand Rapids generating station. A brochure was thrust into our hands by one of the operation's supervisors. It featured a stylized picture of the Manitoba watershed and described Hydro's all-encompassing plans for the diversion of nearly every stretch of moving water in the province, including the Nelson and Churchill rivers.

"We're not even half done yet!" the supervisor boasted.

Wearing yellow hardhats, we were escorted from the top to the bottom of the plant. On one floor, the repair and replacement work being done on the steel turbine blades intrigued us. Under tremendous pressure, the water had worn the steel full of nicks and gouges. At the bottom level of the plant, where the turbines were rotating behind heavy wooden doors, the combined noise and vibration was deafening and ominous.

Water power is always taken at a cost to the natural environment. In central Manitoba, where the topography provides no natural barriers against a dam's reservoir, a vast lowland prairie region had been wiped out by flooding. A high price was paid for the construction of the Grand Rapids dam. The flooding destroyed thousands of acres of wildlife and their habitat and the livelihood of the local native people.

Mrs. Huff, a resident of Grand Rapids, remembered what it was like before the river was dammed. The sound of the water thundering through the gorge was an essential part of the community. She referred to the day when Manitoba Hydro first cut off the Saskatchewan's flow through the gorge as an unforgettable time. The great obstacle at the convergence of the fur trade routes to the northwest had been completely obliterated.

Before we left Grand Rapids, the thoughtful Mrs. Huff tucked homemade sausages, chocolate bars and cookies into every empty pack pocket that we had. She even gave us red T-shirts emblazoned with the slogan "Grand Rapids is a nice place to live," to remind us of our visit to this part of Canada.

It seemed a strange world we paddled through on Cross and Cedar lakes, with their forests of dead timber and thousands of stumps and deadheads. Hundreds of weird shapes in burnished silver wood curved and weaved like writhing snakes. Round stumps resembled black bears and tall slender branches looked like cranes. Some even gave the illusion of men fishing. Solid land seemed to be non-existent. Every island was just a fragile construction of driftwood piled up by wind and waves.

It was quiet on the dusty streets of Easterville that evening when I left Gary with the canoe and equipment to go in search of Christine, the local nurse. The two natives I queried directed me to the far end of town where I found a house opposite the cooperative store. In a village of 800 Cree Indians, Christine was the only medical person. Her husband, John, had introduced himself when we were touring the Grand Rapids hydro plant. In some mysterious way, he had known we were coming and had been on the lookout for us. Since the plant was 60 miles from Easterville, he only had the weekends to spend with Christine. He gave us a bottle of wine to deliver in person. When I knocked at her door, I heard a young boy yell, "Christine, there's a white woman at the door!"

Blonde-haired, blue-eyed and smiling, Christine welcomed me with obvious pleasure. "John phoned and said you would be coming. It was so nice of you to stop. I don't have visitors very often." She accompanied me back down to the lake to assist in portaging our equipment up to the house.

The medical clinic was situated close to the house. By 8:30 the following morning, I noticed that there were already several people lined up outside the door. "Make yourselves at home," Christine said cheerfully as she headed out the door. "And come down to the clinic if you like." Gary and I accepted the invitation.

As the sole provider of medical care, Christine had a tremendous responsibility. Her duties did not begin and end in a normal work day. She had to be available around the clock, which even meant getting roused from bed in the wee hours of dark, cold winter mornings. She acted as a midwife delivering babies, immunized the children, patched up the wounded after drunken brawls and cared for the sick. There was no one to replace Christine whenever she left the village so she trained two native women for emergency situations. In the five years she had spent in Easterville, the first six months had been the most difficult. The challenge and love of her work saw her through until gradually she adapted to the isolation. "You know," she said, "I actually find the reverse is true now. When I leave Easterville, I long to be back."

Easterville had gone through a catastrophic upheaval during the construction of the dam and the subsequent flooding. The original village site, which we hoped to locate, had been situated farther down the shoreline at the point where the Saskatchewan River flowed into Cedar Lake. We were appalled that an entire village of people could be told that they would lose everything— their land, their homes, their fishing grounds—and that they would have to move. A new location was found on limestone bedrock above the high-water level, but it was not the same as the environment they had left behind. The fertile land along the river banks, the fishing grounds and a sawmill; everything that had supported their way of life was washed away.

Walking by small frame houses, some without windows, most with dingy interiors, we waved to the lethargic souls who leaned or sat in the darkened doorways. The lack of response made us uncomfortable. Christine later said to us, "No one knows you two. They are nice people. There are only a few who cause problems. But in some ways how can you blame them?"

We were curious as to what people really watched from their doorways over the course of a day. So we settled ourselves on Christine's porch patiently watching the world go by. The whining, yapping, baying and howling of the village dogs was an ever-present sound of community life. They come close to outnumbering the residents at times. Periodically these dogs have to be rounded up and shot when they form dangerous wild packs. These town dogs were no match for Christine's three healthy huskies. She had left the threesome each a hunk of moose bone to gnaw on and whenever one of the scrawny village dogs approached too closely, a snarling brawl would ensue. Inevitably, the struggle ended with the town dogs coming out the worse for wear. The Indian children fought nearly as much as the dogs, rolling in the dust while others passing by would stop to cheer them on. We watched people come and go from the co-op store and from Christine's medical clinic. Our afternoon on the porch steps left us with the overwhelming impression that, aside from some commercial fishing, the people here simply didn't have anything to do. They were watching life go by day after day without experiencing it. What they once had had to live for had been wiped out by a dam.

After leaving Easterville, we followed the Cedar Lake shoreline westward. Soon we found that the distinctive landforms marked on our map failed to correspond to the surroundings. The effects of the flooding were becoming quite apparent. Moreover, it was very disconcerting to discover that our chart mapped out the area as it had been before the completion of the dam, using a purple broken line to approximate the position of the new landforms. Therefore, the chart was highly unreliable for such a low-lying area where it took very little water-level fluctuation to alter the entire landscape. We had the map spread out between us on the deck of the canoe. As we debated the best plan of action, Gary suddenly looked up to see a church spire piercing through the upper limbs of the forest cover close by. We felt certain that this was the original site of Easterville before the dam's construction. Keeping our eyes on the spire, we paddled toward the marshy land, left the canoe and made our way through thick grasses and underbrush to the higher ground.

A church bell, cracked in half, lay in the middle of the clearing as if representing the broken spirits of those for whom it once chimed. A sign hung over the church door proclaiming, "This is none other than the house of God and the gateway to heaven." We stepped into the gloomy interior. Deep silence. The rows of pews waited for a congregation that would never come again. Farther down the shore, we discovered the remains of the sawmill. Huge piles of sawdust at the water's edge had been carved into strange formations by the waves. These piles had probably once been used to insulate blocks of ice in the summer storage houses. We imagined how different the atmosphere must have been in this village as compared to that of present-day Easterville.

With some misgivings, we left the quiet, forgotten remains of the village and forged ahead into an area of indistinguishable horizons, roughly a thousand square miles of flooded, shallow marshland where very little vegetation grew taller than the height of the marsh grasses. There didn't seem to be any solid land, so we eventually made camp on a twisted pile of driftwood. For a day and a half it stormed and we resigned ourselves to the confines of the tent. On the second evening, just after falling asleep, I was awoken by Gary making a tremendous racket.

"A mother bear and three cubs!" Gary yelled as I scrambled from my sleeping bag in a semiconscious state. In the fading light, we could clearly make out the four bears ambling along the driftwood shore, heading straight for the canoe. Our yelling and waving were in vain, for the wind was driving our words right back into our faces. Gary tried an aerial flare, which we carried for just such a purpose. The mother bear heard it and bounded off into the underbrush somewhere behind us. But the cubs, still young and curious, kept approaching the canoe with the delight of a small child over a new toy. Over and over, thumpity-thump,

the rolypoly hundred-pound black balls of fur played little bear
cub tag, leap-frogging over the hull and slithering down its
smooth sides.

We were in quite a predicament. Somewhere in the darkness
behind us was an anxious sow bear. When the cubs noticed she
had disappeared, they stopped playing and began bawling. Their
frantic cries would bring any mother running to their defense.
Quickly Gary threw some fuel on a tinderbox of driftwood and lit
a match to it, in the hope that we could at least keep them at bay.
Our choice was clear. Either we manned a fire all night, or we
packed up and left. Ordinarily the latter would have been the
obvious course of action, but our situation was not that simple. It
was a pitch-black, windy night. Waves were piling in against the
driftwood. And we had no definite shoreline to follow. Nevertheless, when a confrontation with the unpredictable and protective
mother bear appeared to be a very real possibility, we opted for
the plan of leaving. We hurriedly threw our possessions into the
packs, took down the tent and struggled over the rough uneven
ground toward the canoe, yelling as we went to frighten the cubs
off. As we pushed the canoe into the lake, we turned back and
noticed that the fire we had lit was increasing in size. That was all
we needed to do—start a forest fire. The only accessible con-
tainer was one of our quart water bottles. Gary filled it and
hurried back through the darkness over the jumbled driftwood
fearing he would come face to face with the family of bears. Gary
caught the flames licking the brush behind our campsite just in
time. Two more trips and he finally had it doused.

Since there wasn't a shoreline, we couldn't afford to go too far in
case we became hopelessly lost. A thick clump of bullrushes was the
most welcome harbor we could find. Running the canoe hard into
them, we wrapped a rope firmly around the bunch. Exchanging
place with our packs required some shuffling. Finally, we had them
placed on the seats, the sleeping pads and bags on the floor of the
canoe and the tarpaulin drawn over our heads.

The next morning we spent our time clambering back and
forth between the canoe and the thick mud, half poling, half
pushing our way through the reed beds. We followed up dead-
end channels and poled through marsh, all the while fighting
the urge to return to Grand Rapids. But we were so close to The
Pas we would not accept defeat now.

All afternoon our hopes surged and died. First we found a passage onto the open lake. But it was a vast shallow body of water which could be stirred by the wind into steep choppy waves such as we had experienced on Lake Winnipeg. There weren't any recognizable landmarks on which to pin our bearings. With the reed beds on the south side of us and the lake stretching to the horizon on the north, we paddled west, peering up every channel and scouting every bay looking for an indication of the river. Our prospects for reaching The Pas were dimming. We were getting very disorientated. It was a strange, uncomfortable feeling. On top of this, it was getting colder. Drawing in alongside the rushes, we laid down our paddles. The drizzling rain turned to sleet, then white mushy snow. It spattered on the tarpaulin as we floated, discouraged, hungry and shivering with cold.

"I would consider this dismal enough for emergency rations." Gary hinted.

I beamed with delight. "I'd forgotten about those."

Our spirits buoyed by the sweet taste of chocolate, we set off again. Our hopes soared when we discovered a bit of current swinging through two small, swampy islands. This current indicated that the Saskatchewan River was still hidden in the lake beneath us. But long after forging up the moving water, we were still winding our way around dead-end bays seeking the elusive river mouth.

Suddenly we spotted several white pelicans in the distance and we knew that these birds by nature seek a river current in which to feed. Another storm and four more hours of methodical searching, then a rainbow appeared. Highlighting a spit of land several miles away, the vibrant arching bands of color streamed to earth. It grew in brilliance until a double rainbow had formed.

"Give me the binoculars." I could sense the urgency in Gary's voice. "Joanie, tell me, does that bit of land look any higher than what we are passing right now?" Yes, indeed it did! At the rainbow's end, we found our pot of gold. We rounded a point of land into the mouth of the Saskatchewan River. The last pink glow of evening light waned across the horizon as we collapsed into the tent. We would make it to The Pas in two more days.

Brown water swirled unmistakeably past us. We were in a river again. Embracing us on either side was the thick vegetation of the Saskatchewan riverbanks. A flock of pelicans flew past. The teal and canvasback ducks were rafting up in great numbers in preparation for the fall migration. It was approaching the second week of September and we were barely 80 miles from The Pas.

The yelping and howling of husky dogs could be heard long before we saw the encampment. As we rounded a curve in the river, the deep long hull of a traditional Lake Winnipeg fishing boat came into view. It was partly concealed by an overhanging curtain of willows that flourished along the banks. Then we noticed the four native fishermen staring at us as if we were a ghostly apparition. We broke the spell with a cheerful greeting.

"Where did you camp last night?" asked the large fisherman closest to us. "We didn't see anyone on our way here from The Pas this morning."

"We came from the other direction," Gary said, pointing toward Cedar Lake.

The man looked from Gary to me and back again, shaking his head in disbelief. "In recent times, I have never heard of anyone crossing the lake by canoe." He turned to the others for confirmation. All three nodded their heads in unison.

"Maybe some have gone in but they haven't found their way out to tell the tale," he said, chuckling. "Even we have managed to get lost in there for several days before finding our way out, and we live here." He leaned over the gunwale and extended his hand to Gary. Before leaving, we verified our position on the map with them. We felt elated that these native people, whose forefathers must have greeted the first white explorers, considered our traverse of the lake an achievement!

In the ordinary course of events, our final evening would have followed much the same pattern as any other evening on the voyage. But for some reason, everything seemed to go wrong. First there was the downpour that soaked us to the skin. We were shivering with cold and anxious for a campsite, but it appeared there was none to be had. An impenetrable tangle of alders, willows and poplars overflowed into the river from the slippery banks. When at last we spotted a small clearing, it was a dirty job getting to shore. We shared the space in the bush with the remains of an old cabin. While Gary was busy staking out the tent, I innocently grabbed a handful of cotton-like material from between the logs to wipe the mud off my legs and arms.

"Here, try some of this," I said, handing Gary a piece of this handy cloth.

"That's fiberglass insulation! Makes you itch all over if you handle it."

"Oh, of course." I laughed sheepishly, throwing it aside.

Once inside the tent, we began cooking supper. When the noodles were soft, I leaned out the door to drain them. The lid slipped and the dinner ended up in the grass. I scooped it up, swung the hot pot back into the tent and accidentally rested it on Gary's leg. Quickly snatching his leg from beneath the scalding pot, he upset the noodles for the second time. Meanwhile, what seemed like the entire lower Saskatchewan population of mosquitoes had joined us in the tent. Several escaped with their fill, but most ended their days smeared across our tent wall with the flick of a towel.

"Never mind," comforted Gary. "It's just one of those nights! Have a good sleep."

"I'll try," I said, knowing full well I wouldn't.

Tucking down inside my nylon sleeping bag, I felt as though a thousand tiny needles were prickling me. The fiberglass was taking effect!

As we broke camp and headed upriver the following morning, we were full of edgy anticipation. If all went well, this would be our last day on the river. Flocks of pelicans flew overhead while we slipped beneath huge poplars and skirted beaver-felled trees. At every bend there was evidence of the beavers' handiwork. Pockets of mud had been scooped from the banks to provide packing for their dams and homes. Huge holes and smaller tracks marked the path of a cow moose and her calf foraging along the shoreline. There were always so many new and special things to see. We were finally coming to realize that even the Saskatchewan River had a beauty and appeal all its own. And that the home we were longing for was not a house with a street number, a town or a city, but a longing for our families and an eagerness to tell others of the country we had come to know. Home was also the smell of wet granite, the rustling of loose strips of paper birch, a bed of soft brown pine needles and the crisp clarity of the Shield country lakes. Our life in the canoe was almost over for this year. The realization must have struck us at the same time, for we both slowed our strokes, savoring the final few miles.

A seaplane buzzed low overhead, following the path of the river. When we waved, the aircraft banked and turned back. It passed once more time before landing. We hoped they had not mistaken our enthusiastic waving for a sign of distress. A uniformed RCMP officer climbed out onto the float and hailed us in.

"Welcome to The Pas. Everyone in town is waiting!"

Feeling a little bewildered by his message, we introduced ourselves.

The officer shook our hands. "I'm Sergeant Larsen."

I recognized the name immediately. This was the officer I had been corresponding with for over a year in regarding the arrangements to leave our canoe in the RCMP warehouse.

He smiled and continued, "We were just about to send a search out for you on Cedar Lake. People had bets going as to whether you could get here without getting lost. Congratulations! You have made it with only six miles left to go. What will it take you, another half hour?"

We laughed. "Maybe another hour and a half with this current against us."

Sergeant Larsen waved from the cockpit as the plane rose and circled again. They would be back in The Pas before we reached the next riverbend! The RCMP's official greeting made us feel excited and important. They had flown down the river just to find us. Their gesture was so completely unexpected. We didn't quite know what to make of their allusion to people waiting. How could anyone be waiting when we didn't know anyone there?

Our minds wandered back to practical concerns. Where were we going to camp that night? Would there be frequent trains south to Winnipeg? Would we have to carry the canoe very far through town? The hour and a half passed quickly.

A road runs along the river into town. Many vehicles were strung out along the road, headlights flashing, horns honking. We looked around and suddenly realized that all the commotion was directed at us. On the metal grid bridge spanning the Saskatchewan at the edge of town, people stood waving enthusiastically. As we passed beneath it, we noticed a group of people congregated at the boat launch. Something red came tumbling toward shore. I peered through the binoculars.

"Gary, you won't believe it!" I paused and turned toward him. "They are rolling out a red carpet for us." A wonderful warm feeling swept through us. As we put on a burst of speed, the waiting figures on shore cheered. Rice and confetti were hurled into the air as we walked up the crimson-colored path and were greeted by the mayor, the reeve and the chief of the Opasquia Indian band. They led us into nearby Kelsey Park, which overlooks the broad ribbon of the Saskatchewan River. It all seemed so unreal. Below the Henry Kelsey plaque that commemorates the arrival of the first white explorers into this region, we were presented with gifts: a scale model of a Red River cart, a carving of a trapper and his dog, and two hand-crafted small-scale models of birchbark canoes.

A short while later, we found ourselves on an escorted portage from the river's edge to the RCMP warehouse. Sirens wailed and lights flashed both ahead of and behind our two-man parade. We had expected our arrival into this town to be like that into any other town except that we would not be leaving again the next day. The town's totally unexpected and warm greeting completely overwhelmed us. It was not as though we were a local couple returning home; we did not even have personal contact with anyone in The Pas. The people were simply sharing in our excitement at completing the first leg of a long voyage in their hometown.

"Southward bound on the train to Winnipeg, September 8th," I wrote in my logbook. "We are examining the special gifts one by one. Three periods in the history of transportation in Manitoba are represented here and they are also symbolic of the development of Canada." From the mayor, there was the Red River cart. Brigades of these carts once rattled across the vast western prairies forming straggling lines of human migration. Pulled by horses or oxen, these two-wheeled wagons were the mainstay of the settlers' overland transportation system for a century.

From the reeve, there was the carving of the trapper and his dog. Trapping beaver pelts formed the basis for the early Canadian economy. Later, northern settlers depended upon the winter trapline for the income it provided.

The little birchbark canoes from the chief were the most special of all. To us they represented the ingenuity of the native people who had learned to adapt to this land of impenetrable forests where the lakes and rivers offered the only avenues for transportation. With the help of these people, the explorers and voyageurs who followed learned the only practical way to transport themselves and their cargos.

Already we looked forward to what next year would bring. There had been a new aspect of wilderness in every part of the first year's leg of the voyage, and there were the people. After two days in The Pas, we were leaving behind more special friends that we would look forward to seeing again next spring. Their royal welcome had given us an unforgettable and fond impressions of the journey's midway town, The Pas.

# 10
# The Paddle
# Sings Again

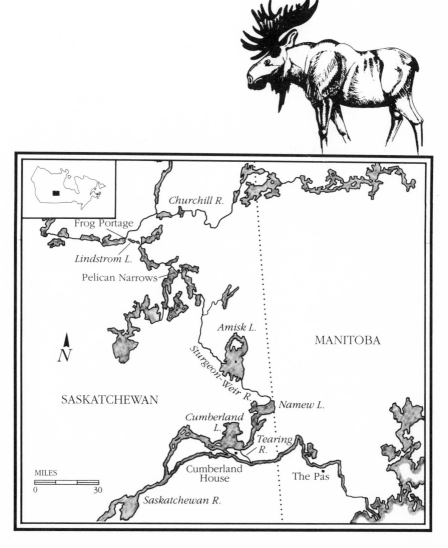

Churchill R.

Frog Portage

Lindstrom L.

Pelican Narrows

Amisk L.

Sturgeon-Weir R.

MANITOBA

N

SASKATCHEWAN

Namew L.

Cumberland L.

Tearing R.

MILES

Cumberland House

The Pas

0          30

Saskatchewan R.

T HE RHYTHMIC BEAT of the swaying railway cars clattering over iron rails drummed out a tune of the Canadian prairies. Peering from the train window, we looked out across the soft green waves of spring fields. Above the lonely, treeless expanse, there was only the vast dome of sky sprawling to distant horizons. The elemental beauty was broken every now and then by the sight of little railside towns and imposing grain elevators. But this view of the prairie provinces—Manitoba, Saskatchewan and Alberta—was only a partial one. North of 50 degrees latitude, which is roughly the prairies' geographical center, the landscape was utterly different according to our maps. It lies on the ancient Canadian Shield.

The extensive waterway system in Canada exists because of the geography of the country. The amount of freshwater surface, the drainage pattern and the Precambrian Shield are the three factors that make possible this country's almost total navigability by canoe. Half of the entire world's freshwater surface lies on Canadian soil, much of which comprises the world's oldest land mass, the Precambrian Shield. Scoured and scraped by the great weight of the moving glaciers, the Shield developed gentle topography for the vast network of drainage patterns. Our route across Canada was, in fact, following a necklace of interconnected water bodies that formed on the steep edges of the Shield. The great arterial routes linking the lakes together, the St. Lawrence, Ottawa, Winnipeg, Slave and Mackenzie rivers, were formed as glacial meltwater and rain flowed over the Shield's edges. They carved paths through the softer soil, eventually ending in the Arctic or Atlantic oceans.

From central Manitoba, the waterway routes constituting the second leg of our cross-Canada voyage were for the most part across or along the edge of the Shield. Our route would follow the northern fringe of Saskatchewan, clip the northeastern corner of Alberta and plunge north through the Territories by way of the Mackenzie River. We calculated that we had no more than three ice-free months to cover the remaining distance of 3,000 miles between The Pas and Tuktoyaktuk. The week before we had contacted Sergeant Larsen in The Pas. His best estimate was that the first lakes we would encounter would be free of ice.

The railway clattered into The Pas on a glorious fresh sunny morning. It was the first day of June 1984. The man in the ticket office remembered us from the year before. His mind was a jump ahead of ours when he recognized our need for a vehicle to transport all our equipment to the RCMP warehouse.

"You folks are going to need some wheels with *this* load," he remarked as he lifted the last of our packs and boxes from the baggage car. "Here's the keys to my van, the brown one over there. Just bring her back when you're done."

Down at the warehouse, the RCMP met us just as we arrived. The doors were opened as Sergeant Larsen welcomed us back to town. Our canoe was carried from its winter resting place and brought into the light of day. A thin coating of Saskatchewan River mud from the previous autumn was plastered to the hull.

The day was spent readying the canoe for the journey ahead. A pop-rivet gun was kindly loaned to us by the local hardware store to make minor adjustments and repairs to the tarpaulin system. Then we carried the canoe across the road and made inquiries at the local Greyhound Bus depot about the possibility of using their special power washer.

The mud, grime and the Saskatchewan River "bathtub ring" soon poured away under the steaming stream of hot soapy water. Beside the hulking forms of 60-passenger buses, our canoe lay shining white. Thoroughly clean, it was then polished and waxed. Now it was ready for the water. Its sleek fast lines inspired us; its unweathered look gave us confidence for the journey ahead. The canoe had survived some incredible ordeals and had come out unscathed. The worries of the past few weeks, the frantic final preparations, the mailing of food parcels and the acquiring of our film supply within hours of catching the train, were now behind us. Soon we would be on the river.

Brown waters swirled past the hull as we launched into the Saskatchewan River's swollen spring current. With some misgivings about the adequacy of our propulsion against this relentless force, we thrust our paddle blades deep and pulled hard. A

west wind was funneling down the river heralding an improvement in the present gloomy skies and spitting rain. A good
omen, but a tough day of paddling lay ahead. A few hardy souls
were huddled together along the boat landing to bid us farewell.
Long after we paddled out into the river, they continued waving
encouragement until we had struggled around the first river
bend.

The Saskatchewan River's silt-laden current carves out a
regular pattern of looping curves. On the inside riverbends, the
silt settling out from the sluggish current creates expansive mud
flats. Sweeping out from the mud flats is a gradual progression of
growth. It begins with the long grasses, followed by the tangled
underbrush of alders intertwined with small willows. Somewhere
higher, the poplars, aspens and spruce trees had established
themselves on firmer ground.

On the river's outside bends, the faster moving current had
stripped away the layers of grass through willows leaving only ma-
ture stands of trees. A feathery curtain of poplar tree roots
dangled from the lip of the undercut banks. Some trees were
leaning precariously, while others had toppled into the river.

The evening's challenge was to search out a dryish place to
camp. The inside bends were out of the question since they were
so thick and gooey. We could just imagine the state of our
equipment and tent after camping there. So we resolved the
problem by deciding to camp on the faster outside bend, even
though it meant climbing the bank. I spied a small clearing
above a half-felled poplar.

"How about that?" I pointed triumphantly.

Gary looked more than a little dubious at the proposition and
suggested we carry on a bit farther. Gliding beyond the over-
hang, we stopped dead at the sound of a solid crash. The
proposed campsite was upended and the landing site beneath
completely smothered by the thick tree trunk and a wide spread
of poplar branches. Our expedition could well have had an un-
timely ending right then and there.

Morning was orchestrated to life with a somewhat inhar-
monious array of twitters, trills, squeals, squawks and lilting
tunes. A persistent beaver was slapping his tail in defiance at our
invasion of his territory. It was not yet fully light, but as I peered
through the bug-proof screen, I could just make out his shim-

mering wake as he cruised back and forth across the surface. A stream of clear, sweet notes came bubbling forth on the cool dawn air. A tiny winter wren was awakening the world. I strained to catch the songs of familiar woodland warblers and flycatchers. The loud, high-pitched song of a yellowthroat poured from a willow thicket. Then we distinguished the sounds of the chattering kingfisher, phoebes, orioles, a yellow-bellied flycatcher and a blackburnian warbler. Quietly we sat cross-legged behind the protection of the tent's screen door and looked out at the droves of mosquitoes alighting and taking off, eager for the taste of warm flesh and blood. Gazing downstream to the eastern horizon, we watched entranced as the sun slowly warmed the sky to a pink glow. Almost imperceptibly, it transformed into a golden light that grew stronger and stronger until the morning sun burst through the uppermost spruce branches. The liquid gold poured down the shoreline and through our little piece of the Saskatchewan River valley.

It was time for breakfast. Gary readied the little cookstove and fired it up while I reached out the door for the pot of water. We were having to alleviate the heavy silt content in the river water by leaving a pot of it to stand and settle overnight. Unfortunately, I failed to notice the thriving water surface until it was too late. Pulling the pot into the tent, I lifted the lid. The water surface was a seething mass of black sandflies. Then I noticed that the ground outside the tent, the inside floor and the sleeping bags were swarming with them. I carefully scooped the living surface from the water and smothered the rest with a few spoonfuls of powdered milk.

Not long after crossing the border between Manitoba and Saskatchewan, we reached the mouth of the Tearing River and the route to Saskatchewan's oldest settlement, Cumberland House. The river tumbled down the boulder-strewn passage that we were attempting to ascend. This waterway linking the Saskatchewan River and Cumberland Lake had been a voyageur route, but since those days something had obviously altered the flow drastically. We struggled with the shallow silty waters in which our canoe constantly bottomed out with horrible grating sounds. An astonished black bear met us at several bends where the river kept doubling back on itself. It was an arduous and troublesome afternoon.

Near evening, we emerged onto expansive Cumberland Lake which was rippling with whitecaps. Farther west, we entered the Big Stone River and proceeded toward the Cree settlement of Cumberland House. This is the oldest permanent European settlement in Saskatchewan. Its beginnings date back more than two hundred years to when Samuel Hearne established the first Hudson's Bay post within Rupert's Land. It later developed into one of the most important distribution depots in the northwestern fur trade. Moreover, this settlement provided a solid foundation for the Hudson's Bay Company's fur trade which was competing with the fur traders from Montreal.

We were bewildered by the strange inland location of the village on Pine Island. There was something unnatural about the shallow, ugly marshland and the thick muddy waters that spread along Cumberland Lake's southern shore. When we arrived at the landing site, I proceeded into town to seek out the RCMP detachment.

The white picket fence surrounding a well-manicured lawn and a clean prefab building made the RCMP detachment clearly identifiable. Then I caught sight of the blue-and-white truck emblazoned with the RCMP insignia parked in the gravel drive. Sergeant Mick Ryan looked up from his work with a smile. I briefly explained our journey. Then I inquired if he knew of a place where we could camp so we could spend the evening exploring the historic town.

"You're welcome to camp back here." Sergeant Ryan indicated the lawn behind the detachment. Later, we gathered around the firepit and spent an entertaining evening listening to the officers recounting their adventures. In so doing, they revealed an RCMP's way of life in northern settlements. Our questions about the lake's condition were answered by the RCMP's special constable, a native Cree who had lived his whole life in Cumberland House.

"When I was a boy, we used to jump from the roof of the Anglican Mission into the lake. Now you can't even see the shoreline!" he remarked sadly.

Gradually, the story of the building of Squaw Rapids dam, 50 miles upstream on the Saskatchewan River, led us to understand the dreadful condition of Cumberland Lake and the frustrating waterlevels that we had experienced on the Tearing River. The lake, and the delta to the west, were once clear waters teeming with marine life. Now much of it was choked out by the excessive silt content. Waves from this expansive lake once lapped the sides of boat wharves in town. But now, little by little each year, Cumberland Lake was disappearing.

The dam had created one major problem—the alternation of water flow during the most prolific month of growth for shoreline vegetation. Ordinarily, the Saskatchewan River would flow very swiftly in July, thus flushing through the naturally high silt content. The dam now pours its greatest load through during late May and June and cuts back in July. With the decreased flow, the silt settles in the delta and along the Cumberland Lake shoreline. Vegetation quickly maintains a firm hold and the shoreline becomes a reclaimed boggy marshland. Willows and alders soon take hold. It is a losing battle as the shoreline extends farther and farther into Cumberland Lake.

Leaving the shallow, murky waters of Cumberland Lake, we entered Whitey Narrows. The swampy shores had given way to flat limestone ledges by the time we reached the southern shore of Namew Lake. After miles of muddy waters, the clear, dark lake was a refreshing sight indeed. Before nightfall, we rolled into the Sturgeon-Weir river mouth on a long smooth swell.

A heavily bearded man standing on shore hailed us over. We recognized Roger Smith from Mick Ryan's description of a jovial character bursting with energy.

"You'd better spend the night here", he said, "or else there'll be some pretty disappointed people."

His statement mystified us but we were grateful for the unexpected hospitality. Roger and his wife, Adeline, ran a busy fishing lodge, store and post office operation single-handedly. Many years before they had fulfilled their dream of motorcycling through the South American Andes. Their appreciation for the clean isolation of northern Canada was so heightened by this experience that they bought a piece of it and set about to establish a business that would encourage others to share in it, too.

Shortly after we made camp, a great strapping fellow came up to the tent. He and his companions were from The Pas. They had been there for the red-carpet welcome the previous year and had heard that we had taken off again. To surprise us, they had planned their annual fishing holiday to coincide with our passing through. The friendly group plied us with supper. On seeing us off the following morning, they cautioned us about the dangers of the Sturgeon-Weir River.

"A week ago, a canoeist went up the same way you're going," said Roger. "He was supposed to return." He paused. "His canoe drifted down just a couple of days ago, all smashed up." The thought of discovering the canoe's lost occupant floating amongst the debris in an eddy below the rapids haunted me for the entire day.

For over 80 miles the Sturgeon-Weir River tumbles from a small group of lakes on the northern edge of the Saskatchewan River watershed. Working our way from its mouth to the headwaters, we discovered a pattern. We began with an ascent of the lower Sturgeon-Weir in what geologists classify as a region of Devonian limestone and paddled our way back to the granite rock of the Canadian Shield.

The river's lower half was strenuous paddling, poling and pulling, because the current tumbles downstream at a rate of four feet to the mile, a delightful downriver run, except that we were traveling upstream! For two days we fought the current and a westerly headwind. The river bottom was fraught with pitfalls, mainly in the form of deep limestone crevasses. Over these flowed a strong shallow current that forced us to pole the canoe up most rapids.

We were not alone on the Sturgeon-Weir. Small flocks of white pelicans were perched on every available shoal amidst the sparkling river. In their quest for food, the pelicans would hurl themselves into the turbulent rapids. Feet and wings flailing in ungainly fashion, they emerged moments later, their bills full. It was not long before we discovered the feeding attraction. I was lining the canoe up a short stretch of rapids, my eyes glued to the fascinating antics of the pelicans rather than on my footing. Suddenly I slipped. Tumbling into a quiet pool, I found myself surrounded by dozens of frenzied sucker fish swarming past me on their way to spawning grounds upstream.

Amisk Lake marks the completion of the first stage of the Sturgeon-Weir River. We negotiated the second section with far greater ease due to the lay of the land on the Canadian Shield. The river fell in a pattern of "drop and pool," which means that the rapids were short and the movement of the water beyond them hardly noticeable by the upstream paddler.

In the heat of a calm June afternoon, we were paddling through an island-studded section of lake at the upper end of the Sturgeon-Weir system when a great deal of commotion and shooting suddenly erupted from a small forested island.

"Ahoy there!" bellowed a voice across the water.

The first thought that flashed through our minds was to whip the canoe around and get out of there. However, turning our backs seemed foolish considering we were well within their range already. So we approached very carefully instead.

Suddenly, without warning, a beer bottle came flying out of the bushes.

"Duck," Gary yelled just as it sliced the air over our heads.

Immediately afterward, an enormous black Labrador came bounding down the rocks and flung himself into the lake. His landing was well executed, and a plum of spray shot into the air and settled upon us like a summer cloudburst. The big black dog hardly gave us a second glance as he surged through the water toward the floating beer bottle. We watched in astonishment as he gently clamped his jaws around it and swam back to shore. Not even waiting to shake the water from his heavy coat, he disappeared back into the woods.

"Lard Jesus," a voice exploded, "that's my new sleeping bag yer shakin' on Shep!"

"They can't be all bad with a fine dog like that!" I whispered to Gary. So out of politeness and curiosity, we pulled our canoe ashore. "Let's go meet them."

After following the path up through blueberry bushes, we laid eyes on a rough-looking pair. Nearest to us was the hunched figure of a man seated on a log. He was dressed in a pair of dishevelled old coveralls. His face might have been handsome in younger years but now it looked rather haggard and weathered. A hook-shaped nose dropped down toward an unruly moustache which melded into a long scraggly beard. Reclining beside Shep, the retriever, was a short dark-haired man who hadn't seen a razor in several days, but still had a reasonably civilized look about him. He was the one who had hailed us to shore.

"We'd sure 'preciate some 'elp in finishin' up this 'ere beer so's we can git on down the Churchill 'fore winter sets in." He swung his arm expansively toward six neatly stacked cases.

Although we had absolutely no intention of helping them polish off all their beer, we accepted their hospitality in the form of a bottle each.

"Just sold the business fer fifty thousand. Me an' Jack 'ere, we're gonna paddle all the way to Hudson Bay even if it kills us. Bought new camping stuff." He stopped and looked around, satisfied. "All new!" he emphasized.

I followed Gary's gaze toward a huge fishing-tackle box polka-dotted with orange price tags. They wasted no time in getting us to admire their outfit. The tackle box was full of everything except fishing tackle. It was stuffed with tools and spare parts for all their various bits of gadgetry. Then we caught sight of two brand new mosquito head nets still in their plastic packages nailed securely to a pine tree.

"Yep, them bug nets sure work great!" one said to the other although he obviously had never taken the opportunity to prove this to be so.

The tent had a big label hanging from the screen firmly announcing On Sale! In fact the price of every piece of equipment in this outdoor-gear display was blatantly visible.

"Look at our guns!" announced Stanley, pulling out four different guns—a 30.30 lever action, a .308 bolt action, a .22 rifle and a 12-gauge pump-action shotgun. These four weapons can be used for a variety of game in all kinds of situations. But, oh no, these were "fer all them nasty bears that'll be huntin' us while we're sleepin. No siree," said Stanley, "I'm never gonna sleep. Gotta be just like a deer. Black bears, grizzlies, polar bears, they're all out thar!"

Gary nudged me with his elbow as Jack, the bearded one, brandished a mask, snorkel and flippers, and of all things, a spear gun! Then with a broad toothless grin, as if saving the best for last, he unveiled their portable meat grinder. Enthusiastically, he explained how he stuffed all the fish through the grinder for himself and Shep.

They weren't finished yet.

"Those are pretty fancy-looking maps you got there." Stanley pointed to Gary's package of topographic maps that he had carried up from the canoe.

"Just regular topo maps," Gary said matter-of-factly, figuring that surely they must know maps if they were heading for the Churchill River. They were looking a bit puzzled so he added,

"You know, the kind put out by Energy, Mines, and Resources, about four miles to the inch."

"Ours don't much resemble those, but I'll show 'em to you."

Stanley tottered over to the tent and climbed inside. I could see the new sleeping bags laid out on top of the firm air mattresses. While he was rummaging around, Jack picked up another empty beer bottle and hurled it toward the lake for Shep who had been growing a bit fidgety for lack of attention.

"Loves 'em, does dat c'azy dog." Shep bounded back into the water and out again. Forgetting to rid himself of the excess moisture, Shep dashed back up through the pine needles and bounded clear past us toward the tent just as Stanley was emerging with an enormous black plastic garbage bag. Bowling Stanley over, Shep landed his great hairy 60 pounds on the new sleeping bags and proceeded to give a long, luxurious shake.

"Chris' Almighty," Stanley yelled, "get this goddam dog off my bed, Jack."

Then came the maps. Stanley rummaged around in the bag and pulled one out.

"Ah, 'ere's the Churchill," Stanley yelled triumphantly, laying it out on the ground. To our disbelief, they were the fancy historic-looking brown maps that usually adorn the walls of roadside restaurants or tourist trading posts, the kind of map that has little diagrams of the rapids and fancy paintings of voyageur canoes, wildlife and other northern memorabilia. In the top corner, there were a few hints about survival in the wilderness and a recipe for bannock. On one map, we were seeing the whole of the Churchill River—from "somewhere" to Hudson Bay. Six hundred and fifty miles were scaled out onto four square feet of paper. "Produced by the Ministry of Tourism" was printed in the bottom right corner.

"What if you come across some rapids that aren't marked on that map?" I asked.

"No problem," drawled Stanley. "That's Shep's job!"

"It's Shep's job?" I mimicked, thinking I had it wrong.

"Dat's right. Th' only reason I let Jack 'ere bring along dat great mutt is 'cause he knows 'is rapids. When he 'ears him, he howls. And dat smart dog, if he's real scared, he jumps out of th' canoe and swims t' shore. See, we sure knows then to paddle like hell fer shore 'er else we're done fer!"

Waving away the offer of another beer, Gary said, "I used to have a dog like Shep. While out duck hunting, I'd send him across the fields to check out some of the local ponds."

Gary had the men's undivided attention. Even Shep's ears were pricked, his head cocked to one side.

"Well, my dog would sneak up on one of these ponds, count the ducks and return. If there weren't any ducks, he wouldn't bark and we carried on. If there were ducks, he would then come back and bark softly. One bark for each duck on the pond."

Stanley asked the inevitable question, as if right on cue. "What happens if the whole pond is covered with ducks higher than yer dog can count? What then, eh?!"

"Well," said Gary, rising to his feet. This was his way of signaling our grand exit. "He'd pick up a stick in his jaws on the way back and just shake it for all it was worth."

"So what does that mean?" Stanley questioned.

Gary tucked our two beer bottles into one of the empty cases. "Well, that's my dog's way of saying, 'The ducks on the pond are so thick you can shake a stick at them.'" They were definitely impressed by this amazing accomplishment.

"Shep looks like a pretty sharp dog. I'm sure you could teach him," Gary finished.

After that show of optimism, they looked around at the shambles of their campsite and then at the tent where a large wet Shep was lying smack dab in the middle of Stanley's new sleeping bag. We wished them the best of luck in all sincerity. But before we left, they managed to unload a bunch of maps on us which were titled "Come to Athabasca Country Where the Sportsman Is King!"

The first thing that struck us about Pelican Narrows was the starkness of the landscape. Like those in old photographs of early settlements, the buildings had been erected on land completely denuded of trees. We pulled in alongside the local wharf near the yellow Hudson's Bay store. A crowd of curious children flocked down to shore, some running, some riding bicycles. They gathered about us intrigued by the canoe and our colorful packs. Our arrival had coincided with the first day of summer holidays from school.

Traipsing through the dusty streets of Pelican Narrows, with twenty-odd youngsters in tow, we felt rather like the Pied Piper of Hamelin. They were fascinated by our camera equipment and the view through each different lens. Each one wanted his picture taken. They pulled faces, smiled, hugged and punched one another. All those who rode bicycles wanted to demonstrate how clever they were at performing tricks off homemade wooden ramps. Taking the roundabout route through the settlement, our tour guides gave us a running commentary on which house was whose. We reported in to the RCMP. While there, we felt compelled to clear our conscience about the twosome coming behind us en route to Hudson Bay via the Churchill. Possibly the RCMP could assist them by suggesting they lighten their load and obtain more detailed maps.

Next stop was the post office where we sent home all our exposed rolls of film for processing. When we reappeared, it seemed the little crowd of smiling, chattering youngsters had grown. We carried on to the Hudson's Bay store to purchase a few supplies. Back at the canoe, we hauled out the food bag and special sealed containers for dried goods. We had never had such a willing team to help us repackage our groceries and see us on our way again.

From Pelican Lake, we carried on up through Medicine Rapids, Wood Lake and Lindstrom Lake. The surface of this shallow, reedy waterway was speckled with bright green lilypads and yellow and white waterlily blossoms. We had reached the upstream end of the Sturgeon-Weir system. Swooshing our way through the water-loving foliage, we approached the historic portage which marks the division between the Churchill and Saskatchewan River watersheds. The portage is so well used that an ingenious cart on tracks has been built to follow the trail. Hoisting our loads and canoe onto the cart, we pulled everything across this important land link to the Churchill River all in one go.

When Joseph Frobisher, a Nor'Wester from Montreal, traveled this way in the late eighteenth century, he was one of the first white men to use this trail. In doing so, he established the all-important link between the northern interior and the southern fur-trading route to Montreal. On this first crossing, he intercepted a band of Indians heading north to the rival Hudson's Bay trading post of Churchill. Frobisher managed to trade with them for their winter harvest of furs; thus the route was originally named Portage de Traite.

Later, when Cree Indians left a stretched frog's skin at this location to mock how the northerly tribes of Indians dressed and stretched their beaver skins, the trail was renamed Frog Portage, the name it bears to this day.

The trail prompted some evocative thoughts of those who had walked this way before us. Certainly there had been the voyageurs, traders, trappers and explorers 200 years before whose diaries and logbooks recorded their travels. But more impressive was the knowledge that native people had been using this portage for thousands of years.

From Frog Portage, the fur-trade route to Fort Chipewyan on Lake Athabasca principally followed the system of rivers which had the longest ice-free season. When the North canoes returned in the early fall after picking up supplies and trade goods at Grand Portage, they turned upstream on the Churchill. From there, the route passed the settlement of Ile à la Crosse and traversed the dreaded 12-mile Methye Portage into the Clearwater and Athabasca rivers. Eventually they arrived back at Fort Chipewyan on Lake Athabasca. In the spring, this was the first route to break free of winter ice; thus it became the principal link between the Hudson Bay and Mackenzie River drainage basins.

Long ago we had chosen to deviate from the fur-trade route at the Churchill River for a number of reasons. We were fascinated by Reindeer and Wollaston Lakes. The route, first explored and mapped by David Thompson, followed these two lakes ending up in Lake Athabasca's eastern end by way of the Fond du Lac River. The route appeared to be the wildest and least-traveled portion of our entire journey.

Also spurring us on to the Reindeer Lake region were the stories Gary's father had told about an exploratory trip that he and two companions had made there over 30 years before. His memories of the clear, clean lakes and rivers, the size and abundance of lake trout and arctic grayling, the natural granite campsites of the Shield country and the sheer wildness and beauty of the region we found enormously compelling.

# 11
# The Wild River
# Is Calling

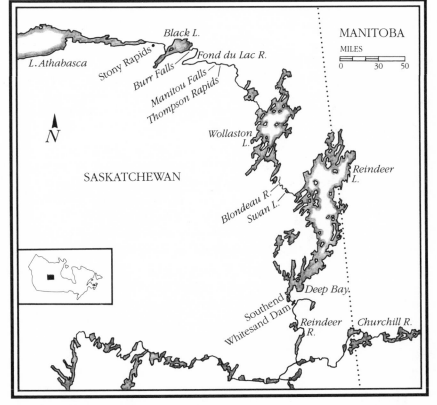

STRONG EASTERLY WINDS funneled through the narrows between Trade Lake and Uskik Lake on the Churchill River in mid-June. Heavy clouds were piling in to fill the void in the featureless, ashen sky. Until we saw the orange tarpaulin, we had not seen any sign of other human beings for several days. As we paddled the canoe toward the scattered remains of a previously inhabited campsite, a freighter canoe came puttering across the bay. The occupant was a young prospector from La Ronge. A floatplane had landed him and his family here the previous day to begin working a claim for copper and gold. They had made camp on the open but slanting surface of the rocky point. It was decidedly uncomfortable, so at the first light of dawn, Dave had packed up his family and moved. Load by load, he was ferrying their month's worth of food supplies and equipment into a wooded campsite at the end of the bay.

An invitation to stop in for tea with a northern prospector and his family was too interesting to refuse. We followed him for a quarter mile around the bay until we arrived on the edge of a steep, heavily vegetated shore. Each of us carried a box of geologists' camp supplies and bushwacked our way through tangled pin cherries and alders. We landed on the doorstep of what I decided was a poor excuse for a campsite. The heavy, dank smell of peat permeated the air beneath the drooping branches of black spruce. Hordes of mosquitoes with voracious appetites were feeding on any exposed flesh. The lumpy terrain was further marred by the presence of knee-high stumps protruding in every direction. A tangle of tree roots intertwined with little stones had been laid bare when they had prepared the ground for their summer residence—a large white cotton canvas tent. Prospectors, survey crews, and native summer camps all use this simple house-shaped tent which hangs suspended over a structure of sapling poles.

Outside the tent, we added our boxes to the growing pile. A two-burner Coleman stove had been placed on a rough-hewn table. Two stumps served as stools. A five-foot pile of disposable diapers leaned precariously against the tent entrance.

"Sara's inside. Go make yourselves comfortable while I put on the kettle," said Dave.

I pulled back the heavy curtain of material and ducked through the opening. It was very light inside because of the white walls, and certainly high enough to stand up in. The tent did not possess a floor so a tarp had been haphazardly thrown across the dirt. Taking up at least half of the area was a large mattress covered in brown corduroy. Our eyes were fixed on the round, rosy-cheeked baby wriggling happily in the midst of it, completely oblivious to the confusion around him. Crouched near the baby was Sara, who was smiling shyly.

Moments later Dave thrust his way in, tea kettle in one hand, mugs, a bag of sugar and a can of condensed milk in the other. Fishing beneath the tarp, he pulled out a plastic tube and emptied its contents on the mattress. We carefully unrolled the scroll of specific geological survey maps and weighted the corners down with anything at hand . . . a tin of tuna, a pillow and some spare diapers. Immersed in a tangy mixture of smells—the fresh leakproof diapers, the heavy aroma of molding canvas and various foodstuffs—we listened to Dave describe what the next few weeks would be like in his pursuit for copper and gold. He had received backing from a company to survey and dig for samples. But the pleasure in the life of the prospector appeared to us to be the search itself, the persistent lure of the elusive prize, rather than the actual find which could change their lives forever.

When we finally left, it was just beginning to spit rain. We pulled the tarp from under the bow and stern decks and fastened it on securely. Fifteen minutes later, we were immersed in a torrential downpour. All we could think of were the cardboard boxes of disposable diapers scattered in piles around the prospector's campsite, gloriously labeled, "Absorbs three times their weight in water!"

On this morning in mid-June, the Reindeer River appeared dark and foreboding. A gusting northeast wind blew the cold, misty air into our already flushed faces. At the river's wide mouth at the confluence with the Churchill River, we drew up alongside a powerless motorboat. The native occupants were happily propelling themselves by a make-shift sail—two red Hudson's Bay blankets tied to a frame of saplings. Our offer of assistance was waved aside graciously. They said they were not concerned about the weather since the community of Sandy Bay was no more than a two-day, 50-mile trip downstream. The positive acceptance of their situation was an attitude we found wonderfully refreshing. Even after having spent such a short time among northern native people, we were learning some very interesting values. Time, for instance, is a lot different to these people. Instead of a clock, which our North American society could not survive without, they still value time in the way their nomadic ancestors did, the seasons and the climate dictating their schedule.

Half an hour later, rain squalls were drifting in slow heavy veils across the expanse of spruce-cloaked hills. Farther upstream, we looked upon the aftermath of a forest fire, the strongest natural force shaping the northern woods. Amongst the charred tree trunks and blackened felled timbers, a profusion of jack pine seedlings were poking their way up through a thick ground cover of fireweed, grasses and raspberry canes. Judging by the spread and height of regenerated plant growth, a fire of amazing proportions had swept through this area within the past few years. In our canoe, we were situated between the mainland and several islands that were at least 200 yards from shore. Both the islands and the land far up into the hills on either side of us had been engulfed in a sweeping inferno. I shuddered at the thought of the terrifying scene—of the intense heat, the crackling and snapping of evergreen trees and the acrid cloud of thick black smoke burning the lungs, bringing tears to the eyes and smothering every creature that couldn't escape in time.

The next morning we awoke to bright sunshine streaming through the tent doorway. The cool night had spawned a heavy dew. Droplets of moisture hung like delicate strings of translucent pearls on the freshly spun cobwebs. We scrambled from the tent, cameras in hand. The beautiful handiwork of nature displayed itself in the vivid green of marsh grasses and the violet arrowhead flowers, the heady fragrances wafting in on the freshly washed summer air. What a day! We couldn't bear to waste a moment.

We hurriedly stowed our gear into the packs. Then we glided out across the marsh. At Devil Rapids, the river narrowed to a bottleneck. The steep-sided channel, lined with black spruce, was shaded and cool. The current came surging around a dog's-leg turn, then the great volume of water plunged over a ledge creating steep-standing waves. Along the eddy lines, powerful whirlpools emitted hollow sucking and gurgling sounds from somewhere deep within the dark depths. There was an eerie feeling about the place, as if the devil of Devil Rapids were growling in hunger. The eddy current was very strong, almost overriding our paddle strokes as we resisted the pull toward the whirlpools. We grasped awkwardly at the shoreline vegetation and pulled ourselves and our canoe up the earthy embankment to the portage. The path through the young birch forest was thickly overgrown and almost impossible to follow. The sun had not yet had time to burn the heavy dew off the leaves so we were thoroughly soaked before arriving at the water again.

Spanning a bottleneck at the Reindeer River's headwaters is the White Sand dam. Some distance below it, we felt the surge of boiling white water. Through each of the five flumes, a smooth tongue of translucent green water came roaring out into the river below. Portaging this dam marked the final carry on the river.

Some distance above the dam, we arrived at Southend where we were going to be picking up our first supply parcel from the RCMP post. Like Pelican Narrows, Southend was located on the edge of the thick forest, yet the buildings themselves stood stark naked on a thoroughly cleared site. Rattling pickups roared past, kicking the road into dusty clouds that settled on our clothes and in our eyes. We could feel the grit in our teeth. The garbage strewn about the streets and between the buildings gave us the impression that we were in an urban subdivision in a southern Canadian city in early spring when the accumulated refuse of winter surfaces with each receding layer of snow. But it was the empty, dark windows from which faces appeared and disappeared in the shadows that left me with a haunted feeling. The windows of a home are like the eyes of a person. Here there were no lights illuminating the cabin interiors. Very few windows were fixed with panes of glass to mirror the outside images. Without light, without covering, I wondered if these dark empty hollows actually reflected the spirit of the lives lived within the four walls.

Closer to the Hudson's Bay store, we were intrigued to find the strange structure of a corrugated, galvanized iron teepee, familiar in shape, but made of very unorthodox building materials. Behind it lay sticks of lumber, an old freezer and several snowmobile engine shrouds. Ironically, a group of healthy sled dogs, in the first stages of summer molt, were tied to the skeletons of long-discarded snow machines. At our approach, they began to howl. Soon all the dogs in town took up the woeful chorus, howling and yapping in various pitches. We were sure everyone in Southend knew that strangers had arrived.

A tiny woman dressed in a faded print dress was coming down the steps of the Hudson's Bay store. Although leathery and wrinkled with age, her ancient face seemed kind. In one hand she dragged a huge plastic bag stuffed with loaves of "enriched" snow-white bread. Under the other arm she had just managed to squeeze a bale of unpackaged disposable diapers.

From the Hudson's Bay store, we went in search of the RCMP detachment. Nobody was in the office but we noticed one of their vehicles parked outside the school. Inside, I was directed to the gymnasium. I innocently stepped through the doors to find a group of people, including three uniformed officers, all staring my way. I hurriedly explained that we had a parcel to pick up.

"Excuse me, Miss, but court's in session right now!" stated an officer from the back of the gym.

Red-faced, I apologized and backed toward the door. On the way out, I noticed the suppressed grin on the face of Corporal Jim Colson. Soon after, we met Jim. He had been waiting for us. The several parcels and letters that had been safely tucked away in their office were now at his home. At Jim's place we opened our mail while he inspired us with stories of the north country we were heading for. Jim had spent two years with the Aklavik detachment in the Mackenzie delta. There was a twinkle in his eyes as he fondly recalled his sled dogs. He brought out his northern outerwear, a combination of RCMP issue and native dress, many pieces of caribou and whalebone carving and most importantly, the relics from his dog-driving days. Wistfully, he recalled setting nets in the delta for fish to feed his sled dogs. He enjoyed the immensity of the land, with the Richardson

Mountains lying to the west, the Arctic Ocean to the north and the barren lands to the east. And in these environments, wildlife like grizzly bears, caribou, muskrat, geese, ducks and whales abounds. In addition, there were the proud people of Aklavik who had, in the face of much opposition, retained their community, their spirit and some of the old customs. We had found it inspiring to talk with Jim. Instead of dwelling on the negative aspects—the worst weather, the most dangerous rapids and so on—as so many people did out of concern for our safety, he kindled our enthusiasm, excitement and anticipation for the journey that lay ahead.

The fresh smell of ozone permeated the atmosphere, along with a dozen other distinguishable odors forewarning rain as we departed from Southend. Our route lay straight north up through the labyrinth of islands in Reindeer Lake.

"That's Birch Point straight ahead, Numabin Bay to the north and soon we'll see the entrance to Deep Bay," Gary called out. Mentally I drew the picture of our position. With only one set of maps, I had learned to make a game of memorizing sections of it. It made the traveling far more entertaining. Sometimes I would visualize our little canoe traversing maps of different scales—the world, Canada, or across the lake or river we were on at the time. Gary's words recalled to me the Y shape of Numabin Bay I had seen on the map, and the circular Deep Bay where a meteorite had landed many millions of years ago, creating a perfectly round bay six miles wide and over 600 feet deep. Legend claims that a sea serpent like the monster of Loch Ness lurks in its depths.

During our time on Reindeer Lake, our only window of calm weather lasted little more than one day. In it we covered over 50 miles, weaving our way through countless shoals and tiny islands. The sun was warm as our paddle strokes lifted and pulled, flashing silver to the passing gulls. Then our opponent, the northwest headwind, came blasting down the 120-mile length of Reindeer Lake. For two days it was like plowing into a constant upstream current, only worse. If we took the slightest rest from the never ending pull of paddle strokes, the canoe would be instantly swung broadside. The result was that we would lose double the distance we would have gained had we kept up the pace. We fought to gain ground against the powerful force that sent its swirling tentacles around islands and into bays. When at last we turned into Swan River, we breathed a sigh of relief. The canoe was no longer pitching, and the howling past our ears had at last ceased. But another challenge lay ahead.

Grasping the gunwales, I hoisted the stern over my head as Gary rested the upturned bow on his shoulder.

"I hope this is the last one," I panted, thoroughly exhausted.

The thick waterlogged vegetation engulfed my boots with each sucking step. I was past caring. For a full 16 hours we had battled the winds, lined the canoe through shallow rock-garden rapids and slogged through the bane of northern portages—muskeg. This spongy, waterlogged surface defied our eager spirits. The mud flats of the Saskatchewan paled by comparison. We struggled on. There weren't any clearly defined portages along the Swan River. Yet every two hundred yards we were forced to abandon our paddles and either walk up through the rapids or portage.

An impenetrable tangle of alders, spindly willows and feathery rushes lined the shores. Growing with their roots firmly fixed in the saturated muck of the river bottom, rather like waterlilies, were bunches of wild calla. Each pencil-thick flower head protruded from a snow-white spathe and was surrounded elegantly by glossy heart-shaped leaves. There were active beaver lodges of colossal size and an abundance of moose tracks lining the muddy banks at the downstream end of the portages. While following these obscure trails, we often wondered if we were not simply on a natural wildlife path. We rounded a bend then stopped short. Gary drew in a deep breath, then exhaled in a contented sigh. Meanwhile, beneath the canoe where I could see nothing, I swatted irritably at the hordes of hungry blackflies.

"Gary, can't we put this thing down?" I exclaimed.

"Oh, yeah," came the distracted reply.

Once the canoe was on the ground, I reached into my pocket for a handkerchief to wipe the oozing blood from behind my ears and neck. Suddenly my eyes focused on one of nature's totally unexpected glories. A band of scarlet burned along the western horizon like a sheet of heated metal. The redness swelled, spilling its intense color across Swan Lake and down the rushing river. The sharp spires of black spruce etched out a neat fringe along the skyline which was broken only by the silhouetted nest belonging to a pair of ospreys.

The following day, we wriggled our way up 13 miles of the narrow Blondeau River. At times, the current had pinched the bends to such a degree that our 18½-foot canoe could only just make the turns without wedging itself between the banks. If I drew the bow around too sharply, the stern would end up resting on a sandbar.

The forest through which we traveled had been burned over in recent years. Occasionally, lanky timbers had fallen across the river and barred our way. If we couldn't sneak under them, we clambered out onto slippery logs. From this very precarious position, we managed to hoist the fully loaded canoe over the obstructions.

The Blondeau's tiny feeder streams converge on the main river channel that flows from muskeg headwaters to Swan Lake. They add to the current's strength and help the passage open. The Blondeau takes the winding path of least resistance. It passes through a glacier-scoured landscape of eskers and marshland. The floodplain is lush and green. The higher ground is dry and sandy. Scores of long skinny hills flowing in a northeast to southwesterly direction are evidence of glacial action. The eskers were formed by the rivers that flowed through the glacial ice sheets and deposited their load of silt on the river bottom. Gradually, as the ice melted and the waters drained away, the accumulation of silt stood as relief against the land.

At the 277th bend (Gary had been carefully counting the bends on the map all day) we disembarked to begin the long haul overland to Wollaston Lake through a series of nine portages and small lakes. The portages were to begin in a break between the path of two eskers. Initially I was dismayed that the only distinguishable landmark indicating the portage's beginning, an old log warehouse, was no longer there as a result of a forest fire. We had been crisscrossing the shore, then climbing higher up the bank toward the blackened spruce trees in search of the building, when Gary suddenly pointed at the charred timbers sprinkled with a thin covering of brown spruce needles. As we rose up over the crest of an esker, we could hardly believe the landscape that confronted us. It was like walking in a lovely, wild parkland because the forest floor was bare.

At least a fine summer day was in our favor when we awoke early to begin the series of portages, the longest being a mile and a half, to Wollaston Lake. Each portage was separated from the next by a small lake which would provide us with welcome relief. Before the advent of regular air service into isolated northern communities, snowcat trains hauling supply sleds kept the Hudson's Bay stores stocked throughout the winter months. Their route into this part of the north had been by way of Southend, Reindeer Lake and overland to Wollaston Lake. The 50-yard-wide trails cut through the bush followed the lowest land between lakes. This land was suitable for winter travel because everything was frozen. We were following these same trails but in the summer months when they are saturated with the accumulated runoff from the higher ground. The land is a virtual sponge lying unshaded in the hot sunshine during the long summer days. It harbors a profusion of wildlife, not least of which were the lowly mosquitoes and blackflies!

Beads of sweat rolled down my forehead and over my eyebrows and trickled into the corners of my eyes. The salty liquid stung. My hair was a crumpled mat squashed beneath a nylon headnet. The netting that kept off the mosquitoes and blackflies also created an aura of hot, steamy, still air about my face and neck. The elastic holding the net in was tied around my throat as tightly as I could bear it. Even so, the occasional fly slipped inside. Pulling down over my shoulders, both back and front, were two packs. In my left hand I carried my camera box and in the other I supported the bottom of the front pack. As I am only five feet four inches tall, this pack hung somewhere over my thighs. Each time I forced my leg up to take another step, the pack would bounce off my knee into my face.

I blew at an irritable pest buzzing around inside the headnet. It was hopeless. The mosquito landed on my neck. Forgetting what I was holding, I swung my left hand up and succeeded in knocking myself in the jaw with the metal box. I cursed loudly while the mosquito continued to buzz. It finally settled just below my eye and proceeded to perform its delicate surgery. As I tried in vain to dislodge it, blowing upward, squinting and blinking, the mosquito clung tenaciously. First the needle was jabbed in and the itching chemical released, then the blood withdrawn. When at last the abdomen had swollen into a red balloon, the mosquito pushed its little forelegs against my cheek as it extracted itself from my skin.

"No way are you going to live!" I yelled, hurling the front pack to the ground and slamming my palm against my cheek. Blood splattered, I hoisted up the pack in triumph and continued on.

Later, on another portage, we were having difficulties with the canoe.

"Come on!" Gary yelled, exasperated. "Why aren't you moving?"

"My legs have disappeared." The echo of my answer reverberated through the upside-down canoe hull.

Gary yanked hard at the bow and took a step forward.

"Whoaaaa!" Splat! My upper body had obeyed, but it was still firmly attached to my lower end which wasn't about to budge. Now I lay face first, the waterlogged vegetation having cushioned the blow. It was so deliciously cool that I just remained there for a second without breathing or moving. Then I felt the canoe being thrown to one side and I was hauled to my feet. Through his netting, Gary smiled tenderly. "I'm sorry. I'll drag it, O.K.?"

Our mirrored glasses were drooping off the ends of our noses when we suddenly caught sight of our own reflections: two soggy bedraggled creatures emerging from the swamp, grass and mud sticking to our hair and our hands swollen with mosquito bites. Each of us was feeling as wretched but looking as funny as the other. Our despairing expressions turned to grins then irrepressible laughter.

Ten hours and eight portages later, we crested the height of land. Below us lay the shimmering silver expanse of Wollaston Lake. Dark, spindly spruce trees threaded their way elegantly along the lake's rim. Jack pine and poplar seedlings had replenished the green lost in recent burns. There was a feeling of the land opening up and of the treeless tundra further north extending its influence southward, rather like the waves blending with a sandy coastline.

Wollaston Lake is a geographical height of land. The Cochrane River, in the lake's northeastern corner, drains into the Hudson Bay watershed while the Fond du Lac River, in the lake's northwestern corner, is part of the Mackenzie drainage system to the Arctic Ocean. Its beauty was in the hilly landscape and interesting shoreline of deep bays and islands. We trolled for lake trout while crossing the deeper sections. In the shallow red sandy coves, we cast our line into clear, sunlit waters where pike were surging around just below the surface.

Shortly past the river opening on Cunning Bay, the lake bottom veered up quickly to meet the surface. The Fond du Lac was so shallow at this point that it resembled an overflowing storm sewer on a cobblestone street. The water flowed in a quicksilver carpet creating an invisible barrier between our canoe hull and the tapestry of round black rocks on the riverbottom. As the current drew us onto a smooth black-tongued channel and swept us toward the white streamers marking the ledges below, we were very high-spirited. There would be no more uphill paddling!

The canoe galloped through the rapids. A quick pry here, a draw, then angling the canoe with a graceful dancing turn, we burst into a quiet eddy to scout the next section of river below. We were on our way to the Arctic Ocean and from this moment on every stroke we made would be across waters flowing toward the vast Arctic Sea at the Mackenzie delta more than 2,000 miles away.

Toward evening, a thin piercing shriek penetrated the sweet gurgle of the river. Swiveling around in our seats, we cast our attention to the distant crown of a white spruce some 60 feet above the riverbank. A large bundle of tangled sticks was thrust into the upper canopy, evidence of a bald eagle's nesting site. A pair of white-headed adults came soaring down, wheeling and diving in a frenzied act of nest protection and intruder distraction. Examining the eyrie through the binoculars, we could readily detect the rough brown heads of large flightless eaglets poking over the edge of their high-rise home. The dramatic aeronautical display continued until the current had whisked us a safe distance downstream.

Early the following morning, as we were carried on the smooth clear current with the sun rising into the sky behind our backs, an eagle descended on vast black wings from the forest ahead. It dove straight toward us. Suddenly it lost altitude; its vicious talons extended from heavily feathered legs. Shattering the glassy surface, it thrust its claws into the sides of a plump, silvery fish. Beating its wings mightily, the eagle lifted the wriggling prey from the river and rose into the dead branches of a nearby spruce. We sat perfectly still, entranced by the magnificent sight. No doubt it was the eagle that inspired me to go fishing that evening.

With one hand I swatted the blackflies and with the other I carried my fishing rod. A small silver spinner dangled from the end of the line. I was confident that one lure was all I needed. I sallied forth to a section of river, leaving Gary to set up camp. All day I had been sneaking little tidbits of information from him about the lives and habits of Arctic grayling, the little fish I had seen locked in those talons.

The words were spinning in my mind as I tied the lure on my line. "Cast it 45 degrees upstream and as you reel it across the eddyline, bang, you'll have one! You have to set the hook fast, because grayling have hard mouths. It'll fight! As it leaps from the water, you'll see the florescent blue spots glimmering on its dorsal fin."

I could hardly wait. All the fishing we had done up to this point on the journey had been trolling and casting for lake trout, pickerel and pike. The grayling was a fish I'd never seen because I had not traveled on such pure, cold oxygenated waters before. With such requirements for survival, grayling can only live in the remote, unspoiled north. Fishing for grayling was a new challenge which required finesse. The techniques Gary had described to me would only work if I understood the habits of the grayling and the river bottom. With a flick of my wrist, I sent the line singing out across the river. Plop, the little lure landed and disappeared. I reeled in quickly. Nothing. Never mind, I knew there were "dozens" out there. I tried again and again.

Then I felt something touch the lure. I jerked the rod up and started reeling. My rod bent double, but no thrashing fish with blue spots appeared. I was stuck on the bottom. How humiliating! And I had only one lure! Well, I couldn't fish without it, so I peeled off my clothes and plunged in to retrieve it. Following the line upstream, I then dove beneath the surface. Something shining flickered from behind a rock. I grasped the lure, lungs bursting, then surfaced again. The current quickly whisked me downstream over a shelf of rough stones.

Shivering, I scrambed from the river clutching the lure firmly. Then a voice from the bushes startled me.

"Now that's enthusiasm!" Gary had come down to the river, curious to find out how I was doing. He fastened the rescued lure back on the line and handed it to me. I cast it out across the river.

"Keep your rod tip high. A bit higher. That's it! Now don't give the line any slack." I reeled in steadily. "You have to be able to feel the current grabbing, pulling and swirling the lure along the river bottom."

Yes, in my mind's eye, I could see the grayling perceiving my little lure to be its next minnow dinner.

Suddenly, the line went taut. The rod tip snapped down toward the water. Before I knew what was happening, a grayling had leaped from the river, the iridescent spots on its dorsal fin glittering. One moment the fish was on the line, and the next it was not. The sudden released tension caused the metal bait, still attached to the line, to go winging off in the opposite direction as if it had been expelled from a slingshot.

"Now this time, anticipate the strike. When it hits, let the fish take a tiny bit of line, then give it a sharp tug to set the hooks."

I cast up just as before. But this time I was ready. Just as the lure crossed a small eddy line running next to a large rock, I felt a strange tingling through me. The moment was perfect. The fish struck hard. I yanked the rod tip up; the hooks were set. My rod buckled wildly as the grayling leapt repeatedly from the river, fighting all the way to shore.

Any hunter or fisherman, in order to be successful, has to identify with the creature he pursues. Taking the time to learn a creature's habits, its environment and the inter-relationship it has with other living things, is to be respectful of its existence. Ever since I had known Gary, he had reinforced and refined my beliefs that mankind plays a role in the "web" of life, and not the role of dominance. This biological perception of the natural world has been around for a very long time.

For thousands of years before the coming of white man to the Americas, native people's lives were defined by the enormous variety of climactic and geographical regions. Each type of people adjusted their way to life to make the utmost of the natural world upon which they had total reliance for survival. The identification with and respect for all living things was the basis of nearly every native religion from the Arctic archipelago to Tierra del Fuego. Despite the thousands of miles separating people, nearly all races developed with the belief that, both physically and spiritually, all living things are related. Their attitude of give and take meant that a hunter never took a creature's life, but rather the animal gave up its life for him. Offerings and prayers (such as those we had seen depicted in Indian pictographs along our route) were a way for the hunter to demonstrate his appreciation to the animal's soul. In return, he hoped this appeased soul would suggest to its fellow species that they should give up their lives for him in future times of need. In this view, everything is interrelated so man can never be thought of as a superior being. The animals, plants, sun, wind and rain were his equally important brothers of the earth; without them his existence would cease. It is believed by archeologists that these ideas were established among the native people at least 1,000 B.C. It is humbling to ponder the thought that if the natives of the Americas had been able to impose their beliefs on the first Europeans instead of vice versa, the entire western world could have evolved harmoniously with nature.

The Fond du Lac lies pristine and remote in the heart of the north Saskatchewan wilderness. From its upper reaches in Wollaston Lake, the river makes a clear swirling descent to Lake Athabasca 170 miles and 600 feet below. It was a relatively narrow channel that was seldom without appreciable current. At Red Bank Falls, I knelt with my legs braced against the canoe sides. We galloped down the wild rocky slope maneuvering our way through the obstacles until the river widened and slowly came to a near standstill.

Our eyes settled on the handsome bull moose wading through a quiet bay full of green arrow shoots and pickerel weed. His head went under, probing for the tasty roots. We dipped our paddles and slipped gently forward. Fifty yards, 40 yards. We stopped dead as his massive rack of antlers appeared, trailing with dripping pickerel weed streamers. Nonchalantly, he buried his head under the surface again. We hurried forward more quickly this time. His head jerked up, possibly in response to the splash of water. He gave us one steady stare, then with magnificent long-legged strides he left the water and melded into the forest with barely a single crack of a tree branch.

Sitting side by side on the bank, we carefully studied the rapids that bear Thompson's name. In 1796, David Thompson was the first white man to survey and document the area between Reindeer Lake and Lake Athabasca's eastern end via the same route we were taking. Working as a fur trader for the penny-pinching Hudson's Bay Company, he was wholly unsupported for this venture. He managed to find two Indians, young and inexperienced in river travel, to accompany him since the Hudson's Bay couldn't spare any men. His journey, combined with the later journey of Malcolm Ross, determined that this alternate route to the Athabasca country was not feasible since the two big lakes were frozen long into the spring, precluding a swift departure from the trading posts.

We felt a kinship with this man whose insatiable curiosity and fascination for scientific surveying led to a life of great achievement. Few explorers have journeyed and mapped as many thousands of miles with such consistent accuracy (up to the limits of the instruments and methods available at the time). Very few men have recorded such a wealth of keen observations and perceptions of nature, wildlife and people as did Thompson. Although not formally educated, he was extremely well-read. Thompson was familiar with the scientific concepts of the time yet he used his observations and knowledge of Indian beliefs to draw his own conclusions. For instance, he believed as the Indians did, that the word "instinct" was created by the scientists to gloss over their ignorance of animal behavior thereby stifling further study of such contemporary mysteries as why caribou migrate.

The high-pitched shriek of an eagle drew our attention back to the present. The sun was bright, the sky intensely blue and the rapids hypnotizing. Ordinarily, we would have launched into them without any hesitation. But out here on the Fond du Lac, where we had only one canoe and were far from help, we scrutinized every rapid carefully before deciding to run it.

Surveying Thompson Rapids, we traced out the route. From far left, we would have to move instantly to far right to avoid a boiling souse-hole. We pondered the alternative scramble over rock and squeeze between prickly conifers. Without saying a word to one another, we both knew we wanted to attempt it.

Taking a deep breath, I thrust the bow through the eddyline. Gary angled her and we ferried neatly above the first ledge.

"Now!" he yelled. My paddle leapt instinctively to make a crossbow draw to assist in pulling the canoe around so it faced downstream. Angling the canoe toward shore, we propelled it forward with short, savage strokes. We just nicked the curling wave below the ledge before bursting into the sluggish backwater. A moment later we were sucked back into the hungry current which rushed furiously toward a second ledge. Just as it appeared that we would go hurtling into that foaming maelstrom, we executed a few pry and draw strokes, miraculously sideslipping disaster by a hair's breadth. The rampaging river subsided into a foam-flecked train of rollicking waves that whisked us downstream. It is that thrill of combining our skills with the forces of nature which never ceases to excite us. A person never "conquers" nature, but can learn to respect the risks and develop the skills to work with her demanding conditions.

Our ears were filled with the rising roar of the waterfall. Manitou Falls is not spectacular by virtue of its height but rather for the beauty of its formation. Above the falls, the swift, clear current comes sweeping around the river bend then surges headlong into a buttress of limestone. This violent onslaught of water climbs the pillar then tumbles back on itself before splitting into two distinct channels. To the right, the current squeezes through a narrow channel then swings in a dog-leg turn to the right. Its sheer white foaming fury plunges through a needle's eye then emerges again to undercut the soft Athabasca sandstone. Left of the pillar, some of the water spills over a long even ledge in a delicate cascade. It was here that David Thompson nearly lost his life on the return journey from Lake Athabasca.

"On our return, about half way up the black river, we came to one of the falls, with a strong rapid both above and below it," I read aloud from David Thompson's *Travels*. "We had a carrying place of 200 yards, we then attempted the strong current above the fall . . ." I continued as we gazed upstream toward the rapid we had just descended, "they [the two Chipewyan Indians, Kozdaw and Paddy] were to track the canoe up by a line, walking on shore, while I steered it."

The two natives ended up arguing about which side of an overhanging birch to pass the tracking line while poor Thompson, sitting in the canoe, was swept helplessly sideways. He plunged over the ledge. The possibility of meeting a similar fate had passed through our minds many times before.

I read again from the log book of this famous early geographer, surveyor and explorer. "In an instant the canoe was precipitated down the fall (12 feet), and buried under the waves, I was struck out of the canoe, and when I arose among the waves, the canoe came on me and buried beneath it, to raise myself I struck my feet against the rough bottom and came up close to the canoe which I grasped, and being now on shoal water, I was able to conduct the canoe to the shore. . . . I had to lay down on the rocks, wounded, bruised, and exhausted by my exertions."

This threesome's adventures were not over yet. They struggled upstream without shoes, change of clothing, shelter or ammunition. The blackflies were thick. One unfortunate incident nearly cost the lives of Thompson and Paddy. At great danger to himself, Kozdaw caught some young eaglets for supper. Moreover, he failed to warn the other two of the effects that the yellow fat in most fishing eagles has on the human digestive tract. Paddy and Thompson came down with violent dysentery which left them in an utterly miserable condition. It was extremely lucky that they came across a Chipewyan encampment. Otherwise they might have died. Thompson concluded his description of this episode on a positive note: "I procured some provisions, a flint and nine rounds of ammunition, and a pair of shoes for each of us on credit, to be paid for when they came to trade, also an old kettle. We now proceeded on our journey with thanks to God, and cheerful hearts."

Thompson recounted the next highlight of the river in his wonderfully descriptive way. "The dashing of the water against the rocks, the deep roar of the torrent, the hollow sound of the fall, with the surrounding high, dark frowning hills form a scenery grand and awful, and it is well named the Manito Fall."

The Fond du Lac River cascades around Burr Falls (Manito Fall in Thompson's writing), then spreads itself across the great expanse of Black Lake. When we reached the lake, its surface had an oily-smooth complexion. Thick storm clouds, building on the western horizon, were smothering the sun. A heavy stillness in the air forewarned us of rain. From the bottom of Burr Falls we had a full 20 miles to go to traverse the southern shore of the lake before we would regain the protection of the river. It seemed like a very long way to go.

The topography of Black Lake was like that of all the lakes located on the southern edge of the glacial advance. Perfectly scalloped sand beaches adorned the south shore while the north side still bore the mark of the ancient Canadian Shield. From our map, we could deduce that the heavily wooded, distant shore was unevenly torn with great incisions and dozens of tiny islands scattered about. A tailwind gusting in from the east was gradually strengthening and piling the tiny waves into whitecaps. In the channel between the mainland and the five-mile length of Fir Island, we rode the swell. It was fast and exhilarating as the canoe rushed along the front side of these cresting waves. Just as the first splatters of rain began speckling the surface, we paddled off Black Lake and into the Fond du Lac River again. At Camp Grayling, we received an unexpected and warm welcome from the first people we had seen in over 200 miles.

# 12
# Je suis un homme du nord

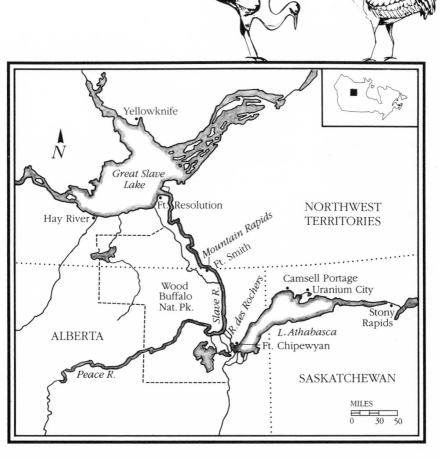

Yellowknife

N

Great Slave Lake

Ft. Resolution

Hay River

Mountain Rapids

Ft. Smith

NORTHWEST TERRITORIES

Wood Buffalo Nat. Pk.

Slave R.

R. des Rochers

Camsell Portage

Uranium City

Stony Rapids

L. Athabasca

Ft. Chipewyan

ALBERTA

Peace R.

SASKATCHEWAN

MILES

0    30   50

T HE VILLAGE OF Stony Rapids, located below the final turbulent miles of the Fond du Lac River before it enters
Lake Athabasca, was where our second supply parcel waited with
the RCMP. The constable, Gord Rogerson, and his wife Heather,
invited us for dinner along with a couple of the local bush pilots.
They were all eager for us to spend some time with them exploring the back country, flying over some of the inland lakes. We
were excited. To view the part of northern Saskatchewan that we
were paddling though from an aerial perspective would be an
unforgettable experience. The weather forecast for the next two
days was for high winds from the west and rain. We were
strangely relieved, for this meant that we could enjoy the
hospitality in Stony Rapids.

Northern bush pilots are a breed apart. No matter how bad,
the weather conditions do not deter them from their plans.
We were interested in the different attitudes the pilots had
toward their work and their varied ambitions. Russ, a tall
blond pilot from Saskatchewan, worked for the local airline,
Aero North. He enjoyed the wheeled aircraft and the journeys
south to the more populated areas of Canada. His ultimate
ambition was to fly jumbo jets to international destinations.
On the other end of the scale was Rob Benz, who also flew for
Aero North and who came from northern Saskatchewan. He
loved the challenge and adventure of flying in the wilderness
where a pilot's eyes, instincts and map-reading skills got him
from one place to another. Despite differences in future ambitions, both these bush pilots relished the independence and
responsibility and the variety of work and people that they encountered as they provided their services to the isolated northern communities. On this particular morning, Rob inquired
if we would like to accompany him on an errand. "I have to
bring Caroline in to do the books this afternoon," he said,
referring to the boss's wife.

Caroline Siemens and her husband, Ben, own and operate Aero North, the largest of several local airlines in Stony Rapids.

Rain was pelting hard against the windshield of the single-engine Beaver as we taxied across the stormy lake. It was not the usual roaring glide followed by smooth lift-off. Heavy whitecaps were sloshing over the floats. Rob thrust the throttle full forward and drew back slightly on the control column. As the aircraft gathered speed, the pontoons managed to plane along the surface. With my face pressed close to the glass, I could barely distinguish between the gray-blue blur of the water and the dark green of the shoreline. Then our pilot pumped the flap control vigorously and drew back the control column to its limit. After bouncing roughly across the wave crests for a few seconds, the aircraft finally left the water. It lifted into the turbulent atmosphere. I noticed that Rob reached for a couple of airsick bags and waved them in Gary's direction. I grinned to myself. The lowly side of piloting with passengers aboard!

We climbed high over the town of Stony Rapids, its white fuel tanks and docks. Toward the heavy western horizon, our eyes followed the river which curled off into the gloom overhanging Lake Athabasca. Swinging east, Rob followed the Fond du Lac River back to Black Lake. It provided a fascinating perspective on the spectacular gorges which we had had to bypass by portaging. Over a 30-mile stretch, Elizabeth Falls, Woodcock Falls and Stony Rapids account for almost a third of the Fond du Lac River's drop from Wollaston Lake. The shoreline of the community of Black Lake was fringed with a most unusual sight.

"Looks like ice along that shore!" Gary bellowed at Rob over the drone of the engines.

He chuckled. "It's spring break-up on Pampers Hill!" We understood. We had already seen enough northern garbage dumps to realize that disposable diapers were not contributing much to the aesthetics of the landscape.

Circling back to the north, we passed over a complex pattern of long sinuous lakes streaming southwest from the northeast. The glacier's handiwork again. Nestled on one of the smaller lakes, the Siemens' cabin was in an enviable location for anyone seeking quiet solitude.

Ben welcomed us at the dock. "Come on up to the cabin."

The eight-sided log cabin was a beautiful piece of architecture. The precise engineering which it must have taken to position the tapered logs so that they spiraled smoothly upward was remarkable. Gary was listening intently to Ben as he proudly described his home and the major difficulties that he and Caroline had had to overcome with just the two of them working on it over several years.

"It's wonderful to know this place is here when things get too hectic in Stony Rapids." Caroline told me. Once, when the pressures of the summer business grew too much to bear, Ben had flown her and their two children to live at the cabin until fall. "It was such a lovely peaceful time to totally enjoy my little girls. We picked berries and looked under rocks together. I read them stories and we played games with natural toys. And you know," she added, "I felt perfectly happy; never lonely. The girls were great company." I smiled and squeezed her arm. I understood and admired her for having done it. City mothers of today don't know what they're missing.

"Here, look at this." Ben tossed Gary a small hunk of dark gray rock. He pointed a geologist's Geiger counter in the rock's direction and we watched in astonishment as the needle shot up into the red zone indicating the ore's rich uranium content.

"I picked this piece up at a place not far from here," he said. "This area has some of the world's richest uranium reserves."

Some time after tea and warm fresh bread, we boarded the plane and returned to Stony Rapids taking Caroline with us. She would spend the afternoon in the office then return to the cabin come evening. Rob flew over the cabin dipping a wing so that we could return the waves of the three tiny figures far below. One last look at the cabin, a pinprick of human habitation in the lonely, wild outback of northern Saskatchewan's Shield country of lakes and rivers. I was sure the tinge of envy I felt just then was not a sentiment that would be widely shared.

Lake Athabasca bears a great resemblance to Lake Superior in general shape, topography and geography, with one particularly noticeable difference. Lining the south shore is a band of vast dunes constituting the most northerly desert in North America. On our map we could see that the southern shore was a series of smooth-rimmed bays, sculpted by the wind and waves. A mirage of shimmering yellow was all we could actually see of the dunes as we paddled along the far shore. The northern shoreline is liberally peppered with tiny granite islands and carved with countless bays. Every now and then, the line of dark green hills is broken by small oases of sand beaches.

The idea of visiting Uranium City and Eldorado had been with us for some time. Ever since we first began planning for the journey, chance meetings had been occuring with former residents of these once-prosperous uranium mining towns. While we were in Stony Rapids, the area's local electrician, Rod Dubnick, extended an open invitation to visit him at his home in Uranium City. We met him again briefly while in Fond du Lac, the village between Stony Rapids and Uranium City. He was halfway up a hydro pole stringing lines. He recognized us and called us over.

"Door's never locked. Just make yourselves at home. This job'll be finished in a day or so and I'll see you then."

So it was that we landed on the shores of the Crackingstone Peninsula, facing a five-mile walk inland with our equipment to Uranium City. Good fortune was with us as two local fishermen pulled into shore just as we were setting off. They offered us a ride, which we gratefully accepted, and dropped us outside a blue bungalow on the far side of town.

"This must be Rod's place. It's the only one that looks lived in!" Gary said, pointing to the neighboring homes with boarded-up windows.

All was quiet. We suspected that Rod was still installing hydro lines in Fond du Lac but that he might be back that evening. We left our equipment and went exploring. The cracked pavement, now encroached upon by weeds, was one sign that this had once been a prosperous northern town. There were buildings, homes, an arena, new structures and old, but very few vehicles and not a sign of life anywhere. Hydro lines, telephone lines and all other services appeared to be intact—but no people. We felt like two lone travelers who had just arrived from a distant planet. Odd bits of debris skittered down the road in the wake of a faint breeze.

Later that evening, Rod returned. Over a dinner of caribou steaks, he talked about his work. He had become something of a jack-of-all-trades since the closing of the uranium mines and his functions included electrician, justice of the peace, coroner, plumber, mechanic and CBC tower inspector. Like the remaining 150 residents of Uranium City, he considers this part of Canada to be his home. The sudden exodus of 4,000 people did not deter Rod or his neighbors from staying in the place they loved.

The next day we piled into Rod's truck and toured the empty streets. The first place we came across was the modern Candu High School nestled comfortably, but forgotten, in the long bunches of swaying horsetail grass and masses of yellow hawkweed and daisies. It was perfectly quiet. I leaned against one of the wooden posts that marked the edge of the school grounds and wondered what it must have been like just two years ago before the uranium mine was shut down. I imagined the laughter and babble of young voices, the field sports and the classes. Rod said they had had a fine woodworking and auto shop.

"It's too bad they had to close it," he said. "That place is full of the most amazing equipment and it just sits there. It's frustrating for someone like me."

As well as the school, we saw the daycare center surrounded by heavy fencing, its playground almost obliterated by weeds. Willowy shrubs of birch clumped together in front of the abandoned medical clinic's windows. The most vivid signs of desertion were the brand new townhouses, their windows boarded up. We were disturbed by what we saw. If the buildings had been old, and decrepit, it would have been different. But they weren't. Everything was as it should be in a neighborhood—little squares of green front lawn, neat rows of wooden- and stucco-sided houses—but no people.

We spent the entire morning with Rod. We had liked him from the moment we met. He was a soft-spoken, easy-going man with a wonderful attitude to the north. He loved this country with its rocky shores and hills and quiet inland lakes and solitude.

"When we first moved here, I used to explore all the smallest creeks by canoe," he said. "I never minded how many blackflies or mosquitoes there were." To us it sounded as though he had carried that canoe and his packs with as much pride and ambition as a coureur de bois. There was an intensity in the way he spoke about his fondness for the country. But much as he wanted to remain, he and his wife were in a quandary. Their son was approaching school age and they were expecting their second child any day. They felt compelled to leave the north in order to provide their children with a solid education. We had seen this pattern emerging with couples who move north then decide to leave when they have families. Maybe some have had enough of the isolation, the harsh climate and the lack of services. Maybe some feel the northern life is fine for very young children, but that they would be depriving their school-age children of educational opportunities if they stayed. Others simply love the life, and never want to go. Although it can be a tough choice to make, there is one very positive aspect to either outcome. Rod Dubnick and all others like him in communities across the north have had the opportunity of living in a way uniquely Canadian. Once most people settle into the high pressure, time-constraining, physically comfortable life-style of the city dweller, it is very difficult to break the ties and "go north."

Among those who have chosen to remain was Philip Stenne. He came from Europe after the Second World War and made his way north to Lake Athabasca. There he met his wife, a native of the region. They lived in the tiny settlement of Camsell Portage, 20 miles west of Uranium City, where Philip was the only commercial fisherman on Lake Athabasca's north shore. The evening we were there, Rod was hooking up the electricity for the Stenne's new frozen storage house. We shared dinner with a large, happy group of children and other community members. The next morning we packed our tent and quietly slipped away.

Later that morning Gary glimpsed a bald eagle swooping low over the cliff tops. It circled, flew back and circled again uttering a distinctly different, repetitious cry.

"Hold on a minute," Gary called out, grabbing the binoculars. He studied a dark, motionless hump on the cobble beach below the bluff. When we drew closer, we discovered the body of another eagle. It was sprawled chest down, its wings outstretched across the sand. When I lifted it, the snowy white head drooped limply on a broken neck. The eyes were clear and the body was still warm. Shortly before our arrival the eagle must have lost control and crashed into the cliff. We presumed it to be the dead mate of the anxious bird winging overhead. I could feel a lump in my throat as I recalled that eagles form a lifelong bond.

*That crag had been his throne.*
*Space was his empire, bounded only*
*By forest and sky and the flowing horizons.* [1]

Never again would they return to nest along Athabasca's north shore together.

Following the shoreline took us in a southwest direction. The landscape was flattening out, an indication that we were approaching the delta region at the confluence of the Peace, Athabasca and Willow rivers on Lake Athabasca's western end. Occasionally we found ourselves poling, or even portaging, through grassy bays on the lee side of islands. This peculiarity in lake level which was not indicated on our topographic map was yet again the fault of man's meddling with nature. Eight hundred miles west of us in the heart of British Columbia, the Bennett Dam had been built to control the Peace River's flow. Its effects were far reaching. The natural flooding which once occured on a regular basis to restore the delta's lost ground has been interrupted. The water level in Lake Athabasca has lowered, revealing bridges of land between islands. The effects actually extend down the Slave River, through its delta, into Great Slave Lake and finally into the shallow upper reaches of the Mackenzie River.

We took advantage of the calm weather conditions and arrived in Fort Chipewyan on the same evening of the day we departed from Camsell Portage. This settlement is perched on a smooth fold of polished granite overlooking the western end of Lake Athabasca. We nosed the canoe into the harbor and pulled up at the nearest pier for the night. While searching for a campsite, we came upon a small meadow with a magnificent view looking out toward the delta and the lake. Despite the wind, we unpacked the tent in unspoken agreement that this would be our home that evening. The tent fly flapped wildly as we struggled to secure the guy lines with heavy rocks. Tired but happy, we crawled into our sleeping bags. I wrote up the log for the day by candlelight, ending with, "This place must surely feel the full effects when the winter tempests come blasting in."

1. From "The Dying Eagle," by E.J. Pratt.

SACRED
TO THE MEMORY OF THOMAS ANDERSON
CHIEF TRADER,
BORN IN NAIRNSHIRE, SCOTLAND,
MAY 3RD 1848.
DIED AT FORT CHIPEWYAN,
FEB. 12TH 1908.

———

AND SO TERMINATED 40 YEARS FAITHFUL
SERVICE TO THE HUDSON'S BAY COMPANY.

The gravestone of solid granite stood firm amid numerous small white crosses and stones tilting this way and that. The knee-high stalks of feathery reed grass made a swishing sound as they brushed against the immovable monuments. The words on that stone spoke not only of one man's life but of an entire era in the history of Canada. They also resonated with significance for us because reaching Fort Chipewyan was a very significant landmark on our voyage of discovery. During the height of the North West Company's fur trade and after its amalgamation with the Hudson's Bay Company, this settlement marked the northern terminus of a vast system of trading posts. At one time it was also the richest post in all of North America because of its proximity to prime beaver and muskrat habitats.

From where we stood high upon a hill we could see the dusty church road that fell steeply to the shore. The unsettled surface of the western bay glimmered in the morning sun. We looked beyond to the hazy blue lumps of High and Lobstick islands. That was the route toward Fletcher Channel and the Athabasca River, the route the fur traders took annually to their rendezvous at Grand Portage more than 2,000 miles away.

"I wonder," said Gary wistfully looking back at the stone, "if Nairnshire looks anything like this."

We headed north from the town toward Rivière des Rochers and the Slave River, beating against a heavy sea and billowing winds. The waters were no longer clear; they were thick with brown silt. We were on the edge of one of the world's largest freshwater deltas, the Peace-Athabasca. It forms where the Peace, Athabasca, and Birch rivers deposit their sediment at the outlet of Lake Athabasca. It is here that portions of the four major North American flyways converge. During the spring and autumn migration, more than a million waterfowl stop briefly to rest and feed in the food-rich delta.

Once back on the water, I caught sight of a strange water craft approaching us at high speed. It was neither boat nor plane. With a tremendous roar, the air boat drew alongside our canoe. One of the three men on board cut the engine and waved.

"Hello!" we shouted in reply. "Where are you headed?"

It turned out they were three biologists from the Wood Buffalo National Park office on their way to the park's interior to make a census of the bison herds of various regions. Wood Buffalo National Park lies just south of Great Slave Lake and straddles the Alberta–Northwest Territories border. The 17,300-square-mile spread of wilderness is the largest national park in Canada and one of the largest in the world. Its territory, which encompasses small lakes, bogs, slow-moving streams and rivers rippling across meadowland and pockets of forest, is home to the world's largest free-roaming herd of bison. We were also thrilled to learn that while paddling the Slave River, the park's eastern boundary, we would be within a day's canoe trip of the only known natural nesting site of the endangered whooping crane.

By noon we had reached Rivière des Rochers, the connecting link between Lake Athabasca and the Peace and Slave rivers. The land here is so flat that it creates some strange situations with varying water levels. The Peace meanders in from the west and when its flow is strong, the current forces water back up its tributaries, like Rivière des Rochers, to Lake Athabasca. When the current is low, the Peace River simply continues on its way past the mouths of these tributaries. This is the reason that Rivière des Rochers can be flowing either south to north, or north to south. At this point, the Peace River enlarges with the increased water volume provided by Rivière des Rochers. Although not really a new river, the Peace has been known as the Slave River from this point north ever since Alexander Mackenzie paddled this way in 1789.

When we reached the confluence of these three rivers, we settled on shore for supper. While we sipped hot chocolate from big plastic mugs, I read from Alexander Mackenzie's logbook: "The Peace River is upwards of a mile broad at this spot, and its current is stronger than that of the channel which communicates with the lake. It here, indeed, assumes the name of the Slave River."

At this very place Mackenzie made the historic wrong turn which led him to discover the Mackenzie River route to the Arctic Ocean before discovering the route to the Pacific. We enjoyed stopping for our evening meal at such significant points along our journey. The scene, as with many others, would be forever vivid in our minds.

The delta silt from the Slave River had settled to form one of the many teardrop-shaped islands. Camping sites were very scarce indeed because of the steep clay banks lining the river. We finally came ashore on a sandbar. As Gary stepped from the canoe and walked away, I noticed with considerable dismay the speed with which the indentations filled with water. Our campsite was barely two inches above the water level! Even an overnight rainstorm could eliminate the distinction between terra firma and the flowing river. As we set up the tent, the pegs disappeared into the syrupy sand and the floor oozed with moisture as the heavy packs were thrown in one by one. As a last precautionary measure, I tied the canoe to the tent. At least we would float away together. A sleepless night would hardly describe the anxieties I went through. Every time I rolled into a particularly wet patch, I sprang awake and peered out the tent door to assure myself that it was only my imagination adrift on the Slave River.

Below Fort Fitzgerald south of the Alberta–Northwest Territories border, the Canadian Shield protrudes from beneath the great weight of Interior Plains sedimentary rock entirely altering the nature of the Slave River. From placidity, the Slave turns savage, hurtling across the 60th parallel, curling and boiling over great ledges of granite and coursing through fractured rock and tiny treed islands. In 20 miles, the waters thunder through Cassette Rapids, Mountain Rapids, Pelican Rapids and Rapids of the Drowned.

We recognized the white pelicans airborne over their curious island habitat, a nesting site in the middle of Mountain Rapids. The biologists from the park office at Fort Chipewyan had described this small flock as the most northerly and the only known river-nesting colony in the world.

We were standing with Don Jaque, the editor of the *Slave River Journal* in Fort Smith on a high point of land overlooking Mountain Rapids.

"This could all be lost so easily," lamented Don as he explained the threat that loomed over the Slave River. The survival of the pelicans was being put in jeopardy by people who wanted to see Mountain Rapids dammed for hydroelectric power. But the detrimental effects would be felt by more than just the pelicans. The fluctuating water levels, the pollution and the drastically altered silt content of the river would seriously damage the ecosystem at the Slave River delta. The prolific population of muskrat there provides a major portion of the native trapper's seasonal income. So great is the volume of water flowing down the Slave River that any significant alteration in its flow would have far-reaching effects on the water levels in the southern end of Great Slave Lake and in the upper Mackenzie River.

Since he was an enthusiastic white-water paddler, Don had organized a kayak club in Fort Smith. For several hours that evening, we traded in our canoeing gear for helmets, double-bladed kayak paddles, spray skirts and kayaks for a more intimate encounter with the river below the final set of rapids.

"Rapids of the Drowned"—the name alone is enough to strike fear into the heart of the most stalwart river runner. The incident after which the rapid was named occured in the late 1700s to a party led by Cuthbert Grant. A very experienced guide led the first party down the raging river. It was agreed that upon reaching the bottom, this party would signal the second party with a gunshot if the channel were safe to run. However, it proved extremely dangerous and they only just made it through without mishap. Shortly after they reached the bottom, one of the men grabbed a loaded gun and fired at a duck winging overhead. His excited blunder signaled the party above. Assuming that the channel was safe, they proceeded to their death in the nightmarish passage.

I was quite alone in the middle of the river. The eddy created in the backwash of an island far above was racing upriver, causing my little yellow kayak to pitch wildly from crest to crest. Feeling like a tiny mouse being toyed with by a cat, I watched an angry whirlpool sweep past, its swirling vortex so deep it could have sucked my entire craft in vertically until it disappeared from view.

Far above me, the chocolate-brown water tumbled and foamed through the islands. The white crests colliding with one another created fountains of foam. These were highlighted by the low angle of the evening sun and contrasted sharply with the bruised-looking sky darkened by a passing storm. Just as I angled my kayak across the current to head back downstream, I glimpsed a flock of white pelicans rising into the black sky. I saw Gary wave from a tiny shoal, camera in hand. Remarkably, he had captured the fleeting moment on film. We hoped this picture would never become a record of a passing legacy.

Below Fort Smith, the Slave River takes on the appearance of a great brown snake coiling and writhing between sand or mud banks timbered with spruce, poplar and willow. It crosses the interior plains region for another 175 miles before it disperses through a wide fan of delta channels at Great Slave Lake. It was already the third week of July and we were anxious to reach the Mackenzie River by the first of August. We seldom left the canoe except to sleep. We were on the water by just after sunrise to take advantage of the cooler paddling hours. Even meals were made in the canoe as we continued drifting northward. In this manner, we covered the 300 miles of the Slave River in just four days.

"Take the Old Steamboat Channel," an Indian trapper in Fort Smith had advised. "Then when it divides, take the Sawmill Channel to Nagle Bay." Although it looked easy on the map, delta channels are as disorienting as the ancient yew hedgerows in England's Hampton Court maze!

While on the narrow Sawmill Channel, where the willows grow thickly to the water's edge, we saw dozens of muskrats swimming beneath the riverbanks. Little tunnels scooped from the bank at water level, half-hidden by overhanging vegetation, indicated the entrances to their secret abodes.

The huge preserve of Wood Buffalo National Park comes to its northern limit 20 miles south of Great Slave Lake. But nature recognizes no man-made boundaries. The same northern prairie, typified by dark muskegs and birch and poplar bush, stretches clear to a shallow marshy shoreline. Great Slave Lake's southern shore has little to suggest the rugged beauty of its northern side. There were only the distant tips of the long curved bays to mark the hours. Presqu'île Point, Sulphur Point, Breyant Point, High Point, Fish Point and False Point—point after point, bay after bay, hour after hour, the miles dragged on. Those were still, summer days and the sandflies swarmed thickly around our heads and in our eyes, ears and noses. In the distance, like thin trails of smoke from a hundred tiny campfires, columns of flies blackened the sky. The shallow waters were warm and murky so there was never a refreshing drink or swim to be had after the wearisome hours of paddling. We were more than eager to arrive at the Mackenzie River headwaters.

Leonard Dion leaned back against the blue fishing dory puffing comfortably on a hand-rolled cigarette. He wore green co-op clothing and heavy work boots. His greased black hair was slicked back and reflected the morning sun. Leonard was a tidy man who ran an efficient fishing operation on Great Slave Lake's southern shore east of Hay River.

"This place used to be packed with fishermen in the days when fishing was good," he said, indicating the concrete platforms at Dawson Landing where fish were once prepared for market. "Now it's hard to fill the nets with anything but suckers and whitefish!"

Climbing back into the dory, Leonard began pounding in a few fresh floorboard planks. We went back to searching among the remains of more prosperous fishing days. Innumerable fishing floats, masses of old nets and empty fish boxes were lying around unused. Leonard had three hired men who left in the wee hours of the morning to haul the nets, take in the catch, then set the nets again. When they returned, we helped them heave several large plastic crates from the dory. We watched with keen interest as they systematically laid out the boxes, shoveled ice from the freezer into the empty ones, then began filleting. Besides their wool jackets and rubber coveralls, the men wore special wrist-to-elbow rubber sleeves and wool gloves without fingers, attire suitable for cold, wet work with slicing blades and slimy entrails. The table was soon a mass of bloody carcasses, and the smell of fresh fish had attracted hundreds of gulls. When at last the fishermen dumped the slimy offal in a heap by the shore, the squealing, yelping medley of the hungry flock was almost deafening. Among the herring gulls I spotted a few Arctic terns, the greatest migrants in the bird kingdom. On slender white wings, they cover a distance almost as great as they would circling the globe during their annual migration between the Antarctic and the Arctic.

"Eleven hundred miles to go," Gary called merrily from the stern as we swung the canoe past Point Desmarais. The silty brown lake was now infused with the refreshing green water of Canada's mightiest waterway, the Mackenzie River.

# 13
# Land of Wandering Spirits

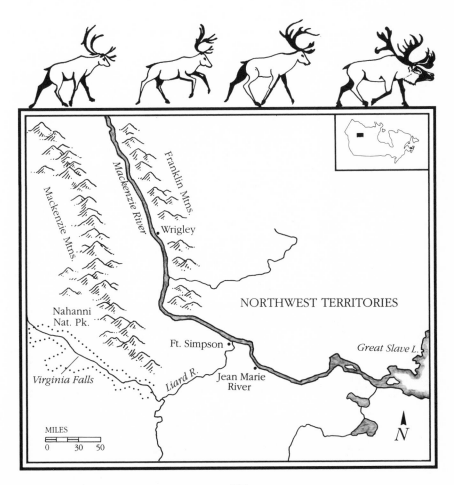

B EYOND GREAT SLAVE LAKE, two broad arms of the Mackenzie River embrace Big Island, then merge into shallow
Beaver Lake. The river widens and slows until it is once again
squeezed through the lake's western end. Here we passed Fort
Providence, a Slavey Indian community which commands a wonderful view from its location high upon the plateau above the
river banks. From Fort Providence, numerous swift channels
break from the main one, weaving around Meridian Island, then
again converging in another large shallow water body called
Mills Lake.

Second only in size to the Mississippi–Missouri River system in
North America, the Mackenzie's drainage basin encompasses some
700,000 square miles. For 250 miles beyond Great Slave Lake, the
broad ribbon of river bears west until it collides with the foothills of
the Mackenzie Mountains. But nothing stops the unrelenting flow
save winter's deep freeze, so northward it swings following a valley
carved out by the glaciers. Spruce and birch crowd the riverbanks.
At its northern extremity in the mouth of a vast delta, the river ven-
tures into the barren lands and is shortly thereafter consumed by a
polar sea. We were heading more and more due north, and only
one month remained in the Arctic's brief summer. We would experience as much as a 70-degree variance in temperature and
noticeably shorter days. Our journey would take us to the Arctic
Circle and 400 miles of paddling beyond.

West of Mills Lake, the river makes its slow methodical way
through low-lying land, gradually picking up speed until it surges
past the Slavey Indian settlement of Jean-Marie River. At this
location, nothing could pass on the river unnoticed. A few
people gathered along the banks as we turned in towards shore.
One man waved. He was friendly and outgoing and introduced
himself as Chief Ernest Hardisty.

Obviously very proud of the community in which he lived,
Chief Hardisty asked if we would be interested in a tour of the

village. Jean-Marie River has managed to retain many of the old customs. The quality of life here was apparent to us in the brightly painted buildings, the playground, the school, the log homes, the happy faces and the activity all around us. There were several stretched moose hides tanning in the sun with lard pots hung on a peg beside them. In another corner of the village, carpenters were busy putting down the floor for a new building. Nearly all the buildings were constructed from logs, unlike the dismal prefabricated shacks that had often dominated the scene in native communities farther south. Surrounding the homes was a green park-like area. The air smelled fresh. In other communities where unpaved roads carve up the terrain, young people cruise the streets incessantly, kicking up clouds of choking dust into the air. In Jean-Marie River, there is only one road. It links the village together but does not lead to the outside. Access to Jean-Marie River is by water and air only.

Chief Hardisty led us up the hill where we stopped at his mother's cabin. Here we had a view clear across the green hillside and out over the broad shining river. The two wooden steps leading up to the door were indented and worn smooth with age. His mother had just left to spend a few days in Fort Simpson where she could sell her handiwork of beaded gauntlets, moccasins and moosehide jackets to the artists' cooperative store.

As we looked around us, we were surprised at the lack of color and decoration in her little home. The kitchen boasted nothing more than a plain table, two chairs, a small wood cookstove and a fridge. There were two tiny bedrooms. Ernest disappeared into the pink one. A single bed, a dresser and a night table filled the room. From his mother's dresser drawer, he pulled out a sewing basket containing the simple tools of her trade, a few curved needles, bags of colored beads, thread and scissors. Ernest proudly showed us examples of her artistry. On two pieces of moosehide, destined to become the tops on a pair of moccasins, she had beaded a pink rose pattern. Each woman has her own design which distinguishes her work from that of other artisans. Chief Hardisty was proud of the artistic talents of the women of Jean-Marie River, talents for which the village has become well known.

Ernest pulled out a photo album, the binding of which was held together by many yellowing layers of tape. He turned the dog-eared pages one by one, revealing faded black-and-white photographs. There were pictures of sled dogs, old buildings and people, spanning the years of his mother's life. One yellowed photograph from the 1940s of the residential Catholic mission school was strangely disconcerting. The students, the priests and the Grey Nuns were all gathered on the front steps. Ten priests filled the foreground. The "Blackrobes," as the native people called them, had large crosses dangling from their necks. Behind them stood a group of eleven Grey Nuns flanked by several dozen Indian children all dressed in black, the girls in dresses on one side, the boys in knickers and long stockings on the other. It was attire fit for a funeral procession. Some smiled, some frowned and some were distracted. The photograph was a testimonial to the time when native family life and customs were sacrificed as the white man imposed his beliefs and values upon them. However, the mission's schools were only the final straw in the havoc wrought upon the native people by the missionaries.

In their dedication to the end of saving souls, the missionaries lived very close to the native people. Ironically, their presence delivered far more than salvation, since they carried with them the deadly Old World diseases for which the Indians had absolutely no immunity. When people first populated the New World via the Bering Sea landbridge at the end of the last Ice Age, the diseases of the Old World did not follow. Anyone afflicted could never have survived the harsh Arctic conditions. So there were no widespread epidemics in the New World before the coming of the white man. Many thousands of years passed before Old World inhabitants ventured out to explore the oceans and eventually settle in the Americas. However, once they did begin arriving, the effects were catastrophic. Tens of millions of people perished in an epidemic of far greater proportions than the Black Death, which swept away a third of the European population in the fourteenth century. It took less than 100 years to reduce the native population to a mere tenth of its former size. Unlike the Europeans, they never recovered.

Chief Hardisty could put a name to all the faces in the photograghs, no matter how fuzzy or faded. He remembered them as children and he knew where they were and what they were doing now. He could tell the story behind every picture because they represented his heritage.

Good weather and a strong current combined to help us complete the Mackenzie River's first 250 miles to Fort Simpson in just three days.

While picking up our food and film parcel at the RCMP depot in Fort Simpson, we spoke with one of the guards who was native to the region. He had many an interesting native legend to relate. Two of them involved curses put upon the land by the Dene, the native people.

Because they were once driven from the north shore of Lake Athabasca, the medicine men used their magical powers to curse the land, declaring that people would never grow and prosper or settle into this area long enough to ever call it home. Recent evidence of the efficacy of this curse was Uranium City. As we had seen for ourselves, it was a ghost of its former self, with fewer than 100 of its original 4,000 inhabitants left.

Another legend involved the Dene coat of arms which depicts three arrows by the Mackenzie River. It is said that these arrows are hidden somewhere in the valley and if they were ever disturbed, life along the Mackenzie River, as it is, would cease to exist. Our friend suggested that the arrows may already have been disturbed and the Mackenzie Valley's days numbered. The landscape had been scarred by survey lines, intruded upon by roads and was now faced with the development of the oil pipeline from Norman Wells. We imagined what could be so catastrophic as to annihilate life along the river. If an earthquake were to occur, it would create a chemical nightmare in the vulnerable wetlands of the delta. The flora and fauna of the Arctic may be attuned to a harsh environment, but they are extremely sensitive to petroleum poisoning.

In Fort Simpson we also met Ted Grant, the owner and operator of Simpson Air. He was flying into the Nahanni Mountains west of the village to deliver a load of lumber to a long-time resident, Gus Kraus. As we flew with Ted to Gus's cabin on Little Doctor Lake, two large pyramid-shaped mountains appeared to converge straight ahead. Ted flew the Platus Turbo Porter so low over the trees that the floats almost brushed the upper branches. This aircraft's short takeoff and landing capabilities make it ideal for traveling between and landing on the mountains' lakes and rivers. The aircraft touched down and came to a stop in a very short stretch of water. Then Ted reversed into Gus's beach.

After we helped Ted and Gus unload the lumber, Gus's wife Mary and his granddaughter Jennifer made tea. We sat in the quiet dark cabin, the light filtering in through a large window which overlooked the lake. Eighty-five-year-old Gus talked quietly, but there was an intensity in his blue eyes that I had never seen before in a man of his age. For over 50 years, he had prospected and trapped, surviving, living and loving the Nahanni wilderness. Looking out across Little Doctor Lake toward the mountains he knew so intimately, Gus told us a little of his life. He described the past winter—a visiting grizzly and an encounter with a large bull moose. Finally, he spoke of the place below First Canyon at Clausen Creek labeled Kraus Hotsprings on our map. During the Second World War, a war which must have seemed very remote to him, Gus made his home in these mountains. He met an Indian girl, Mary, and they made their home by the hotsprings. Although the sulfur stench was not pleasant, the heat provided the warmth for their home throughout the coldest winter months. A tropical zone of several hundred acres surrounded the cabin, allowing them to grow vegetables otherwise impossible to cultivate in the short summer. Later when Kraus Hotsprings came within the boundaries of Nahanni National Park, they moved to Little Doctor Lake.

Following Jennifer behind the cabin and through the bush, we arrived at a lush vegetable garden overflowing with potatoes, peas, beans and carrots. She pointed out the reddening Saskatoon berries, then took us to the teepee playhouse and swing bars Gus had built her. Gus and Mary were teaching Jennifer at home. Books of all kinds lined the cabin walls. It was fascinating to hear the legends of the Nahanni River from a couple who had experienced it so intimately throughout their younger lives, before the cloak of mysticism had been drawn back by the advent of frequent boat and aircraft travel. Finally we waved goodbye to Gus and his family and took off to fly up through the Nahanni River canyons.

A giant pillar of limestone rose majestically like a great shark's tooth from the thundering cataracts below us. Ted swung the aircraft in a wide circle. With our noses pressed against the glass, we were mesmerized by the power of the water as the river split around the column and plunged almost twice the height of Niagara Falls into the raging gorge below. The spray caught the

sun and refracted it into circular rainbows. This was Virginia
Falls, the highest in Canada. The Athapaska Indians aptly named
the Nahanni "Nahadeh," meaning Powerful River. It surges, boils
and flows through the deepest river canyons in all of Canada.

Swinging southeast, we followed the river down through twisting gorges with such ominous names as Funeral Range, Headless
Creek and Deadman Valley. At times we flew on a level with the
banded dolomite walls and limestone bluffs, but we were still
4,000 feet above the swollen current. The flat plains capping the
top edges of these deeply carved valleys are representative of
what this area looked like several million years ago. This ancient
watery passage was young then, winding across a landscape with
no more topography than some worn old mountains. Gradually
as the land began shift and fold, it buckled upward at the same
rate as the river carved downward. We gazed down upon the
Nahanni and imagined ourselves descending the swift waters by
canoe. The vision of steep walls rising around us and the mystical
beauty of the canyons streaming by filled us with wonder at
nature's artistry.

The Mackenzie River flows over a region once submerged by a
succession of inland seas going back 600 million years. In the
immense time period of 550 million years, a bed of sedimentary
rock composed of thick deposits of sand, shale and limestone
was laid down. Unfathomable amounts of plant and animal life
decayed here, leaving the rich deposits of oil and natural gas that
are found all the way from Texas to the Beaufort Sea. Indeed,
the Mackenzie River is the corridor to the western Northwest
Territories. Its integral wealth in the form of petroleum oil was
now being exploited through development of a pipeline stretching from Norman Wells to northern Alberta.

On our way to Fort Simpson, we had seen the first signs of the
installation of the pipeline. A 50-yard-wide bulldozer swath had
swept back the trees and unfolded the earth in ugly scars on
either side of the river. The previous winter, a mile-wide channel
had been blasted beneath the river bottom through which the
controversial Mackenzie Valley pipeline was threaded.

We left Fort Simpson and our route now lay directly north.
The mighty waterway had come up hard against the flanks of the
Camsell Mountains. At this point, the river makes a firm decision
to drive northward to its destination, the Arctic Ocean. The main

channel separated, braiding around low teardrop-shaped islands. We chose the eastern channel around McGern Island quite by chance. It was developing into a very calm, hot day on the river. Twice we had soaked our T-shirts and hats, letting the evaporation of the water cool us off. Then along came *Skoocum II*.

A shallow green river scow was moving at a snail's pace toward us. As it drew closer, the white-bearded captain at the helm called out, "I sure wish I was going in your direction." Ernie Werbecky was traveling on a wing and prayer with one motor dead and the other dying occasionally.

"I can't just drift to Fort Simpson from here," Ernie laughed. The motor coughed. "Keep chugging, *Skoocum*," he said in response. He turned to Gary. "Other one's on the blink and I'm off to get it fixed."

With his head cocked to one side and his brows knitted in a frown, Ernie listened with intense interest as Gary told him briefly about our travels.

"The boys at Willowlake Creek would be very keen to meet you. How about stopping in? It's our base of operations while we survey and mark the lines through this area of the Mackenzie." He paused, then looked back at the motor. "I wish I didn't have this motor to play with," he said, irritated. "I'd have liked to escort you there myself. And don't forget," he yelled as he chugged away, "get yourselves a good meal while you're at it!"

When we arrived at the camp, we saw over two dozen red-and-yellow striped fuel barrels strewn haphazardly about the landing area. They had arrived via the barge only a few days before. The fuel would be consumed quickly, most of it by the camp's flying workhorse, the Totem helicopter. Two people emerged from the doorway of a nearby camp tent. They introduced themselves as Bruce, the mechanic, and Brian, the pilot. Their business involved transporting supplies and equipment and flying the survey and line-cutting crews into regions west of the Mackenzie River. They had to begin picking the crews up from the bush and transporting them back to the camp for the night. Would we, they asked, like to see where the pipeline was being built?

The rotors began to whirl, then we lifted off, sending a cloud of dust in every direction. Our map suddenly sprang to life. There were the islands, the broad brown Mackenzie and the sparsely treed McConnell Range.

Below us, the lush green foliage surrounding Willow Lake Creek stood out in stark contrast to the spruce forest blackened by fire for miles around. Only isolated pockets in the valleys had been spared. We could see the clear, dark creek flowing into the Mackenzie and sneaking along the shore for a quarter of a mile before being absorbed by the opaque waters of the mighty river. There were the survey lines crisscrossing the surface in every direction. From our vantage point in the big transparent bubble of the helicopter, we could see the marks of progress extending in two long narrow scars northward and southward. One was the start of a new road while the other running parallel to it was the unfinished link in the Mackenzie Valley pipeline. More than 300 miles ahead lay Norman Wells where the pipeline originated. Many hundreds of miles south was its destination in northern Alberta.

We do not pretend to have great knowledge of the pipeline and the countless effects good and bad that such development contributes to the north, but we have talked to the people and we have seen the changes that roads generate in the villages. It was not so much the physical scars across the landscape, but the alterations in the way of life that the roads bring. Roads make places accessible to a transient population, one which has no vested interest in the welfare of the community. The towns consequently lose their identity. All of a sudden people no longer know their neighbors. In the summer, the streets bulge with curious onlookers who drive north to see native Canada.

The particular road that we were flying over was unfinished because the people of Wrigley had taken up arms against such an intrusion. They have seen what has happened to places like Fort Simpson. They want to be in control of their own destiny, not under the thumb of some powerful development company or tourist bureau.

The torn edges of steel-wool clouds swept across the band of sky over our dark, watery corridor. The reflection of the gathering gloom was all about us in the stormy river that tossed our canoe on agitated waves. Cobblestone beaches lined the shores below dark hills smothered in black spruce. The view to the McConnell Range of the Franklin Mountains, which towered 3,000 feet above the river, was obliterated by the high riverbanks.

Clearwater streams appeared either gushing from the forest and fanning out across the cobbles or trickling down the hillside creating a clatter of tiny stones. An incessant headwind moaned past our ears. That day the miles stretched on forever. Then we saw the kayaks. Without hesitation, we altered direction and headed shoreward.

Two lone figures sat side by side on a log warming their hands over a small fire. Their yellow tent pitched behind them was like a dapple of sunshine on the beach. For a moment, I saw Gary and myself mirrored in the couple. The image emphasized all the more the immensity of the landscape. My humbling thoughts were interrupted when the woman waved, got up and walked down to the river's edge. All we could see beneath the brim of her floppy green hat was a glowing smile. The expression welcomed us as truly as any words.

"You look like you're ready for something hot to drink," she said. "Won't you come and join us?"

We pooled our biscuits and honey with their hot chocolate while we talked and shared our experiences of paddling the river. Instead of continuing on, we pitched our tent beside theirs and enjoyed the companionship of fellow paddlers that afternoon. Together we explored the beaches, shuffling through the cobbles and sand. Our beachcombing turned to gold panning with the aid of our cooking pot in a nearby stream. We didn't strike it rich but we had fun. George and Sylvia led us up to an old trapper's cabin they had found hidden far above the Mackenzie's edge. By day's end, the weather had changed. Salmon-pink fish-scale clouds reflected a sun already hidden below the horizon. Sylvia stirred a thick vegetable stew that bubbled in a pot over the fire. George sat in the sand opposite Sylvia, downwind of the trail of smoke. But they hardly seemed to notice. His arms were wrapped about his knees and his black eyes stared into the flames. He was telling me about his family.

A family devotion for wilderness travel was obvious. Although they lacked much money to purchase good equipment, their ingenuity led from one adventure to another. George had three sons, George, Chuck and Andrew who all shared his enthusiasm for adventure. They had rowed a leaky rowboat down the St. Lawrence taking turns rowing and bailing, sleeping and steering. They had patched it up with driftwood and roofing tar when it began leaking faster than they could bail. Another time they had ridden a home-built bicycle for three around Lake Ontario.

"Some ingenious soul cut an old 28-inch Raleigh in half and had lengthened it out with one-inch galvanized plumbing pipe, upon which he welded three seats. It was always breaking down."

"I'm not surprised!" I chuckled.

George continued, embellishing the story with more details. "Spokes broke constantly, the front fork crumbled from hitting too many bumps, and the rear drive wheel broke from the stress of three of them pumping up the mountains on only one gear, but Georgie patched it up and they got to the White Mountains and home again."

Being professors, George and Sylvia had their summers off. They had decided to spend this one kayaking down the Mackenzie River. While they were here, two of their sons, along with a cousin and a girlfriend, had decided to paddle down the Albany River to James Bay in Ontario, probably with thoughts of tremendous fishing and white-water canoeing dancing in their heads. George and Sylvia laughed and smiled at one another.

"Andrew has a motto," Sylvia grinned. "It is better to burn out than to rust away."

I could picture them all very vividly. Although they lived apart, they shared a spirit of family togetherness through the anticipation and participation of outdoor adventures.

Gary was listening but he was also ensconced behind his camera lens. Crouching nearby he was capturing these wonderful moments. What had started out as a funereal and gloomy morning had been transformed into an unforgettable scene of friends brought together by chance on a wilderness river and blessed by a fine northern sunset.

The next morning we woke to the steady drumming of rain on the tent fly. As quietly as possible, I pulled on my rainsuit and unzipped the door. I heard a rustling in the warm sleeping bag behind me, then a sleepy voice said, "Better wait a while, Sylvia and George will still be sleeping."

"I wanted to be up first and light the fire," I said eagerly. But hearing the sound of a rattling pot, I knew I had missed my chance. Sylvia and George had already been up beachcombing for an hour. I looked at my watch . . .7A.M. on a rainy day?!

We were once again gathered about the campfire when Sylvia
pointed to a huge boat coming around the far bend. As it drew a
little closer, we realized it was the coast guard. For a full 10
minutes it came chugging upstream through the mist. We
watched, joking thankfully that our voyage was downstream.
Soon I could make out the name, *Dumit*, stenciled along the
foredeck.

"I've seen that name before . . . ." Gary paused. "I know, it's on
the map. It's the name of an island just below Sans Sault Rapids."

Suddenly a voice hailed over the loudspeaker on board the
ship. "Is there anyone on shore by the name of George?" A
curious expression came over George's face. I hardly gave it a
second thought as I was intent on photographing this exciting
event. Gary laid his hand on my arm as our friends walked
toward the gangplank that was being lowered from the boat's
side.

"Joanie, something is wrong. I know it."

I turned and looked at Gary. His dark eyes were focused on
the boat, not the couple. His brow was creased, his lips set firmly
together. He was very worried although I had no idea about
what.

"Come on, let's go on board too," I urged.

The rabble of comments left us puzzled and concerned.

"Something about a canoe found in James Bay . . . ."

"Ontario police have been contacting all the RCMP detachments along the Mackenzie . . . ."

"I don't know really except we have been looking for this
couple for days! . . ."

Up on the foredeck, subdued conversation was being carried on around the captain's radio. Not wanting to interfere,
we busied ourselves looking at hydrographic charts of the river
downstream and the obstacles ahead. Then the captain came
over. He was a handsome white-haired man who had a passion
for collecting unusual rocks from along the Arctic coast. He
showed us one of the window ledges in the control room. It
was jam-packed with pieces of fossilized wood, fossils in rock,
golden agate rock and rocks of all kinds. In between handing
each piece to us and expounding on its special characteristics,
he gave us a short explanation of their mission to find Sylvia
and George.

"Ten days ago, the Ontario police called our base in Hay River and a message was forwarded asking us to find them. It is feared that their two sons have drowned."

My stomach tightened into a ball as the captain went on.

"No one is quite sure how far they got before they capsized, but their canoe was found in James Bay."

Then it occurred to him that we might be traveling with George and Sylvia. Gary explained a little of what we were doing and how we had come to be camping with this couple.

"But they couldn't have drowned," Gary said emphatically. "Something else must have happened."

We glanced across the control room to where Sylvia and George had collapsed to the floor, their backs against the wall. Their faces were completely drained of color, their eyes wide, sunken and staring straight ahead. They were lost in their separate worlds of despair.

Then, looking straight at us, George said in a flat detached monotone, "My sons are dead."

Gary mustered up a calm but determined reply on the strength of his conviction that they should not accept this as final since only the canoe had been found. "Joanie and I could return to Ontario and make a thorough search of the lower Albany. They must be alive, waiting on the river bank somewhere for rescue."

George would not be swayed. Whatever the police had told him had made him lose all hope. We led them quietly back to camp to collect their equipment. The little campfire, once the center of our friendly gathering in the rain, added no comfort to the situation now. When they were ready to leave, Sylvia handed us a book about the Mackenzie River.

"You two can make more use of this than we can. Please take it." She pressed the book into my hands. "And paddle the river for us." She looked so forlorn that only Gary's belief that their sons could still be alive prevented me from bursting into tears.

"Don't give up hope, Sylvia." Gary hugged her. We walked down to the boat together. Then they pulled away from shore, moving slowly against the current. It would be a long journey to Wrigley, then Fort Simpson and home to Ontario. We stood at the water's edge without speaking until the boat had disappeared from view. We felt utterly helpless. Wordlessly, we turned back to camp, methodically packed our gear as we had done hundreds of times before, launched the canoe and paddled away. I couldn't look back.

It would be some weeks later before we would receive a firm report from a CBC correspondent that, indeed, a party of canoeists had gone missing on James Bay. Two canoes and some gear had been recovered. There were no survivors.

# 14

# To the
# Arctic Ocean

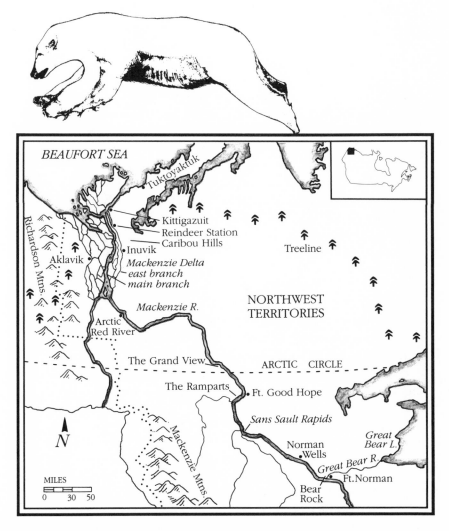

# H

ALFWAY DOWN THE Mackenzie, the mountains appeared greener and more distant and rose in contrasting sweeps of dark green and hazy blue. Several major rivers and many smaller creeks came pouring out of the McConnell Range to the east and the Mackenzie Mountains to the west. The clouds were high and unthreatening. A fresh breeze whisked us along on the already swift current. While having lunch we allowed the canoe to drift, exposing its full length to the wind. Chattering yellowlegs swooped down upon us in agitation. Water pipits dashed back and forth along the beaches on spindly little legs. Several sandhill cranes rose in flight, beating their great wings and cackling loudly.

While returning upriver after having reached the Arctic Ocean in 1789, Mackenzie wrote in his log of a curious phenomenon that we had heard of but never seen: ". . . we saw several smokes along the shore. As we naturally concluded . . . that these were certain indications where we should meet the natives who were the objects of our search, we quickened our pace; but, in our progress, experienced a very sulphurous smell, and at length dis-covered that the whole bank was on fire for a very considerable distance. It proved to be a coal mine, to which the fire had communicated from an old Indian encampment. The beach was covered with coals, and the English chief gathered some of the softest he could find, as a black dye; it being the mineral, as he informed me, with which the natives render their quills black."

During the winter the warm air rising from this seam of burn-ing coal forms a white cloud of condensation over the hills; hence their name, the Smoking Hills.

Paddling by the mouth of the Great Bear River, where oil seeps and sulfurous springs ooze from the hillside, we gazed up at the towering sentinel of Bear Rock. On its face are three red patches. They are explained in this native legend. "A giant after having suffered a cold and hungry winter, killed three beaver. He ate them and then stretched their pelts on Bear Rock. These pelts are the red patches on the cliff face."

Below Bear Rock, we paddled on a current that was sharply divided between the Mackenzie's own brown silty color and the clear green of the icy-cold Great Bear River. Behind us the magnificent MacKay Range towered along the southern horizon. Since we had passed Fort Norman, the temperature had dropped considerably. A light drizzle developed into a steady rain and then sleet. It was time to head for shore. We were thankful we had been able to pick up the special overbags for our sleeping bags at the Fort Simpson detachment. No doubt we would be seeing a lot more weather like this.

The following morning I could feel the frost in the air even before we left our sleeping bags. The tips of our noses were red and icy cold. When I pressed my hand against the wall I felt the nylon tent crisp with frost. Outside, the Carcajou Range seemed bright for early dawn, especially considering the sun had not yet appeared. Gary held the binoculars to his eyes.

"I knew it felt like we should be skiing this morning. That's snow up there!"

A shaft of sunlight bursting over the crown of the Norman Range behind us illuminated the distant snowy crests. Far below them, near the river's edge, a band of vertical clay ridges caught the morning light. Separating these light-colored stripes was a uniform pattern of dark stripes formed by the shadows cast in the deep gulleys.

Although it was only mid-August, it felt more like mid-October as we briskly packed up camp. Pausing to warm our hands, we listened intently to the faint sound of honking trickling up the valley. As it grew in strength, the great migrating V of Canada geese, southward bound to warmer climes, poured into view. The snow may have been 2,000 feet above us, but it was cold enough to spur us all on.

For the first time our clothing packs were almost empty. To combat the chill of the north wind, we donned three layers of clothing. We even wore our home-made nylon paddling mittens called pogies. It was another hour before the sun penetrated our cool shadowy passage below the eastern band of mountains called Discovery Ridge. And still longer before swift paddling pumped warmth into our chilly feet and tingling fingers.

A flock of sandhill cranes signaled our arrival at Norman Wells. With a flourish of wing beats and loud trumpeting, the birds lifted off from shore behind the first offshore island. This strange hump of gravel was no ordinary island. Like the five others in this part of the river, it had been built artificially to provide a platform from which to drill for oil in the Mackenzie River bottom. The islands had been well engineered to withstand the tremendous forces of spring breakup when house-size plates of ice come tumbling and grinding down the river. They were teardrop shaped, their prows facing upstream and reinforced with concrete blocks. Each one was erected upon a substantial gravel pad which extended from the river bottom 30 feet below to 30 feet above the water level.

Unlike the other Mackenzie River settlements which had their beginnings in the fur trade, Norman Wells began with the discovery of immense oil reserves in the early 1920s. During the Second World War, the Canol Pipeline and Highway were built from the Mackenzie River, through the mountains, the Yukon, and into Alaska to provide fuel for Allied ships in the north Pacific. The tremendous undertaking had only just been completed and operations begun when the war ended. The pipeline was disassembled and the rest fell into ruins.

Norman Wells boomed again during the construction of the Mackenzie Valley pipeline. But once in place, it takes relatively few people to keep it operating. The transient, non-native population of Norman Wells was already dwindling. The pipeline was built to serve the interests of southern Canada without providing much for the region itself.

At the Norman Wells docking facilities, we watched the great balloon-tired landmovers trundling down from Hamer Mountain carrying their contribution of gravel for building up the artificial islands. Despite the size of the machines, each load they carried seemed a miniscule amount. Back and forth these machines moved, hauling gravel and demolishing part of a mountainside. We likened them to a colony of ants, which they were, in relation to their surroundings.

"This is where the oil will begin its long journey southward once the pipeline is completed." Mike, the RCMP corporal, was pointing down a long, green laneway sliced out of the northern bush. "Instead of using pumps to draw the oil out, highly purified water is pumped into the well. This displaces the oil, thereby recovering it far more efficiently."

Near one end of the site, a tongue of fire roared continuously from a pipe. Thousands of dollars worth of natural gas, a by-product of the oil drilling, has to be burned off until the pipeline is complete. At that time, the proper equipment will be installed to harness this energy to provide power for the plant and other facilities.

We walked to the graveyard from which we could look out over the river to the west and to the ravaged white rock of Hamer Mountain to the east. The gravestones had some interesting stories behind them. One tall gray one was engraved with the word Hamer and over the name was a prospector's pick and shovel. We gazed up at the mountain that bore the same name and recalled the story we had been told.

Every winter, Hamer headed up to his cabin in the mountains ignoring people's concerns regarding his age and health. The pilots always flew low and tipped their wings to greet him. In his seventy-third year, he didn't appear for several days. Finally some men went up the mountain and found him flat on his back in front of the stove, arms outstretched. No one cared to reposition him to fit the standard coffin, so they built one around him.

East Mountain and West Mountain stand like two great sentinels at the entrance of the Sans Sault Rapids. Above us, the glowing white peaks of the Carcajou Range, the Bat Hills, the Gibson Ridge and Beaver Tail Mountain reached far above the treeline to heights of 1,200 to 1,400 feet. Standing in the canoe, we struggled to comprehend the immense landscape. The river dropped away from us and we were unable to see beyond the horizon that it formed. Over the roar of the wind, we strained to hear the rush of moving water below that mysterious horizon. On the gravel bar where we landed, the sand was being swirled into tiny twisters. We walked across it, coming to the edge of the San Sault Rapids. The distance to the far shore was deceptively close. Then we sighted the tugboat, a reference point of size. Dwarfed against its surroundings, the tug was barely making progress pushing one barge against the mighty current. We could see the rest of its barge train below the rapid waiting to be taken up the river one by one. While watching the tug, we realized in astonishment that the white crests marching down the river were monstrous in comparison to how they had first appeared to us. We returned to the canoe and launched it into a safer channel, a small stream spilling through the gap which separated the gravel bar from the mainland.

If we had been able to fly above the river at this point, we would have seen hints of the approaching delta. Snafu Creek and the Ramparts River, visible to us only on our map, were surrounded in an area polka-dotted in tiny lakes and squirming creeks. Beyond the Sans Sault Rapids, the river thickens. Patterns of low-lying and underwater sand shoals in the middle of the river are hard to make out from a distance. If we tried to follow a straight path, it invariably led us onto the sandbars or into the backwater eddies behind them. So despite the added distance, we quickly discovered that it was far more efficient to follow the main deepwater channel twisting through the larger river.

In the pewter light of dawn, the Ramparts loomed ahead. On the horizon, a vertical wall of clay appeared to block the river's passage. But as we slowly drew closer, a dark void appeared indicating the entrance to the narrowest section of the Mackenzie River. Sheer clay walls rise 200 feet on either side while the two-mile-wide river is squeezed into a quarter-mile-wide channel. If the water level was low, the river would be surging through the gorge creating great sucking, boiling eddies on either side. The darkened doorway beckoned us to discover what lay beyond.

We quickly snapped on the tarpaulin and zipped up our life jackets. There was little time for contemplation. Our muscles tensed, our senses tingled with both fear and exhilaration. Then the current had us in its grasp, sucking us through the open doorway to the Mackenzie. The cliffs closed in around us. There was no turning back now.

We quickly discovered our fears were unfounded, and the water level was high. After the initial tug, the current steadied and we simply drifted through. On the walls, weird limestone formations jutted out like castle turrets. A piercing wail reverberated off the walls; our startled eyes registered a streak of feathers banking back toward a nest high up on a ledge. Then the bird swung back and plunged toward us like an arrow. We glimpsed the blue-black moustache drooping down on either side of the sharp beak and the angular wings half closed to cut the wind. Masters of aerial speed and agility, peregrine falcons are one of nature's swiftest creatures. Catapulting down on prey in flight, peregrines reach lightning speeds of up to three miles a minute. Obviously disturbed by our presence, the falcon continued shrieking and diving. We slipped quickly downstream out of its territory, feeling privileged to have caught sight of such a rare creature.

The broad river squeezes through the canyon walls, swings below the settlement of Fort Good Hope, then flows westward to cross the magical latitude and officially enter the Arctic. A quite ordinary looking Roman Catholic church overlooks the river from atop the bluff at the great river bend between the Ramparts and the Arctic Circle. We quietly drew back the green wooden doors of the church and stepped in. Colorful frescoes and paintings combining native culture and images of Christianity adorned the walls, windows and altar. The church's artistry was begun by Father Emile Petitot, a remarkable priest, who in the late 1800s explored and mapped the area northeast of the Mackenzie and documented the lives of the Loucheux Indians. The beauty of the church was further developed by the generations of artistic priests who succeeded Petitot. From the roseate window of the church, we peered down on the mission house. It was late afternoon and a group of native people had turned up for mass. Orginally, they held mass up on the Ramparts where a small shrine of Holy Mary is poised on the cliff face. But the effort of getting there is too much for most of the older people so this was no longer the practice.

Of all the settlements we had paddled by on the Mackenzie River, Fort Good Hope was undoubtedly the loveliest. There was the natural beauty of its location near traditional fishing grounds above the Ramparts. It was a quiet village, unspoiled and not yet intruded upon by roads and pipelines. The people had pride in their village, which they expressed in the homes they built. Timber harvested from islands in the Mackenzie River is abundant. The trees grow large since there is not the permafrost affecting their growth as there is on the mainland at this latitude. A number of industrious residents were constructing log homes. The focus of community life was a large circular log building. Inside, a friendly atmosphere prevailed as the people talked and played cards. On one side of the building there was a large wooden platform built for the purpose of ritual drum dancing. The residents had passed a law prohibiting alcohol in the community. This law was a sure sign of the respect the people had for themselves and each other. We felt that people here had formed a more open society than life in our cities. Although all was not perfect, the residents generally cared far less for personal appearances and material possessions yet much more for community gatherings. Living close to nature seems to induce a healthy atmosphere and spirit of goodwill among people.

On August 17, I scribbled in my logbook, "Today we crossed that magical imaginary line, the Arctic Circle. At 66 degrees latitude, the summer days are very long. When sunset finally comes, it is but a short stretch of twilight before sunrise creeps across the eastern horizon and announces another exciting day in our travels."

Although we were still 250 miles from the Mackenzie Delta, the river was already starting to swell. Like a snake whose belly distends after swallowing a frog whole, the Mackenzie's girth encompasses huge islands. These islands are divided neatly into separate pieces by persistent gnawing channels. Below the Arctic Circle, the mighty river swings north again, thickening against the high bank of the western shore at a place known as the Grand View. While in Fort Good Hope, we had been told to watch out for a special encampment where young native people were taught the skills of their forefathers.

We thought we had found it when we spotted a pale brown tent-shaped structure in the distance. But it seemed out of proportion with the surroundings. As we drew closer to shore, we realized it was a colossal pile of sawdust. We were astonished to find a sawmill operating north of the Arctic Circle. Even more surprising was the size of the logs being sawn into lumber— spruce trees of a girth that I could only just wrap my arms around. Not far off stood a home that was newly constructed, judging by the look of the rough-sawn wall boards. We were 70 miles away from Fort Good Hope. There were another 200 miles before the next settlement. We were very curious to discover more about the people who had managed to wrest a living as well as a home out of this wilderness.

The front door was open. Inside, a red-haired woman in a red checked shirt and jeans was stirring a large kettle on the cookstove. When I knocked, the woman turned quickly, the startled look immediately softening to a beaming smile.

"Well, I'll be. Visitors! Come on in!" Irene explained that her husband Fred and the rest of the family were out fishing. She led us into a spacious room, a true "living room." The family was building a new home because their previous one had burned to the ground the year before. Irene was optimistic about the matter, though. She was grateful that no one had been hurt and that because the mill was so close at hand they had been able to build another home fairly quickly.

Irene and Fred Sorenson had been here a good many years and had once operated a sawmill even farther north in Arctic Red River. They cut their timber on the Mackenzie River islands where the permafrost is far below the surface. The rich siltation, abundant water source and long daylight hours encourage the trees to grow to a good height and girth for this part of the world. We were traveling in a valley where the river moderates the climate to create conditions less harsh than those found much farther south and east.

"I'd like you to sign my guestbook," Irene said. "This is one of the few things I saved from the fire." Leafing through the pages, we were surprised how few entries there were considering some dated back more than 12 years. But Irene had plenty of stories to tell and vividly recalled each visitor as if they had been there yesterday.

It was very late when Fred, his two sons and a daughter-in-law got home. While Irene set about cleaning and cooking their catch, Fred plugged the television set into the generator outside. A break-dancing routine was lost somewhere in the purple snow of static. Every few minutes Fred would say to us, "Pick a video . . . go ahead, pick one! Bet you're surprised to see TV in the wilderness." It was not the first time, but the incongruous sight always surprised us.

At early dawn, when the mist was still rising from the river and the sun was a yellow ball already far from the horizon, we slipped quietly away. Some miles downstream, we glimpsed the triangular white shapes of canvas tents, the ones we had been seeking the night before. As we drew closer, we could see smoke rising from the stovepipes that poked out in an elbow-shaped curve from the back of each tent wall. Several very old square-stern canoes were pulled ashore. A ragged group of veteran huskies lifted their graying faces. When I spoke softly to them, they settled back to sleep. There were lengthy racks of drying fish. We wandered up to the doorstep of an immaculate white tent. Square timbers had been laid out to enclose a piece of ground. The feathery spruce bows carpeting the area were definitely a woman's touch.

Two faces peered out from the doorway and wished us good morning. Soft-featured Sara with long black hair and broad smiling Alfred took a seat on the edge of their timber wall. We knelt down beside them. Together we shared a few moments of the morning without words. There was the smell of woodstoves and smoking fish, the sounds of camp pots clanging and the lilting rhythm of native speech. I reflected on the unhurried atmosphere and camaraderie that we always felt among these people of the north.

Alfred Masozumi was an artist of Japanese–native Indian ancestry. For most of the year he lived in Yellowknife. But this summer, he had organized a special summer camp for native children, most of whom were from Fort Good Hope. Its purpose was to rekindle interest in the lost traditions among the young. By bringing together teenagers and skilled native people, Alfred was attempting to bridge the gap that was growing between the oldest and youngest.

Behind one tent, an elderly man was busily fashioning a pair of snowshoes. In a special smoke tent, a woman was hanging fillets of whitefish on a rack over a smoldering fire. Some of the young boys were out setting nets while others were in the eating tent devouring stacks of pancakes. When they saw us, they pushed aside their plates and made room at the table. One brought us a steaming pile of hotcakes smothered in butter and syrup. Another supplied jugs of juice and a pot of coffee.

We felt an enthusiastic energy among the people. No one was idle. We felt certain that the interest generated here would be carried back into the communities.

At Point Separation, the main trunk of the Mackenzie River begins its 100-mile journey through the largest delta in Canada and one of the largest in the western hemisphere. Constantly shifting and changing within the bounds created by the

Richardson Mountains that rear up to the west and the lower-humped Caribou Hills to the east, this oblong-shaped labyrinth of submerged and emergent islands twisting channels and silver-surfaced pools is one of the most striking physical features of the north. The river and the delta finally end in true arctic tundra at the edge of an icy sea.

Regularly during our journey down the Mackenzie, we had been speaking with CBC Radio in Inuvik. The afternoon program's host, Pam Petrin, had ended each interview with an invitation to anyone living or traveling along the Mackenzie to join us for a stretch. In the end it was Pam herself who joined us, along with a fellow broadcaster from the station, Paul Andrew. In Inuvik, a few of the other native announcers had been translating the story of our journey into Loucheux, Hareskin and Inuvialuktun, the three native languages broadcast by CBC Inuvik.

A cloud of dust billowed from behind the blue CBC truck as it pulled into the ferry operator's trailer site on the east side of the river opposite Arctic Red River. Pam and Paul had driven 80 miles south from Inuvik on the Dempster Highway. They unloaded their aluminum canoe and two monstrous packs. In addition to a healthy supply of meals, Pam carried a large tape recorder. This was a working holiday.

Pam and Paul were our first and only canoeing companions to travel with us in the second year of the journey. Early on the morning of August 20 we departed from Arctic Red River. Although the storm-tossed Mackenzie was dark and foreboding, cheerful spirits and joking between friends waylaid any reservations we might have had about setting off.

The 100-foot shale cliffs of the Lower Ramparts lined the shore below Arctic Red River for several miles forming a steep corridor that was home for a population of sparrow hawks and peregrine falcons. They descended on arrowtip wings from the shale cliffs, circling and swooping in great plunging dives. We stopped paddling and watched a peregrine streaking earthward in a high-speed attack. It had singled out a swallow which it plucked from the air with deceptive ease. It appeared the prey had been dropped unintentionally, when suddenly another falcon swooped in from below and plucked the falling ball of feathers before it dropped into the river.

The agitated waves were really rolling now. White spray hissed off the crests as we climbed each mound and sliced through the top, balancing and careening down into the next one. We were finding tremendous enjoyment in sharing each other's company. As Pam's canoe pitched about in the wave troughs, it seemed very small in comparison to the immensity of the river. We could well imagine as we watched her and Paul how often we had looked like a tiny speck to others.

From the sprawling Middle Channel, we broke off into the narrow winding East Branch just as a pale lemon sun shed whispers of warm light across the bleak landscape of low clay banks and gnarled black spruce. On the marshy point ahead, we were greeted with our very first sighting of the elegant whistling swans. Through the binoculars I could see the black bills marked with a yellow teardrop below the eye and the slender white necks that grew straight and taut when the swans saw us. Then they were off pattering across the marsh and launching themselves into the air on powerful wings. High-pitched hooting drifted down from above as our canoes glided silently by.

We drew our canoes in for the evening on a slippery mud flat. There was plenty of driftwood for a fire and a light covering of grass on which to set out tents. Pam hauled her bulging pack to the edge of the campfire and proceeded to dump out the contents. There was a grill, fry pans, a large pot and cutlery. A few bottles of cold cider, steaks, potatoes and mushrooms were lined up along a slab of driftwood. Then in her fine delta-trip tradition, Pam pulled out a bottle of her homemade Irish Cream liqueur. Full of bubbling laughter, Pam was the ideal canoeing partner. Not only did she create one of the most memorable meals of our voyage, but her camping equipment was extremely well organized.

Paul was the perfect silent sternsman. He smiled and nodded. When he spoke, it was in a very soft monotone. But despite the lack of inflection, what he had to say was always interesting.

The East Branch swung in lazy loops along the edge of the delta. On our second morning together, Pam set the tape recorder on top of her pack and turned it on to record our surroundings—the swoosh of the paddle blades across the water surface, Gary's imitation of a loon call, a gabbling straggle of snow geese passing overhead or the wind rustling softly in the moose maples and alders that clung to the riverside.

On the next river bend, a log cabin came into view. A woman was standing high on the bank overlooking the bend beckoning us over. As we drew alongside the dock, she hurried down to greet us. Pam had told us a little bit about this delta couple, Lucy and Jimmy Adams. We climbed up the bank and arrived in a clearing. Several part-husky dogs were tethered on the edge of a large vegetable garden. They practically tore the stakes from the ground when they bounded forward barking loudly before being pulled to an abrupt halt at the end of their chains.

"Quiet!" Lucy called out. Then she asked if we would like to help her hang the fish out to dry. At the river bend upstream from the Adams' cabin, we could see where the fishnets had been strung out to harvest the annual winter feed of whitefish. Smoked and dried, the fish was a staple of the northern diet and provided a change from moose meat or small game.

We went into a small wooden building where a smoldering fire in the center of the earthen floor produced a steady stream of smoke. Lucy showed us how the fish were filleted. It was similar to our own technique except she removed the sides of the fish from the bone without separating them at the tail. Thus she ended up with fillets that could be hung like tea towels over the smoking and drying racks. Lucy was so cheerful and gregarious. Her long black hair, streaked with gray, fell far below her shoulders. The corners of her mouth turned up in a wonderful warm smile. But the charm of a true smile is in the eyes. Lucy's danced and sparkled, the little crow's-feet in the corners curling upward when she laughed.

"Come have some tea," she insisted, hoisting some large stumps out from underneath the plywood table. "You can sit on these." Overhead an orange tarpaulin rustled in the breeze, protection from the sun or rain. "You never tried smoked whitefish?" Lucy asked in her sing-song voice. "I'll fix that!" She disappeared behind the rack of dried fish then reappeared moments later with a large fillet of striped pink meat. Pam tore a sinewy strip of greasy fish off then passed it on to me. I took a cautious nibble. The flavor was distinctly smoky but savory.

The dried, smoked whitefish were stacked rather like small bales of hay. A modest little storage shed, surmounted by a NWT tourism polar bear flag flapping in the breeze, contained all the fish bundles until they were needed.

Lucy sat on the stump next to Pam, her elbows resting on the table. She was telling us the story of the time during the last fall's hunt when the bull moose had walked right into camp.

"After they shot him, I gutted and cleaned him," she said. "And then there's the bible. Each page has to be cleaned really well." After some questioning, we finally figured out that the bible must be part of the moose's stomach.

Meanwhile, Paul and Gary had gone to assist Jimmy and their son in the excavation of a deep pit. A cross-piece held in place by two posts straddled the hole. From this simple structure, a pulley system had been rigged. While one man shoveled thawed black muck from the bottom of the hole into a bucket, the other hoisted the bucket to the surface and emptied it. The twosome were digging a pit to preserve fish for the dogs. The permanently frozen ground provides an ideal natural freezer. But the process of building one is very time consuming. It had taken them all summer to build the fires, melt the frozen turf and scoop it away to create a hole eight feet deep and six feet across.

The fish placed in this pit would not be filleted for the dogs. Much of it would turn into the foul-smelling delicacy known as "stinkfish." Meant not only for the dogs, the native people once relished it, too. Two generations ago, making stinkfish was tradtion. They dug a small pit in the ground and the un-gutted fish was thrown in to fill it up. A wood and mud covering was laid over the fish for the summer. Eventually, when they reached a ripe stage where the flesh was soft and mushy, the fish was consumed.

Surrounding the camp was a rustling forest of willow, poplar and spruce that filled the air with sweet smells. Pam had discreetly started her tape recorder when Lucy turned the subject toward their "summer children."

"It took Linda only three tries to learn to fillet the fish. Her first try was OK, her next even better, but by the third, she had a perfect fish. Fastest one to learn." Lucy and Jimmy took on several teenagers over the summer. Like the young people in Alfred Masozumi's camp, they came to learn the old skills.

Our arrival in Inuvik felt like a premature ending to the expedition. A gathering of friendly faces greeted us as we pulled into the pier with Paul and Pam.

Pam and another CBC broadcaster, Dave Tait, treated us to a feast of Arctic char in Inuvik's Finto Inn. Then we trundled down main street to the town's famous barnboard-sided Mad Trapper Inn. It was dark inside but as our eyes grew accustomed to the low light we realized that the walls were papered from top to bottom with one-dollar bills. It was a tradition from long ago for trappers to leave money on the wall. If they returned flat broke, they could still buy themselves a drink. Grabbing a pen and a dollar bill, we scribbled a message about our canoe trip. Like the trappers, we too hoped to return, perhaps at a time when we would be embarking on another expedition.

Broad grins were spread across Pam's and Dave's faces as they each slid a parcel from behind their backs.

"Open them," they urged.

Tearing the wrappings away we found two blue T-shirts. I held mine up. The words "CBC Inuvik Salutes" encircled the "exploding pizza" logo on the front. Gary chuckled as he turned the T-shirt over and read, "The World's Longest Honeymoon!"

Meeting up with Pam, Dave and other broadcasters from CBC Inuvik had been like a reunion of old friends. None of us had ever met before now, yet we knew each other's voices very well. Apart from our wonderful weekly chats with Alan Millar of CBC Radio's Ontario Morning program, we had also been making regular broadcasts with CBC Inuvik. In fact the morning of our departure from Baie Comeau, Dave Tait had manged to track us down and do an interview before we ever made a paddle stroke. His closing remarks were, "We'll look forward to seeing you in Inuvik next year."

We lingered awhile outside the Mad Trapper, watching life go by in Canada's largest town north of the Arctic Circle. An assortment of vehicles passed by on the main street. There were pick-ups and transports, old Volkswagens and 40-foot motorhomes. The latter usually had a small vehicle in tow. After having been pulled 500 miles up the dusty Dempster from Dawson City, these cars were so plastered in dirt, they were recognizable only by shape.

Pam knew the Dempster. She had described to us her journey down it on a motorcycle. It sounded spectacular—wild empty

plains and mountains, migrating herds of caribou and the occasional grizzly bear, a rough road following river valleys, carving
through mountain passes that grow steeper and greener with
each passing mile.

Although the main street was paved and the sidewalks were no
longer wooden boardwalks, and although Inuvik was only a
quarter-century old, it still gave the impression of being a
frontier town. Inuvik began life in a unique way. It was not the
site of a native encampment or a Hudson's Bay post as most
other northern villages along the Mackenzie River were. Inuvik
was not at the confluence of rivers. The salmon didn't spawn
here and whales did not frequent the channel. It was not even a
major thoroughfare for migrating caribou. Inuvik was simply a
sparsely treed wilderness on the edge of the tundra where some
natives laid their traplines. The town was conceived in the minds
of federal politicians who believed that a substantial com-
munications base with educational, administrative and transportation facilities was necessary north of the Arctic Circle.

Many obstacles were overcome but probably the greatest of all
was figuring out how to build a southern town on permafrost.
Lying just beneath the tundra was blue ice, which is permanently
frozen ground. Steam pile drivers forced hundreds of wooden
pilings into the ground. All buildings were erected high off the
ground on top of this enormous "children's playground" in order to insulate the permafrost from their warmth. Otherwise, if
the ground melted beneath the buildings, they would simply
topple over. Snaking through the town, linking the buildings,
was a strange box-like corridor called a utilidor. Its shiny
aluminum exterior encased the insulated pipes that provided
sewage removal, water and heating. Because the pipes could not
be buried, they traveled above ground.

We explored local buildings inside and out. Our Lady of Vic-
tory, the igloo church, is one of the most recognized man-made
landmarks in the northwestern Arctic. On Sundays, an overhead
projector beams the words of the hymns onto the white sloping
ceiling. After visiting the church, we admired parkas fringed with
delta braid and appliquéd with colorful northern scenes in the
small back kitchen of a talented elderly artist. The day ended in
a memorable baseball match between the CBC crew and the
Northern Transportation Company. When a row of huge fellows

came marching across the field, we turned to one another thinking we really had some competition. It was a hard-fought game with plenty of action and determination on everyone's part. Each time Tommy Ross slid into home plate with dirt flying from beneath his moccasin rubbers, we cheered loudly. Tommy was an Inuit broadcaster and an avid canoeist. During the '67 Centennial Canoe Pageant in which Joe Meany had raced across Canada in a three-man kayak, Tommy had traveled with the Northwest Territories team. Several team members gave the ball walloping smacks which resulted in home runs. Twice Gary emptied full bases with hits that sent the ball soaring beyond the field and under the pilings of the public-school building. The end result was that CBC won their first game of the season.

That night, the north wind off the Arctic coast whistled through the town out of a dark threatening sky. After a late and wet start from Inuvik the next day, we had covered about 30 miles of the twisting delta passage when we discovered the abandoned village of Reindeer Station tucked below the Caribou Hills. The orange sun, dropping noticeably earlier these days, appeared briefly between the ceiling of cloud and the horizon, spreading a rosy glow over the once-bustling village. We came ashore to explore the dilapidated frame cabins and sheds and a couple of homey-looking two-story wooden buildings.

A Bombardier snow machine, with its rounded dark blue roof and rows of porthole windows, had crawled to its final resting place in the long grass after years of winter travel. I climbed into the driver's seat of this strange vehicle with its caterpillar tread and peered out the front space where the windshield once was. I imagined the bundled-up passengers in the seats behind me, their faces pressed against the blurry windowpanes, which were now also empty holes. At the time when it crunched across the creaking Styrofoam-like snow in the dead of an Arctic winter, the snow machine provided the only warmth for miles around. Inuvik had not even been conceived of and there were only dreams of a northern highway such as the Dempster. The Mackenzie delta was still a very remote region, with Reindeer Station the only populated village in the southeastern delta.

Gary discovered an underground cellar, once common in settlements constructed on the permafrost. We drew back the weather-beaten door covering the entrance. A wave of cool air gathered about the square plywood-lined hole. Swinging my legs over the edge, I stepped onto the first rung and descended into the dark hole. Gary followed with flashlight in hand. The beam of light struck a huge mound of solid ice which had formed in rolling folds at the base of the wooden chimney. Shining the beam around, we found ourselves in a room with an ice floor, ice ceiling and ice walls with ice shelves. The permafrost had been dug out using the same tedious process that we had encountered at Jimmy and Lucy Adams'. This cold room was a natural underground freezer where the meat and perishables for the village were once stored.

After wandering up an overgrown path lined with raspberry brambles, we entered one of the two-storey homes where we found the evidence of the last occupants—a cookstove, a wooden table and chairs. Upstairs we discovered old beds precariously balanced on rickety floorboards which felt like they might cave in at any moment. There were a few dishes, a couch and some other articles of furniture. Children's school books were scattered around the home. The sight of the books made us think that the occupants left, planning to return but never did.

We left the lonely, forlorn place behind and followed an eroded sandy path up to the high ridge of the Caribou Hills behind the village. Brushing past the willows and yellowing poplar, we arrived at the edge of the tree line. The full force of winter's long and icy blast keeps the vegetation here from growing any more than a couple of feet high. From 500 feet up, we gazed across the delta where channels and lakes shimmered like liquid bronze. Through the stand of golden poplar along the forest edge, we could see the East Branch coiling its way northward toward the Arctic Ocean. Thinking back on the empty house, we found ourselves reflecting on the rise and fall of this northern village. Reindeer Station was once home to the Mackenzie delta Inuit who had altered their nomadic existence to become reindeer herders like the Laplanders. The government had wanted to get the native people managing and harvesting a natural resource with profit to both the people and the animals. By the early 1920s, easier and easier access to wild places and the introduction of high-powered rifles had contributed to the demise of wildlife in this part of the Arctic. Therefore the Department of the Interior began to investigate the possiblity of reindeer herding. By the spring of 1929, the Lomen

Reindeer Company in Alaska had been contracted to deliver 3,000 head of reindeer to the Mackenzie delta. It was to be, at most, a two-year undertaking. The 10 men who set off on the 1,000-mile drive, as the crow flies, had no idea they would actually cover 2,500 miles over a vast, dangerous and unexplored territory of mountains and barrenlands. They faced avalanches, death from exposure, semi-starvation, and lost their way for months on end. But the greatest challenge that they had to overcome was the very strong natural instinct of the reindeer to return home to Alaska.

The Lomen herders consisted of some Lapps and some Inuit. The Lapps were there to teach the Inuit how to herd; to change their basic philosophy from being nomadic hunters to being pastoral herders. After five years of driving the animals eastward, the herders arrived at their destination, a reserve of nearly 30,000 square miles in the Mackenzie delta region. Over 2,300 animals were delivered, but an astonishing 90 percent of them were the result of the annual fawnings during the journey. Only 300 animals of the original herd actually survived the trek.

Within one year, one-third of the herd had borne calves. Within the next five years, the herd had multiplied three-fold. The long-range plan was to divide the government herd up so that it could be managed by separate native herders. Where once the Inuit families roamed the Arctic coast and the frozen delta plains for wild game, they now followed the reindeer as a shepherd might a flock of sheep. While the herders herded, their families lived in the settlement at Reindeer Station enjoying the best of a northern community. With a Hudson's Bay store and a school, the community provided a comfortable life compared to their previous nomadic existence. Why then was it abandoned? For one thing, the reindeer herds did not expand as much as had been expected. But the real problem probably lay with the people themselves. The nomadic element in the Inuit's character was as inbred as the farmer's love of the land and the fisherman's of the sea. If this nomadic quality did not take them away, then other more lucrative opportunities were presenting themselves with the development of the western Arctic. Trapping was becoming more profitable and interesting than following a herd of reindeer.

That evening we decided to sleep in one of the small cabins near the shore, which seemed to have been kept up by the local river users as a common shelter. On the porch, barring the doorway, was an archaic outboard motor, probably one of the first ever made judging by its design—one which resembled an industrial mixmaster more than the sleek outboards of today. Hoisting the motor aside, we swung the door open. Inside it was very chilly. But we quickly lit a fire in the cast-iron stove. This solved the problem so well that even before the soup was boiling the room had become unbearably warm. We flung open the door and sat on the porch step in the cool evening air. As we munched on the last of our fresh vegetables and the final chocolate bar, we felt in high spirits. During the night a northerly wind arose and whistled through the cracks in the cabin walls. I woke up once. The end of my nose felt as cold as an ice cube. Gary got up twice to investigate some strange noises. We had heard that barren ground grizzly bears occasionally visit the river's edge in the Caribou Hills. Each time he returned, he threw an extra stick of wood in the firebox and fluffed up his down bag for a little added insulation. Muffled in the warmth of his bag was Gary's weather forecast: "It's getting pretty cool out. It's going to be long underwear from here on in!"

The next day we struggled against the gusts from the north which threw whitecaps across the river. They were stronger than any we had experienced before. In four hours, we barely made 10 miles. In the northern sky, the clouds had lightened from a steely gray to a yellow ochre with pink tinges. But there was something very strange about their appearance. Their wispy fingers were reaching into the hills like filaments of white gauze obliterating the scene before us.

"It's snowing!" I gasped in amazement.

"It's certainly cold enough," Gary said putting down his paddle and slapping his hands against his thighs to get the blood going again.

Suddenly we were engulfed in a swirling tempest. The wind tore the tops from the wave crests in long ragged streaks. Bowing our heads against the stinging flakes and hunching our shoulders against the cold that seeped down the back of our necks and up our sleeves, we fought our way to shore. We drove the canoe up into the ooze at the river's edge. I leapt out as Gary scrambled over the packs from the stern end to help me. We didn't dare risk getting our footwear soaked. We were already freezing cold. Fumbling through the packs with numb fingers, we hauled out the tent and set up camp.

Later on, while Gary studied the maps and updated the logbook, I went exploring. The Caribou Hills were very steep and rose straight up only 50 yards behind our camp. I was scrambling though the thick reindeer lichen and scraggly black spruce when a clear lilting tune stopped me dead in my tracks. It was a robin. I couldn't believe my ears. I crept forward eagerly. When at last I saw the orange-red breast, puffed out but growing duller with the coming of winter, I smiled, then laughed softly with delight. The presence of this brave little creature, who had no tent for shelter and who would be setting off soon on a long journey under wingpower alone to more southerly climes, was an inspiration.

Just an hour before, the emptiness of the country had been having a depressing effect on me. The cold ate at my stamina. But now I felt thoroughly rejuvenated! I hurried excitedly back down the slope to fetch Gary. Not surprisingly, the robin had disappeared by the time we returned, so we continued up the slope. We broke through the final shelter of trees. Soon only a thin scattering of bushes remained. Then we were standing on the crispy gray-green tundra. All around us was a brilliant array of earth-hugging plants, their tightly bunched leaves made brick red, amber and deep crimson by autumn's frosty touch. Bare hills rolled eastward toward the barren lands that sweep across the eastern Arctic to Hudson Bay. To the south, west and north lay the delta, streams and pools forming an endless crazy quilt in pewter gray. Far to the west where the sky had cleared was the hazy outline of the Richardson Mountains.

As we were starting down, Gary stopped and stared intently toward the delta. "Belugas!" he cried excitedly.

Entranced, we watched half a dozen smooth white backs undulating in playful formation in the channel below. They were still some distance downstream from our campsite when they turned back toward the open sea and disappeared. Sighting the belugas brought back memories of that day at the mouth of the Saguenay River when we had found ourselves among them on the tidal current. We had begun our journey with the belugas and we would end it with them.

Despite our eagerness to continue, we were pinned to land for another day and a half. The wind tore at our tent in wild gusts, thumping the walls like a palpitating heartbeat. It was almost impossible to sleep. All we could think of was that the Beaufort Sea lay ahead, 30 miles of open ocean coastline between us and Tuktoyaktuk. In Inuvik, in the Mad Trapper Inn, a stout sourdough had urged us to hurry. "It only takes a strong north blow to lock her in fast for winter."

Near the delta mouth, the river swings in a wide loop around a point of land which was once used during fall roundup as a place to corral the reindeer, prior to swimming them to the winter range on the mainland. Because the region was so remote, we were astonished to find a large sign which read "Swimming Point Botanical Garden," with an explanation of the display of native arctic plants. This garden had been planted for the purpose of displaying the arctic flora native to Richards Island in the delta. Little plaques with the Latin and English names written on had been thrust into the ground beside several species, including the shrubby cinquefoil with its crinkled, notched leaves and the pasqueflower's feathery seed heads, both of which were not in bloom. We were feeling the effect of being little more than 100 miles south of the polar ice cap as the frigid wind cut through every gap in our clothing. This quaint little display of plants huddled close to the earth was much better adapted to the arctic climate than we were. After taking a few pictures we hurried back to the relative warmth of the canoe's tarpaulin.

The few meager stands of willow finally petered out and all that remained were thin scatterings of bushes and tall swaying grasses. Amid the vegetation high above the river's edge, we spied an abandoned cabin. It stood so solid and proud in this land of no trees. The fact of its construction would have seemed strange if it were not for the tumble of driftwood strewn along the shore. We decide to camp, for the cabin was on the lee side of the riverbank. It would provide a windbreak for our tent.

On investigating more closely, we discovered that the cabin had no ceiling except for a couple of planks. A ridge-pole ran the length of the one-room home. Window and door frames were wide open to the elements. It was difficult to tell if the cabin was growing out of the grass or the grass out of the cabin, for the sod roof hung like heavy eyelids to meet the vegetation stretching upward. One side of the dwelling had caved in, but from the front it looked almost livable, although extremely desolate. We were constantly amazed at the signs of human activity popping up out of nowhere in this vast, harsh environment.

With the wind and the noise of the drumming surf rushing past our ears, we ventured cautiously past the abandoned village of Kittigazuit. The native people believe that spirits still lurk among the forgotten rows of driftwood grave markers. As we shivered with cold, we could feel nothing but respect and pure admiration for the people who had once survived in this land for 12 months of the year enduring some of the toughest living conditions on earth. What's more, they did it with cheerful love of family and abundant respect for their natural surroundings.

The tree line was far behind us by the time we made our first sighting of the strange pingos. These 200-foot hills of solid blue ice are carpeted with tundra vegetation, except at the peaks where expansion has broken away this insulating layer to reveal the core of ice. Melted by the summer sun, they look like small volcanoes. They are the only exception to the flat waterlogged delta plain surrounding Tuktoyaktuk.

Our final camp was pitched on a tundra meadow overlooking Kittigazuit Bay. We had never felt more exposed to the elements than while taking a brief exploratory walk. Cheerless, icy waves tumbled in off the ocean on one side while the hummocky tundra all around made walking very difficult indeed. We were worried about the possibility of an unexpected encounter with a barrenground grizzly bear. Our eyes were always moving, with good reason. There are optical illusions in this landscape where the tundra horizon appears much more distant than it actually is. We were crouched down in the soft spongy peat among the crimson bearberry leaves and arctic willow when Gary gestured toward the southeast. Antlers appeared, then the entire body of a caribou rose in silhouette against the flat white sky. For a moment we were entranced, but then the thought suddenly registered . . . what if it had been a grizzly?

That night was a long anxious one filled with restless dreams. The wind took the tent in its teeth like a mad dog and shook it hard. The flapping of nylon made it impossible to hear anything else. Our red eyes the next morning made it obvious we had had little sleep. We were so close to our destination yet we still felt so far.

The wind had subsided slightly by the time we took off, but the rolling swell was steep enough to force us far from shore. The scalloped bays were shallow, much like those of our first days on the St. Lawrence River. A brooding skyline seemed to meld with the angry sea and the coastline was littered with sharp gray shale of all shapes and sizes. Low banks lining the ocean separated it from the frozen tundra. At Whitefish Station, an Inuit summer encampment, a few fish-drying racks clung to the land, meager reminders of the human presence. Survival is a matter of treading the fine line between life and death out here, where the land is so immense, so naked and exposed, so powerful yet in many ways so very fragile. We were very aware of our utter insignificance.

Suddenly Gary called out, "Look, there's Tuk!" Two strange ear-like protrusions poked above the eastern horizon. Directly below was the white dome of the DEW Line. The brief sighting was quickly wiped out as stinging snowflakes filled the air. We struggled to keep a straight course in the crazy bouncing swell. The wind suddenly picked up extra force, shrieking in off Kugmallit Bay, and the waves now began to engulf the canoe. Rearing up in long corrugated strips, they tumbled forward, blasting into the hull. It took all our effort to brace the canoe with the paddles and not tip over. Our situation was becoming extremely perilous. Gary lifted his paddle and pointed toward shore.

"There's an opening," he bellowed over the wind. "Let's go!"

The "opening" was a break in the shoreline surf that led into a protected bay. Veering the canoe downwind, we rode the swell in fear. More than one expedition has ended in disaster just when success seemed imminent.

Once we had landed safely, our adrenalin rush subsided. Disheartened, hungry and freezing cold, we began to wonder—if this was an arctic fall, what would winter be like? We rubbed our numb hands and stomped our feet to get the feeling back into our toes. As we danced about, Gary noticed a long string of bleached whale vertebrae lying in the gravel.

I scrambled up the bank with Gary to survey the desolate country. It had occurred to me that there might be an alternative route to Tuktoyaktuk. As Gary held up the map, we noticed an obvious inland lake route between Split Hill and Ibyuk Hill. A thin spit of land would separate us from the sea once we neared the town. Few words were needed to express our joy. Gary put an arm around me, squeezed tight and said, "I think we'll get there today after all."

We ran back to the canoe, hauled out the packs and began the slow portage over the lumpy ground. Gary's long strides and good balance were ideal for tundra travel. He loped along, barely weighting one foot before springing off on to the other. Meanwhile I tripped and struggled with the front pack bouncing off my knees. Sometimes I ended up on my knees, other times flat on my face as the large pack on my back hurled me forward. We did the trip back and forth once more to carry the canoe, sprinted across the small lake to the next shore, portaged again—then our final stretch of water lay before us. Gary climbed to the summit of Ibyuk pingo. Our course was clear. He dashed back down the slope and leapt into the canoe.

Winter was sweeping across the landscape in thick white curtains that completely obliterated the surroundings. Then mysteriously a pair of whistling swans appeared. They sailed into view like ghostly ships through the snow and passed within yards of our canoe. Their long slender necks stretched skyward as they lifted themselves from the water on beautiful white wings. A thick blast of snow obscured our vision momentarily. When it cleared, these arctic summer residents had vanished; they were winging their way southward. Suddenly and profoundly, our perspective on this harsh land softened.

A narrow gravel spit, like many others we had already seen, was the last place we would be pulling ashore on our journey. The windward edge was being pummeled with saltwater surf from the Beaufort Sea. The leeward edge rippled with cat's paws, gray-green in the strange stormy light. The thrum of the pounding waves and the clinking of stones falling against one another were all that we heard. Behind us, the pingos stood as frozen sentinels, symbolic witnesses to our journey's end. The wind ripped away our excited yelps of triumph. The lone pair of swans barrel-rolled in off the north wind and whistled overhead. Like the swans, we too would soon be flying south again. And like the swans, we would return.

# Epilogue

O UR DESTINATION was reached once we paddled into the Beaufort Sea, but for obvious reasons the nearest community, Tuktoyaktuk, served as our landfall after 6,000 miles and 10 million paddle strokes. Constable Dave Grundy, of the RCMP, and his wife, Elaine, welcomed us into their home for several days while we made preparations with Beaudril to fly our canoe and ourselves south to Edmonton. The mayor of Inuvik, on behalf of the town, arranged our passage home to Ontario from Edmonton since they had so enjoyed sharing in our adventures through the weekly interviews with CBC Inuvik. One morning, shortly after arriving in Tuktoyaktuk, we did our 35th and final interview with Alan Millar on CBC Ontario Morning. As a wonderful surprise, Bob Burt, the producer with whom we had paddled on the Ottawa River, arranged for our parents to be on the line. Their voices, full of warmth and pride, filled us with a longing to be home with them again. In the past months, their understanding and undying support for us and the expedition had been a real source of inspiration and courage when we most needed it.

In the twilight hours, as we flew out over the Beaufort Sea, southward bound, the millions of delta lakes and creeks lay gold and glittering far below. Our faces were pressed against the windows eagerly seeking familiar landmarks as the plane followed the Mackenzie River valley toward Great Slave Lake. Upstream and downstream, across lakes and oceans, we had made a personal discovery of where rivers run. The final vision we held in our minds as darkness fell, was of an Arctic, still beautiful, wild and beckoning to be explored.

Following our canoe voyage, we undertook a 7,500-mile expedition by bicycle, spanning the country from Tuktoyaktuk to L'Anse aux Meadows, on the northern tip of Newfoundland. By way of a northerly route, our journey linked three oceans—the

Arctic, Pacific and Atlantic—traversed both territories, all 10 provinces, and encompassed widely varying geographical regions through all four seasons.

In the near future, we are aspiring to undertake a 3,000-mile high-Arctic route by canoe, linking Tuktoyaktuk, on the Beaufort Sea, with Chesterfield Inlet, on Hudson Bay.

So much to behold, so much to share! Many adventures swirl through our thoughts daily, and we intend to live out our lives following our hearts and dreams in pursuit of them.

# Acknowledgments

T HE FOLLOWING organizations, institutions and companies assisted us in both planning and undertaking the journey. But these groups are made up of individuals; many of you are known to us personally, and some are not. To all of you, we are most grateful for your faith in us and in our expedition:

Our principal thanks must go to the Labatt Brewing Company Limited which provided financial and other support. Having an enterprising and enthusiastic company behind our expedition was a very valuable asset.

Pentax Canada Inc., which provided the excellent camera equipment with which all the photographs in this book were taken and 5,975 more!

Brian and Vicki Dorfman, of the Grey Owl Paddle Company, who provided us with paddles, listened to our technical feedback and who have continued to support our endeavors wholeheartedly.

Alex Tilley, of Tilley Endurables Inc., with whom we share the spirit of adventure, for his personal enthusiasm in our expeditions.

Gulf Canada Resources Ltd., and especially Jim Guthrie and the employees working out of Tuktoyaktuk for the offshore drilling division; and Beaudril Ltd., for without its assistance we would not have been able to transport our canoe out of the Arctic.

Sawyer Canoe Company

Nike Canada Ltd., which supplied us with clothing and, above all, their excellent lightweight hiking boots.

Bill Hughes, of Filmworks Inc., who supplied Kodachrome 64 film for the expedition.

Woods Bag & Canvas, division of Woods Canada Limited, for the suspension-system packs, sleeping bags, clothing and tent which kept us warm and dry.

Fitzwright Manufacturing Company, which donated Bare wetsuits for early spring on the St. Lawrence River.

Winchester/U.S. Repeating Arms Co., Inc.

Kettle Creek Canvas Company.

Magic Pantry Foods.

Brunswick International.

Black Water Designs, for providing us with Sierra Designs foul-weather clothing, tents and sleeping bags for all our expeditions since the completion of our canoe trip.

Trailhead, Ottawa.

Budget Rent A Car of London, for supplying a van to transport our canoe and equipment to the east coast to begin our voyage, and to Jack Mills for returning the van to London.

The *Toronto Star*, the *London Free Press* and the *Bracebridge Herald Gazette* for publishing regular photographs and reports as our journey progressed.

The Royal Canadian Mounted Police detachments along our route were of tremendous service, doing everything from storing our canoe in their warehouse, to holding parcels and mail, and keeping track of our progress from one settlement to another. The friendliness displayed by individual members will always be warmly remembered.

In regards to the production of the book itself, we would like to thank the following:

Biz Pro Ltd. in London, especially Jim Jearvis, who loaned us a word processor and typewriter (which was a great improvement on our 40-year-old manual typewriter!).

Doug Gibson, for his faith in our project and for acquiring an Ontario Arts Council Grant which assisted in the writing of this book.

We are also most grateful for the support of the following people:

Tanya Long and Kathy Fraser, who helped us organize our thoughts on paper.

Jack McClelland, for his encouragement and faith in the writing of this book.

Ted Currie, for providing ideas for the prologue.

Audrey McDonald, a long-time friend and artist who has been a good teacher in the skills of drawing and painting.

Ken and Elsie Fisher, of the London Canoe Club, and Nova Craft Canoes for their send-offs and their homecoming welcomes during the expedition.

The CBC Radio crew, especially Bob Burt, producer, Alan Millar, broadcaster, and Steve Starchev, technician, who deserve special mention for making all those weekly broadcasts so much fun!

We would also like to acknowledge Wayland Drew for enlightening us on the world of book publishing. We have greatly admired Wayland's writing on Canada and his wilderness philosophy.

It was not just traveling through the wild vastness of our land that made us proud of the country we live in. It was when we realized the greatness of the people that lived within it. Although we have done our best to acknowledge everyone chronologically, we apologize if any names, no less deserving, have been omitted:

Leone Pippard, Ste. Pétronnille
Ross & Arlene Breadner, Bev and Jane Dekay, Gerry Timmerman, London
Alain Bourassa, Baie Comeau
Lisette and Claude Tremblay, Ste. Thérèse de Colombier
André Tremblay, Tadoussac
the mayor of Bois Chatel
Denis and Giselle Comptois, Ste. Marthe du Cap
Jean, Rivière Ste. Anne
Carmen Dodaro, Toronto
Tim and Chantal Pychyl, Ottawa
Clayton McGuffin, Nepean
Hermann and Christa Kerckhoff, Lac Rocher Fendu
Art and Betty Appleby, Braeside
the Leblanc family, Westmeath
Phil and Lynn Chester, Betty and Les Culpepper, Bob and Jean Lucier, Deep River
the Zimmerman family, North Bay
St. Clair Dokis and family, Charles Balwin, the Lacasse family, Chuck and Shirley Hansman, French River
Mr. and Mrs. E. Dittmer, Kerri and Chris LaFrance, Algoma Mills
Meredith and Richard Walker, the Kelleher family, Theo MacKay, the St. Joseph Channel
Buck and Terry Archambault, Sault Ste. Marie
Betty Russell and Gayle Davey, Gros Cap
Ann and Gordon Wyllie, Wawa
George and Tija Luste, near Michipicoten Island
Bonnie Breadner and Don Farquhar, Marathon
Stephen O'Donnell, Neys Provincial Park
Marlene and Don Simonson, near Simpson Island
Roger and Susan Bailey, Swede Island
Mary and Dick Gosling, David and Barb Olafson, Cloud Bay
Mr. and Mrs. Osmond Parsons, Donald Ford, Grand Portage
Joe and Vera Meany, Lac la Croix
Allan and Darlene Toffan, Fort Frances
Ralph and Joy Nelson, Mr. and Mrs. Patterson, Jim and Gail Crackel, Valerie and Cheryl Hamilton, Mr. and Mrs. Les Ivall, Rainy River
Ernest and Mary Klassen, Lake of the Woods

Hugh and Teresa Dennis, Sue and Terry Johnson, Kenora
Pat and Gordon Kabaluk, Lac du Bonnet
Bill and Ryan Safruik, Pine Falls
the Monkman family, Gladys Oddleifson, Tom Monkman, Loon Straits
Mrs. B. Huff, Grand Rapids
John Andrews and Christine Thomas, Easterville
Sgt. Larsen, The Pas RCMP detachment, Dan Hill, Myrna White, Kevin and
    Colleen Nicholson, The Pas
Mick and Terry Ryan, Cumberland House
Roger and Adeline Smith, the "Namew Lake Nimrods," Sturgeon Landing
Ralph and Alma Tompsett, Bonnie and Dean Tait, Amisk Lake
Brian and May Gudmundson, Brent and Judy Poncelet, Pelican Narrows
Dave and Sara Partridge, Churchill River
Jim Colson, Sally and Kerry Wisser, Southend
Dick Chrysler, Henry Bird, Reindeer Lake
Brian and Sharon Elder, Kate Bragg, Rob Askin, Ivan Robertson, Wollaston
    Lake
Ted and Sandy Jackson, Waterbury Lake
Glen and Agatha Mockford, Black Lake
Ben and Caroline Seimens, Russell Balman, Tom Brown, Rob Benz, Gord
    and Heather Rogerson, Stony Rapids
Andrew and Dixie Butler, Fond du Lac
Rod Dubnick, Uranium City
Philip and Mary Stenne, Camsell Portage
Dave and Christa Blair, Judy and Dan Frandsen, Fort Chipewyan
Don and Sandy Jaque, Diane and Lou Gauthier, Fort Smith
Leonard Dion, Hay River
Phil and Sharon Callan, Fort Providence
Chief Ernest Hardisty, Jean Marie River
Ted Grant, John Sheehan, Diane and Russ Gregory, Colleen and Dave
    Hart, Harvey Lewis, Sgt. Goodridge and the RCMP detachment, Fort
    Simpson
Gus and Mary Kraus, Little Doctor Lake
Ernie Werbecky, *Skookum II*, Bruce Nesbitt, Brian Dougherty, explorations
    camp, Willow Lake Creek
George Grinnell and Sylvia Bowerbank, Mackenzie River
Dave Felbel, Karen Tsukamoto, Fort Norman
Mike Floyd, Brian and Cindy Dawson, Norman Wells
Jim and Carol Nieman, Fort Good Hope
Fred and Irene Sorenson, Grand View
Alfred Masuzumi, near Fort Good Hope
Joseph Kocian, Gordon Robertson, Charlie Remhold, Arctic Red River ferry
Lucy and Jimmy Adams, Mackenzie delta
Pam Petrin, Paul Andrew, Dave Tait, Jim Robertson, Inuvik
Paul and Barb Schram, Dave and Elaine Grundy, Brian and Laurette
    Sutherland, Carol and Ed Henderson, Jack Alonak, Tuktoyaktuk

Finally we would like to thank both of our families who provided the place and the space to write this book, who read the rough manuscript and offered suggestions and ideas for improvement and ultimately provided the incentive to keep the whole thing going. They are the only ones who really know that writing this book proved more of a challenge at times than the journey itself!

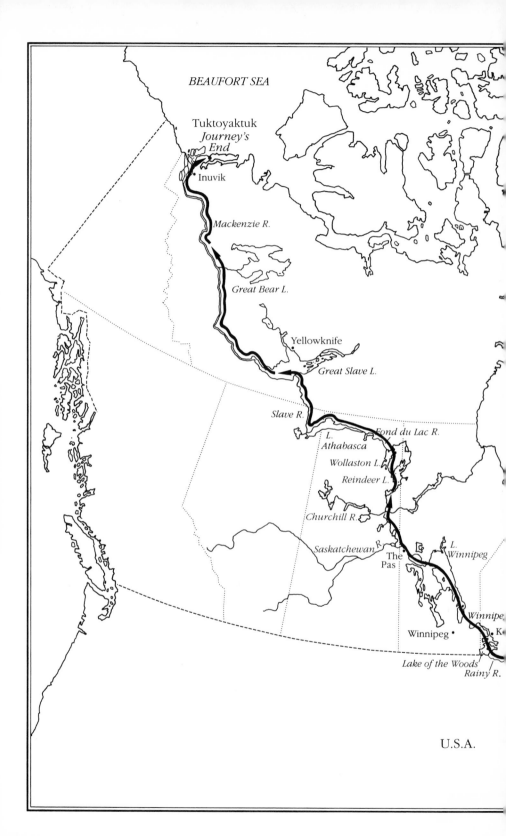